HONOUR
AND THE
SWORD

From sale and profanation
Of honour and the sword,
From sleep and from damnation,
Deliver us, good Lord.

G.K. Chesterton

I dedicate this book to my grandchildren, Euan and Katie,
and Ciaran, Elliot and Lily,
hoping they will grow to be honourable and honoured

HONOUR
AND THE
SWORD

The Culture of Duelling

Joseph Farrell

Signal

Signal Books
Oxford

First published in 2021 by
Signal Books Limited
36 Minster Road
Oxford OX4 1LY
www.signalbooks.co.uk

A catalogue record for this book is available from the British Library

ISBN 978-1-909930-94-0 Cloth

Cover Design: Tora Kelly
Typesetting: Tora Kelly
Cover images: Duel de Charles de Lameth et du marquis de Castries, le 12 novembre 1790 (Musée Carnavalet/Wikimedia Commons; reddit.com
Printed in India by Imprint Press

CONTENTS

INTRODUCTION

The lawyer Alfieri, born in Sicily but American by citizenship and culture, takes on the role of narrator-cum-chorus in Arthur Miller's modern tragedy, *A View from the Bridge* (1955). As he watches the unfolding catastrophe of Eddie Carbone, an Italo-American longshoreman and 'a good man',[1] he is torn between foreboding and optimism. He ponders that 'in some Caesar's year, in Calabria perhaps or on the cliff in Syracuse, another lawyer, quite differently dressed, heard the same complaint and sat there as powerless as I, and watched it run its bloody course.' At the same time, he takes comfort in the fact that modern beliefs and consequent conduct are gentler: 'Now we are quite civilised, quite American. Now we settle for half, and I like it better.'

Eddie and his wife Beatrice have brought up Beatrice's orphaned niece Catherine, but Eddie's feelings for her develop beyond the paternal as she grows into an attractive young woman, and degenerate into vicious jealousy as he sees her fall in love with Rodolpho, a relative and an illegal immigrant to whom they had given refuge. He denounces Rodolpho to the authorities, an unpardonable infringement of the community's code, and his own. His death at the hands of Rodolpho's brother Marco, in retaliation for the denunciation, has the feeling of an almost suicidal duel in expiation of this violation. Alfieri's doleful closing words are a futile repetition of his earlier declaration that 'I think it's better to settle for half.'

In history, the duel was the recourse of men, or gentlemen, who were incapable of settling for half. The men who participated in duels - and it should be stated from the outset that, despite the existence of female duels, which will be recounted later, the history of duelling is a study of male conduct, male power and male self-image - felt themselves obliged by outer or inner forces to risk their own lives or to break that one law recognized by all moralities and all cultures,

1

the commandment against killing a fellow human being. Anthropologists have not discovered any ethical code which condones murder unless in conditions of warfare or as part of some primitive religious rite. In Evelyn Waugh's words, murder is 'the accepted token-coin of extreme wickedness',[2] yet it was for some centuries by wont and custom condoned in one form in western society, even if condemned by Church and State. The ecclesiastical condemnation was an expression of the Ten Commandments, and this was an ethical imperative to which duellists themselves made official obeisance, even when they conformed to the *code duello*, the Italianate phrase used in all languages and all western cultures to refer to the recognized rules of conduct that governed duels.

It is not sufficient to dismiss this breach as a form of personal hypocrisy, the one sin still condemned by post-Christian society, for the issue is more complex. In 'affairs of honour' the standards of religion and of society were at odds. Christ taught that the man who had suffered a blow to one cheek should turn the other, but in ages dominated by the code of honour - the idea that underpinned all duelling - this particular Biblical precept had little appeal. To meekly accept an insult was to allow one's honour and standing in society to be demeaned, and in a competitive world where alterations in the hierarchy of power or in public standing were decided by the observance of the social etiquette of the day, by evidence of seigneurial favour or disfavour, or even by the inability or inability to keep up with changing fashions in dress or expression, the failure to respond to a deliberate slight could be ruinous.

A duel was therefore not a mere brawl between drunks or hooligans. It was an act of violence disguised by formalities, courtesies and a ritual as rigid as a liturgy of worship, but these protocols took time to develop before being eventually laid down in writing in 1777 in Ireland.[3] Offence having been given, honour demeaned, apologies demanded and refused, it was then required that seconds be appointed, cartels exchanged, weapons chosen and an appointment fixed. A stoic insouciance in the face of death was required. The smirking pre-duel request for 'pistols for two and coffee for one' may never have been actually spoken, but its currency is significant and it sets the right tone. Once swords were crossed or shots exchanged, an injury or death might be inflicted. Normally, a fatality would be ignored by society, but if the law did intervene the duellist would be arraigned before a jury of assenting peers and, most commonly, a verdict issued which was an acquiescence by like-minded men in the view that the alleged crime was no more than a misfortune occasioned by the performance of gentlemanly manners.

No study of western history in recent centuries can be complete without some account of the duel and the code of honour, even if duelling is now uniformly judged as outlandish and incomprehensible. Primo Levi in *The Drowned and the Saved*, his final meditation on the Holocaust, wondered whether the world of the concentration camps could be revived by some future despot, or whether it had been definitively consigned to history, 'like slavery and the code of duelling'.[4] There is no emerging revisionist trend of thought urging reconsideration of conventional judgments of the barbarity of duelling, nor will any be offered here. The sheer incomprehensibility of the once widespread and (largely) socially condoned practice is the stimulus behind writing this book. The question this book sets out to examine is - what made *homo sapiens* all over Europe, from Sicily to Ireland, from the Urals to the Atlantic, in the Americas from Ontario to Patagonia behave in the way he did during a period which can be approximately dated from the Italian Renaissance to the late nineteenth century?

If the code of honour, the basis of duelling, was theorized by the Renaissance humanists, the duel's development also owed something to another historical phenomenon, the medieval code of chivalry, and the tournament and joust. There were essential differences between the joust and the duel, even if they were both forms of single combat, but it can be briefly stated that the joust was either a form of sport or a theological activity where God, whose omnipresence was the prime fact of life in the Middle Ages, was on hand to ensure the victory of right, at least in principle. The duel on the other hand was a part of a civil, secular code. It was a dominating feature of European life and culture, but the terms, duel and honour, require investigation, especially now that all notion of 'honour' and its connotations have passed from observance as totally as the cult of the gods of Lower Egypt. The study of duelling requires of the twenty-first-century reader the suspension not only of disbelief but of incredulity, since it involves an examination of canons and creeds which were once dominant but are now as beyond recall as the beliefs of the ancient Egyptians. The visitor to the Nile will marvel at the great pyramid complex at Giza or at the paintings in the Valley of Kings, but will puzzle over the creeds of which these monuments are an expression. A reader today of the etiquette governing the *code duello*, of the wording of challenges, of the poignant messages left to wife and family by a man who crept out of his home at dawn to face another man in the knowledge that he might shortly kill or be killed, will experience similar feelings of bafflement.

Given that most duellists, but by no means all, preferred to avoid publicity, and that most duels involved private citizens who were of no interest to the press of the day, it is impossible to give accurate figures of the number of duels actually fought or aborted on the field. At times it will seem that, especially in the late eighteenth and early nineteenth centuries, there was scarcely a personage of note in politics, the law, public administration, newspaper publishing, or literature who did not issue a challenge or who was not 'called out'. Some of the more ardent duellists racked up participation in an astonishing number of duels, either as principal (duellist) or as second. Many do not figure among the great and good of history but may have enjoyed some local celebrity and commanded a few column inches in local publications or in court records. However, prime ministers, presidents, Cabinet ministers, lawyers, accountants, generals, colonels, landowners, clergymen, roués, gamblers, counts, earls, dukes, writers, artists and even some sovereigns made their appearance at dawn on the field of honour to 'blaze away', in the Irish expression. As late as 1967, Gaston Defferre, socialist politician and Mayor of Marseille at the time, fought a duel with René Ribière after an exchange of insults inside the French National Assembly. A much truncated list of prominent duellists in history would include the astronomer Tycho Brahe, the fabulist La Fontaine, Giacomo Casanova, Pushkin, Lermontov, Vice-President Aaron Burr and former Treasury Secretary Alexander Hamilton, President Andrew Jackson, a Lord Byron (uncle of the poet), the banker John Law, Marcel Proust, Victor Hugo, Gabriele D'Annunzio, the Duke of Wellington, Clemenceau, Canning and Castlereagh, the celebrated poet Giuseppe Ungaretti, Sir Alexander Boswell, the Duke of Hamilton, Prosper Mérimée, Richard Brinsley Sheridan, baronets and colonels by the score - the list could be extended enormously. Mark Twain was almost engaged in a pistol duel but wriggled clear.

If one added duels fought on stage or in works of fiction, the list would be longer than Leporello's catalogue of Don Giovanni's conquests. Starting with the combat between Mercutio and Tybalt, duels proliferate in Shakespeare, even if Falstaff delivers a jeering dismissal of honour itself. The description of a duel does not necessarily imply that the writer approved of the event, but it does imply that he, occasionally she, found the drama of the duel irresistible. It raised the stakes in melodrama. The Sicilian actor, Giovanni Grasso, quarrelled bitterly with Luigi Pirandello when he found that the playwright refused to include a duel in a play he was to perform. He had a point, in that a duel gave vent to his histrionic talents and was box-office gold. Pirandello himself was anything but averse to dealing in duels, and not only in fiction. His father was a notorious duellist, and he himself challenged an actor whose performance in a one-act play of his had displeased him. In one of Pirandello's short stories, *The Turn*, the duel is ironically handled, but in other works, like *The Rules of the Game*, there is a more serious, off-stage duel.

The duel was an integral part of the action in Walter Scott's *Ivanhoe*, but in general while Scott manages both to lend a certain romantic glamour to the duel, he also calls it into question. In *Pride and Prejudice* Jane Austen allows

Colonel Brandon to make no more than a mention of his duel with Willoughby, although both had emerged unharmed. Richardson's *Clarissa*, Stendhal's *Scarlet and Black*, and Dumas' *The Three Musketeers* contain scenes of duels, as do Thackeray's *Barry Lindon*, *Vanity Fair* and *Henry Esmond*, but the attitudes of these authors differ, or are hard to decipher. Russian literature contains many examples, most notably the famous case of Pushkin who depicts an imaginary duel in *Eugene Onegin* and later was killed in an encounter: Lermontov, author of *A Hero of our Time*, hero-worshipped Pushkin, and underwent the same fate. Other fictional Russian duels occur in Tolstoy's *War and Peace*, Dostoevsky's *The Brothers Karamazov* and Turgenev's *Fathers and Sons*. Chekhov's short story *The Duel* features the plight of a luckless man dragged against his will into a duel, happily aborted, but Chekhov was fascinated by the duel and wrote that he could not conceive of a play without at least one pistol shot, fatal in *The Three Sisters*, missing its target in *Uncle Vanya*.

There are specific national characteristics to the duel. It had its roots in Renaissance Italy, spread to France where the concept of honour was elaborated, was militarized in Germany, or Prussia, made distinctly upper-class in Britain, and democratized in the United States. The Wild West shoot-out, like the *Gunfight at the O.K. Corral*, is a linear descendant

The aristocratic and the democratized forms of combat: Jacques Caillot, *Les Caprices*, c1620, Wikimedia Commons: E.W. Kemble, *The Duel*, 1887 (Library of Congress, Washington DC)

of the duel, but without the ritual. Conrad's *The Duel* has heavy undertones of disbelieving irony, skilfully maintained in Ridley Scott's film adaptation, *The Duellists*, while the duel that never was in G.K. Chesterton's *The Man Who Was Thursday* is overt pastiche. The duel made an elegant leap from prose and theatre to opera. The savage death-struggle in *Cavalleria Rusticana*, provoked by sexual jealousy and preceded by the ceremony of ear-biting, has roots in a Mediterranean folk culture which predates the code of honour, but the reference to Alfredo's duel in defence of Violetta's good name at the end of *La Traviata* is more gentle, even pathetic.

The history of the duel has a beginning, a middle and an end, like a well-made play. In *Officers and Gentlemen*, one of the novels which make up Evelyn Waugh's Second World War trilogy, *Sword of Honour*, the question of honour is raised in ironic tones. As the British officers on Crete prepare to escape, deceiving their men and abandoning them to the advancing Germans, Ivor Claire takes Guy Crouchback aback with an abrupt, unexpected question.

Guy, what would you do if you were challenged to a duel?
Laugh.
Yes, of course.
What made you think of that now?
I was thinking about honour. It's a thing that changes, doesn't it? I mean, a hundred and fifty years ago we would have had to fight if challenged. Now we'd laugh. There must have been a time a hundred years or so ago when it was rather an awkward question.
Yes, moral theologians were never able to stop duelling - it took democracy to do that.
And in the next war, when we are completely democratic, I expect it will be quite honourable for officers to leave their men behind.[5]

This exchange crystallizes cultural dilemmas at the heart of any analysis of honour and duelling. What were the factors which for hundreds of years would have made it 'awkward' if not unthinkable for gentlemen like Waugh's characters to refuse a challenge to a duel? The dialogue ends with a deliberate anti-climax: 'Ivor stood up saying, "Well, the path of honour lies up the hill," and he strolled away.' The great questions are unanswered. What were the forces that made issuing a challenge necessary? What was the change in sensibility that caused duelling to be viewed as simply ridiculous? To what extent did a code of honour determine behaviour? And what was honour anyway? In their discussion, Ivor and Guy wryly question the nature of honour, its central value in a cultural cosmos which has now vanished but one which once drove men, gun in hand, to take up positions face to face with each other, at a distance which allowed them to see the colour of their adversary's eyes. As Waugh recognizes, the very idea of honour, which is at the heart of the culture which upheld the duel, has been stripped of its power. Any attempt to recover the once dominant mind-set and complex of values which made the quest for, and defence of, honour an imperative is almost as demanding as accurately imagining the life, culture, professions and pastimes of the human beings whose charred bodies have been excavated in Pompeii.

In assessing the reasons for duelling, it is hard to identify how much weight to give to personal motive and individuality and how much to the power of social conformity. In many cases, there is nothing in the previous life of individual duellists which will offer enlightenment on why they 'went out', gun or sword in hand. Even in the 'golden age' of the duel, there were always critics of the practice in Church and State, and indeed a few unfortunate or scapegoated duellists were hanged for their part in duels which seem no different from others that were condoned or even applauded. Equally, there were many stout champions of the practice as well as enthusiastic practitioners, some of whom participated in multiple duels and were prepared to issue challenges on pretexts which seem to posterity slight, ludicrous or downright preposterous. Some men had a pathological fondness for duelling and might now be diagnosed as near-psychopaths. US President Andrew Jackson showed a disconcerting enthusiasm for the activity, as did the Earl of Mohun, who features as a villain in Thackeray's *The History of Henry Esmond* and who both in that fiction and in life fought with the Duke of Hamilton. Both men died of their injuries. Others seemingly addicted to duelling include the nineteenth-century Italian poet and politician, Felice Cavallotti (1842-98), one of the Thousand who made up Garibaldi's expeditionary force for the invasion of Sicily and later an anti-monarchist politician. He fought more than thirty duels before his career came to an end in a duel in Rome with Ferruccio Macola, editor of a Venetian journal. There are streets, piazzas and a multiplicity of plaques in his honour all over Italy. One plaque in Campo S. Stefano in Venice pays homage to the 'Soldier, Legislator, Poet' who gave 'his sword to Liberty in sad days, and his eloquence to Justice in tranquil days'. No one will be surprised at the omission of all reference to his end, sad or tranquil, but anyone who stops to read those grandiloquent words might be taken aback at the incongruity of the setting. Cavallotti had no connection with the *Serenissima*, unlike the man who ended his life, whose home it was. Macola seemingly had no intention of killing Cavallotti, and was given a mild sentence but was ostracized by society and driven to taking his own life.

Some critics suggest that, once the folderols of ritual are stripped away, the real roots of the single combat lie in the human, male psyche and in the quest for individual revenge for wrongs done. Max Weber saw the history of civil society as a chronicle of the struggle of the State - monarchist, aristocratic, dictatorial or democratic - to win that 'monopoly of violence' which he judged indispensable to its existence. One of the State's prime tasks, he wrote, was to ensure that its organs, courts, militia and police forces, will not only defend the individual from violence, injustice and the unwarranted intrusion of superior strength, but also assume responsibility for righting wrongs inflicted. A more recent writer has stated that the belief in community justice and the thirst for individual revenge are more closely related than is comfortably believed.[6] This was not the view of

Francis Bacon, who famously declared that 'Revenge is a kind of wild justice, which the more man's nature runs to it, the more ought law to weed it out.'[7] Bacon pitches law and nature against each other, nature straining to react according to individual dictates, law seeking to restrain such impulses in the name of the common good. The duel represents a rejection of State rights and State power. It is a desire for individual vindication of a wrong genuinely or supposedly suffered.

It is at times hard to identify the weight to be given to personal motive and individuality. The balance between individual choice and social conformity, even in extreme cases, is a precarious one. How free is the individual of the environment he inhabits and of that form of ethical conditioning now called culture? There were reluctant duellists for whom it can almost appear that duelling was in the air, part of a code of behaviour to which they were required to conform with no more ado. The unwelcome conclusion might be that culture instils a habit of mind, comparable to fashion, and it is worth recalling that fashion was itself recognized in other times as a powerful intellectual force, not only a mode of conformist attire. David Hume wrote of the 'contagion of fashion', and in his *Pensées* Blaise Pascal remarked that morals too are subject to fashion - an especially intriguing statement coming from so deeply Catholic a thinker, one who believed in an eternal moral code. Pascal did not suggest that moral edicts in themselves can be varied, but that individual precepts acquire greater or lesser force according to the circumstances of particular ages. What is the force that made slavery or duelling quite acceptable once, but repugnant today?

At this point, the modern reader will find the notion of 'culture' to hand, but it does not explain everything, and it was not always in use. The word employed in other times was 'custom,' a term which had the same force and a similar, if not identical, meaning. The use of the word 'custom' was a plea in mitigation; it was an appeal to the habits of mind of a people, and thus, it was implied, a justification of practices whose moral basis was recognized as being shaky. In the Christian tradition, there was always a recognised clash, which will be referenced several times in this work, between the commandment forbidding killing and the community code which countenanced duelling, and at those times, particularly during a legal case, it was common for men to appeal to ways which were sanctioned by wont and familiarity, by custom. The word suggested a certain permanence, it made the choice of a course of action more than individual, it inserted it into the life of the tribe. A man had, of course, an obligation to Christian codes, but the customs of the nation, class or caste to which he belonged expected or at least tolerated actions or reactions which seemingly ran counter to the otherwise dominant code. In western societies, custom required of a man compliance with the code of honour, so what was a man to do?

The emergence of the term culture in its modern sense is fairly recent, perhaps dating from nineteenth-century Germany. In its current sense the word may be of Latin origin, and originally it had a purely agricultural sense, like cultivation, but it later acquired its metaphorical, modern meaning in the writings of men like Johann Gottfried Herder or Johann Joachim Winckelmann. From the very outset, the term was confusing since it was given two conflicting meanings, a purely aesthetic sense and a more anthropological sense. The earliest Prussian meaning was aesthetic, but gradually the word evolved to carry the wider sense of an amalgam of social beliefs and customs, underwritten by usage but not arrived at by rational process. Culture came to stand for those activities and convictions which are of their essence pre-rational, taken for granted, are coterminous with common sense, and which coax or coerce people to act in a certain way because everyone else does, because it has always been that way. Perhaps the dynamic relationship between prejudice and reason serves to give body to a culture. There are sanctions against anyone who deviates, not necessarily painful, punitive measures but subtler signs of disapproval which can lead to the ostracism and isolation of an individual who shows too obvious a dissent.

From a notion of culture, *Kultur*, as expressing the distinctive *Weltanschauung*, or world view, of a people, the idea came to denote a complex of values and laws that human beings live by, and whose observance endows a man or woman with the respect of his peers and enables them to live at peace with themselves. It is a recognition of refinement, of status, of conformity to standards and values which with time hardened into a code of common sense, beyond discussion, denied only by criminals, eccentrics or adventurers. In recent times, historians have awoken to the shifting or even cyclical nature of cultural dictates. If the duel was not made necessary by law or duress, there was an element of compulsion of a different order. In the abstract, a challenge did not have to be issued, or having been received could be refused, but on another level, it simply could not. A man had to do what a man had to do, as the jocular line runs. What is the power of cultural pressures as such, how completely do they determine the behaviour not only of convictions but of styles of behaviour which the individual considers freely chosen? In all human society, freedom is circumscribed, but the limits of freedom are determined not only by jurisprudence or politics. The question of negative individual restrictions or positive requirements is not limited to that liberty 'which no good man loses except with his life', as the Declaration of Arbroath (1320) has it. Nor does it involve the right which was, together with the right to life and the pursuit of happiness, 'self-evident' to the Founding Fathers. It does concern a supposed freedom of action, asserted or submitted to in the face of subtler drives and temptations if one is to be really a man, endowed with the private self-respect and public reputation which accompany that title. This is a freedom which has to be won in, or at times against, the prevailing culture and the norms which constitute it.

A code of honour, once it became part of cultural law, imposed styles of conduct, even when they were potentially self-destructive. It required a man in certain circumstances to issue a challenge to a duel under pain of forfeiting his social standing, and required a man who received such a challenge to accept or decline under pain of being an outcast or branded as a coward. In his deeply moving testament written the night before he went to his fatal duel, Alexander Hamilton wrote that he felt he owed Aaron Burr the opportunity to shoot at him. It was a duty, not an option. It may be that a man of his well-established reputation could have refused, especially since Hamilton was anti-duelling, but then in the Earl of Rochester's penetrating maxim, few men have the courage to display cowardice.

The analysis of duelling may seem of antiquarian interest to a modern reader, but the aim is to establish not only what duellists did but why they did it (and why they eventually stopped doing it). In addition, the acceptance of the custom by so many for so long should invite an examination of contemporary customs and habits which are not currently subject to questioning but which will appear outrageous or ludicrous to succeeding generations. The duel was once an expression of codes of belief and conduct in an identifiable age of western history, and the task is to examine the moral codes and social etiquette of the duel and duellists. This book has no ambition to take its place alongside the many systematic histories of duelling. It contains the narration of individual duels combined with an analysis of the polemical treatises, articles, reports, books, sermons and speeches produced over the centuries by people on both sides of the debate about the techniques and morals of duelling. It also examines the literary representation of this particular form of combat, analysing the motives and emotions conjured up by writers who were also themselves sometimes duellists.

It is not possible to give neatly precise dates for the first or last recorded duel. It was the expression of a cultural mood which was long in the making and slow to disintegrate. In consequence, this work, while not ignoring developments in their historical context, does not follow a strictly chronological order. It is book-ended by two dramatic and illustrative duels, those involving Giacomo Casanova and Alexander Pushkin. The duel was well established before Casanova fought Branicki, so he was conscious of operating inside a tradition and his first-person account of the event affords valuable insight into the mind of the duellist. The tradition was still a force in Russia in Pushkin's day and his response to gossip and slanders illustrates the enduring power of the social and cultural pressures brought to bear on a gentleman anywhere in Europe. There were other duels after his death, most notably the one fought only four years later by Lermontov which brings the book to a close. But by then the hold of the culture and tradition of duelling was weakening, as attested by the writings of Alexander Herzen, Lermontov's acquaintance and contemporary. Disputes were settled in more peaceful ways.

I owe a debt of gratitude to many people, but I put my gratitude to my wife, Maureen, in a category by itself. I cannot say how much I owe her for her patient help over many months.

Thereafter, I would like to single out Paul Selfa and Cormac O'Cuilleanain for their meticulous reading of what I wrote chapter by chapter, bringing genuine expertise to the task of eliminating errors and improving the style, presentation and narrative.

I am also grateful to Andrew Wilkin, Paolo Puppa, Anna Holloway, Paola Bottalla, Neal Ascherson, Marilyn Suckle, Vincenzo Barbarotta, Al Selfa and Tom O'Hara for much appreciated suggestions.

1 Arthur Miller, *A View from the Bridge*, London: Penguin, 1961.
2 Evelyn Waugh in *G.K. Chesterton: A Half Century of Views*, edited by D.J. Conlon, Oxford: Oxford University Press, 1987, p. 72.
3 The Irish Code Duello is a set of twenty-seven formal rules for duelling that was agreed and adopted at the Clonmel Summer Assizes of 1777 by gentleman delegates from Tipperary, Sligo, Mayo, Galway and Roscommon.
4 Primo Levi, translated by Michael F. Moore, *The Drowned and the Saved*, in *The Complete Works of Primo Levi*, London: Penguin, 2015, pp. 1418-9.
5 Evelyn Waugh, *Sword of Honour*, London: Penguin, 1999, p. 421.
6 Susan Jacoby, *Wild Justice: The Evolution of Revenge*, London: Collins, 1985.
7 Francis Bacon, *Of Revenge*, in *Essays or Councils Civil and Moral*, edited by Brian Vickers, Oxford, Oxford University Press, 1996, p. 14.

1

FOR THE HONOUR
OF VENICE
CASANOVA'S DUEL

On 5 March 1766, Count Franciszek Branicki, scion of the purest
of blue-blooded Polish aristocracy, *podstoli* or chamberlain of
the royal court in Warsaw, Knight of the White Eagle, general
in the Polish Army, chosen counsellor of King Stanislaus II,
arrived at the arranged time at the Warsaw residence of Giacomo
Casanova. The count was seated in a grand coach and six and was
accompanied by a uniformed retinue befitting a man of his rank.
There were ten retainers in his suite: two mounted grooms with
two additional horses preceding the carriage, two hussars and
two *aides-de-camp* taking up the rear, together with four other
mounted servants. The carriage, with the coachman up front,
had seating for four, but was occupied only by the count plus
one military officer. Casanova was impressed by such grandeur,
but also embarrassed by the extent to which it overshadowed
his own modest retinue of two servants, and so, unwilling to
lose face over this inequality, he preferred to dismiss his own
men. The count advised him against this course of action,
suggesting that Casanova might well require their services
later, but Casanova waved aside this objection saying that he
was confident the count's men would provide any assistance he
might require. Branicki was pleased to offer reassurance on this

score and promised that should it become necessary, Casanova would receive better treatment than would he himself. The two men shook hands on this pledge.

Casanova did not know precisely where they were headed, and felt it inappropriate to enquire, but he knew the day's business. He has left two accounts of the day, the first in a pamphlet, *Il duello*, and the other in a chapter in his Memoirs.[1] The pamphlet is written in the third person with Casanova referring to himself, significantly, as the Venetian, but that apart the two accounts differ only in trivial details. The central fact is that the two men were driving together to a spot outside Warsaw where they would face each other pistol in hand for a duel in which each would attempt to kill the other.

Victor Hugo, as part of his campaign against capital punishment, wrote a short, passionate work on the last night of a condemned man, but a convicted prisoner is in a different situation from the intending duellist in that the prisoner has no power of independent choice. His penalty has been decreed by a judicial authority and will be executed by a representative of the state. On the other hand, a man *en route* to a duel has the option, in principle at least, of a change of heart or escape, and indeed might be comforted by the awareness that there will be at the appointed place two seconds whose task even at that point is to invite the duellists to reconsider. Certainly his seeming freedom is not absolute, for he is bound by accepted cultural protocols, by recognized duties as a gentleman, by a sense of responsibility to himself, by a socio-ethical code of honour bolstered by a fear of shame.

How powerful were these forces? Their grip has loosened or been dissipated since that March day in the eighteenth century, making it almost impossible to assess their hold, but it is valuable to make the intellectual effort to recreate the ethos that drove men to engage in duelling, and specifically to make the imaginative effort to reconstruct the mood in that carriage. How great was the intensity of the inner turmoil these particular men may have felt that day, torn between the socially imposed imperative of maintaining *sang-froid* and the primal fear that every human being must feel in the face of ceasing to be? This was the Age of the Enlightenment; both men were highly educated and well versed in the culture of the age of Voltaire and Montesquieu. In the coach, the two sat wordlessly for a time but the silence became oppressive, awkward or even ill-mannered. It is written in the Book of Ecclesiastes that there is a time to keep silence and a time to speak, and Casanova decided it was time for conversation. He did not broach some great matter of state, but decided trifling items of small talk were in order, so he politely asked the count if he planned to spend spring and summer in Warsaw. This question was bathetic or eccentric since his aim was to end his opponent's life a few hours later on the field they were driving to. The count was evidently taken aback, but recovered his composure sufficiently to say that passing summer in Warsaw was indeed his plan, unless his companion made that impossible. Casanova reassured him that nothing could be further from his mind than incommoding the count in that or in any way. Now that conversation had begun, Branicki felt called on to continue, and wondered if his companion had ever been in the army. Casanova replied that he had, but was curious to know why the count had made that particular inquiry. Plainly disconcerted, Branicki admitted that the query had been made merely for the sake of having something to say. In his Memoirs, Casanova has the conversation fade out at this point, but in the pamphlet, *Il duello*, he records that the count grew testy and brusquely cut off the exchange. If this is so, such discourtesy in those circumstances is surely comprehensible and pardonable even in a gentleman of his rank.

The bizarre incongruity of Casanova's willingness to enter into small talk is baffling to the contemporary mind, making it hard to know whether to sympathize with Branicki's impatience or to be impressed by Casanova's display of aplomb and nonchalant civility. It is already difficult to empathize with the full ramifications of the *code duello*, as it was known, but the Branicki-Casanova encounter provides an excellent starting point for any enquiry, largely because Casanova's account of his experiences, however self-serving, provides posterity with unrivalled access to the beliefs and conduct of a participant in a gentlemanly duel, as well as a unique insight into duelling itself, its code, its protocols, its morals, its rituals, its fantasies, its complex contradictions and into what it is appropriate to call its etiquette.

Most duellists spent what they feared might be their last night on earth saying prayers, writing letters to their loved ones, drafting wills, attending to outstanding business, particularly to creditors. William Pitt the Younger and Alexander Hamilton like many others drew up letters, explanations of motive and even an apologia the night before engagement in a duel, but only Casanova has left a first-person, calmly thought out, autobiographical account of the social events and mental processes which led up to the duel. Nothing in Casanova can be regarded as merely typical or wholly indicative of wider trends, so while his thinking on duelling may be idiosyncratic in its approach to the moral complexities of the question, it does also offer some valuable insights. His account covers the reactions of society, the proceedings on the day and his own post-factum justification of his acts. As such, his pamphlet, structured like a novella, is unique and invaluable. Precisely because of the subtlety of Casanova's intellect, and in spite of his heightened capacity for self-aggrandisement and self-deception, his narrative of his duel is of singular value in the quest to uncover what once drove men to accept the risk of injury or death.

It may be a surprise to find Giacomo Casanova at the age of forty-one in Warsaw, but he was a tireless traveller, either on the run from agents of the law or spurred on by his own adventurousness or insatiable curiosity. 'A man born in Venice into a poor family not blessed by fortune and with none of the titles which in cities distinguish certain families from the normal run of humankind but educated, as it pleased God, in the style of those who are destined for something better than the way of life followed by ordinary people...' With these words, Casanova, who had a high sense of self-worth and a conviction that he belonged to an élite of intellect if not of blood, opens *Il duello*. To discover him fighting a duel will come as a shock to those who link his name to less sanguinary activities, but John Masters, the supreme Casanovist, believes that the duel in Warsaw was an event 'comparable in importance in his life only with his escape from the Leads'.[2] The latter feat is recounted in the *Histoire de ma fuite* (Story of my Escape), another of the few works published in his lifetime. The two events occupy a central position in his life as he lived it and as he shaped it for later generations.

Posterity has made the very name Casanova a synonym for serial philanderer, but the man himself was also gifted with an acute, highly refined intellect, was imbued with the new thinking that was the Enlightenment, and had debated as an equal with Voltaire and Rousseau. His psychology has been endlessly analysed by observers, biographers, novelists and film directors, and while the reliability of his autobiographical writings has been questioned, there is also a contemporary school of dedicated Casanovists (one of whom was a priest who had taken a vow of chastity), who have dedicated time and energy to combatively establishing the reliability of his narratives. These scholars have scoured archives and parish records to establish the real identity of women whose names he had concealed behind asterisks or pseudonyms and have in the main verified what appeared to be arbitrary or invented fictions by comparing them to facts soberly recounted by contemporary chroniclers. They have triumphantly rejoiced in discovering that although dismissed as a braggart or a fantasist, much of what he wrote was in fact accurate.[3]

Few human beings have written more about themselves, but while his name has become in common parlance synonymous with Don Juan, the *tombeur de femmes*, the womanizer, the sexual prowler, the arch-sensualist, the inner man always eludes satisfactory diagnosis. Some see in his cult of sex an almost metaphysical quest for the eternal female, others find in him a suppression of a homosexual urge, while others again identify the roots of his being as lying in a quest for the mother who, preferring to leave his care to others while she pursued her own dream of success on the stage, abandoned and refused him the maternal affection he craved. Casanova's boyhood was troubled as he was moved from one lodging to another. He was consigned by his mother to a flea-ridden boarding house in Padua, and his education entrusted to Dr Gozzi, who took pity on him and brought him to his own house. One other member of the household was the tutor's sister, Bettina, who in Casanova's account ensured that he was kept properly clean but who used the occasion of washing him to inspect his private parts and to seduce him. He was aged eleven. Casanova was then and was to remain a sensitive moralist with a need, shown later in his examination of the events which led to the duel in Poland, to ponder and justify his every act. The first demonstration of his wayward but acute mental faculties came in his reflections on how he was treated by Bettina. Being a woman, she was, he concluded, a weaker creature who needed an outlet for her compassion, which she found initially in assisting him.

Casanova moved back to Venice, and in 1741 took four of the ecclesiastical minor orders which would normally be the first steps to the priesthood. The vow of chastity would be required only with the conferment of the major orders, the sub-diaconate and diaconate, and Casanova never went that far, although he did consider, and others considered for him, a career in the Church. Once he even contemplated becoming a monk in the Abbey of Einsiedeln in Switzerland. After receiving the minor orders, he was entitled to be known as *abbate*, a clerical title which did not impose many obligations and carried with it certain privileges, including, paradoxically, the right to decline all challenges to a duel. For men of the upper classes, the refusal of a challenge issued by a peer normally exposed a man to contempt and opprobrium. Perhaps his lowly background gave him a keener sense of the need to assert his honour, but in any case he did not avail himself of the exemption from responding to unwelcome challenges to his honour, or indeed from issuing challenges. He fought various duels in the course of his life, the first with Count Celi in Padua in 1749. He defeated his opponent, whom he left for dead, although he in fact survived.

Unsurprisingly, the majority of the duels, but by no means all, involved women. Recovering from a frustrated love affair in Venice with a Countess A.S., who was removed from his attentions by her father and married off, he returned to Padua and took to gambling in the house of one Ancilla, a dancer by profession. The standards at the gambling table were not of the highest and Casanova accused one of the players, Count Tommaso Medini, or Medin, of cheating, an accusation which led inevitably to a challenge. The two men fought with swords, but the duel was only until first blood, which was drawn by Casanova. In Paris in 1752, he fought with the Chevalier de Talvis, also known as de la Perina, once again after he believed he had been cheated.[4] Even in old age, in the dismal days as librarian in the Castle of Dux in Bohemia, engaged in a bitter epistolary quarrel with the majordomo, he was still thinking of challenging him 'if only we lived in a land where duelling was tolerated'.

Casanova served an apprenticeship in swordsmanship as well as in the arts of love-making, while also accumulating knowledge of esoteric practices, associating with the occult sect known as the Rosicrucians, as well as the Freemasons. Such membership may have been in part responsible for the accusation of authorship of irreligious material which led to his arrest in Venice in 1755 and imprisonment in the *Piombi*, the Leads, the prison on the far side of the Bridge of Sighs from the Ducal Palace. It was supposedly impossible to escape from there, but after a brief period of despair Casanova set to devising a plan. In his pamphlet, he described in detail his patient, ingenious scheme which involved scraping through the floor of his cell and dropping into the palace, and if some carping critics have doubted the entire tale and allege that Casanova merely bribed his way out, it is enough to note that he was at liberty by the end of October 1756. He crossed into France and made his way to Paris where, as was the case wherever he fetched up, he had no difficulty in being admitted to high, indeed royal, society. Over the following years, he traversed Europe, from court to court, gambling table to gambling table and bed to bed, leaving behind him broken promises and unpaid bills. He was convinced of his own probity, and in regard to his affairs could boast that 'Virtue had greater attractions for me than vice', where the virtue in question was not his own but that of the women he fell in love with, or at least made love to.

In Paris in 1759 he fought with a man who had stolen his ring, wounding him severely but leaving him alive. He arrived in London in the summer of 1763 and spent nine precarious but highly active months there, including an escapade with no fewer than five sisters who constituted a private seraglio, but after they went their way he contracted an unspecified illness from another woman. He was yet again cheated over a gambling debt, accepting in payment a note which turned out to be forged. To his dismay, he discovered that under English law anyone passing a false promissory bill, even in good faith, was liable to death by hanging. He fled to Berlin, where in 1764 he met Frederick the Great and tried to find a post in the royal household, but although he was a frequent guest at aristocratic tables, he could not find a permanent source of income, and so the following year he moved to St Petersburg. He met Catherine the Great on three occasions, and discussed with her the advantages of the Gregorian calendar, which Russia had not introduced, and attempted to interest her, as he had with Frederick, in one of his favourite schemes, setting up a lottery, but he was rebuffed.

In October 1765, he moved to Warsaw. Armed with letters of introduction, he made for the royal palace, once again hoping for some kind of official, salaried position. Not a wealthy man, he lived on his wits and was remarkably successful in making friends or finding patrons in every city he visited. He was well received in Poland and was given regular gifts of money by the king. His only entitlement to move in noble circles was his possession of the Roman Order of Knighthood conferred on him by Pope Clement XIII, although he himself set little store by this bauble. While aware that such a distinction was 'of great help to a man', for him it was no more than a 'respectable decoration which impresses fools'. However, since 'the world is full of fools, and they are all inclined to evil,' it is as well for a man to flaunt any conferred dignity he may have.

There were other Italians in the city, most notably three renowned female dancers. Warsaw had been a Mecca for Italian performers since the days of the *commedia dell'arte*, and they were made welcome. One of the performers was Anna Binetti, another travelling Venetian whom Casanova had originally met in Padua in 1747, and again in Stuttgart in 1760 when she assisted him in his escape from creditors. On that occasion too he was unable to meet gambling losses and had been enclosed in a room by a group to whom he owed money. Anna visited him and, having smuggled in some of his clothes and possessions under her skirt, helped him clamber down a rope and then drove off with him. In Warsaw, she delighted the king and was given a year's contract to perform, but there were two other Italian ballerinas, Caterina Catai and Teresa Casacci, already in town. Relations between the women were not sisterly. Binetti and Catai had both fixed themselves up with highly placed admirers, Catai with Count Carlo Tomatis, an Italian who was Master of Entertainments at the court, while Binetti had found favour with Count Branicki, Royal Podstoli, the title by which Casanova refers to him in his writings.

One evening, there was an unseemly, un-aristocratic brawl between Tomatis and Branicki as the two men left the theatre. Strangely Casanova omits all mention of the event in *Il duello*, but gives a detailed account in his later Memoirs. Perhaps he saw in retrospect the 'point of honour' at stake between Tomatis and Branicki as a counterpoint to his own encounter with Branicki. The *podstoli* had attended a performance by Catai and went to her changing room to compliment her. Having exchanged pleasantries, he then escorted her to a coach standing outside the theatre, but that coach had been reserved by Tomatis. Branicki helped her in and then took his place alongside her, to the annoyance of Tomatis, who refused to allow the coach to move off. Branicki peremptorily ordered one of his servants to strike Tomatis on the face, which he did. All codes of duelling were unanimously of the view that to strike a gentleman on the face was an offence of such gravity that it required the offended party to demand satisfaction. In the immediate aftermath, Tomatis behaved with unexpected tranquillity, or undue cowardice. He got into another carriage and rode off.

The following day Warsaw society was in a turmoil. How would Tomatis react? Who was really at fault? Tomatis had rudely told a nobleman to get out of the coach, but on the other hand Branicki had invited himself into the company of a lady who was unquestionably in a relationship with Tomatis. The king might have settled matters, but he declined to take sides, and there were other factors which complicated Tomatis' personal dilemma. He had financed the performance with forty thousand sequins of his money, a sum he expected to have reimbursed from the royal exchequer but which he feared would not be forthcoming if he exacted some form of revenge on a man who was an *habitué* of the royal court. In the eyes of men of that age, honour was a prize beyond gold, or at least beyond most sums of gold, but all scales can be adjusted. Tomatis vacillated. Branicki maintained that he had repaid one offence with another, but although he had his supporters he was generally considered to be on shaky ground. Casanova entertained no doubts. Whatever he may have thought at the time, by the time he composed his Memoirs he was convinced that the initial fault was Caterina Catai's for entering the coach on Branicki's arm, but that was a female miscalculation and not the central issue. His final judgment was uncompromising:

> I believe that Tomatis should have killed the servant, even at the risk to his own life. That required less courage than he had displayed in ordering the Podstoli to the Crown to get out of his coach. I considered Tomatis much at fault in not foreseeing that Branicki would respond to the affront with violence, and consequently in not being on his guard at the moment when Branicki suffered the affront.[5]

The casualness of Casanova's statement that the servant should have been murdered on the spot is chilling, at least today. In less than thirty years, revolutionaries in France would be calling for Equality, but that was in the future and Casanova expressed a standard view that a servant was expendable and that, even when obeying orders from his employer, he had no rights, not even to life. Nor was Casanova impressed by the conduct of the women, but they were ultimately bystanders. The main players were male, and they were expected to act in accordance with accepted social codes and with notions of honour, meaning that Tomatis was exposed to criticism, or even contempt, for his passivity. In the aftermath, Casanova confessed himself also taken aback by the reaction of the actress Anna Binetti. His own mother had been a member of a theatre company, and he believed that this gave him unique insight into the quirks and foibles of actresses. 'A woman of the theatre when exposed to competition, longs with such anxiety for victory that she makes herself the declared enemy of all those who fail to help her triumph and overcome anyone who stands in her way.' Binetti had failed to take Tomatis' side mainly because, in Casanova's view, she was motivated by jealousy of the other Italian performers. He suspected that she might even have incited Branicki to offend her main rival, and he went so far as to wonder if she was anxious to see Casanova himself caught up in a similar affray. She had, he was informed, complained to Branicki of Casanova's lack of appreciation of her and invited Branicki to find an opportunity to humiliate him.

The occasion soon arose, and it involved the same cast. Casanova had been invited to dine

Anna Binetti by Louis-François Marteau, c1766, National Museum Warsaw (Wikimedia Commons)

at the royal table and was there encouraged by the king to come and see the best of Polish theatre. He was reluctant to go along since he had no knowledge of Polish and feared boredom, but a king's words are orders. When he took his seat, he may have been surprised to find that the performers were not Polish but the Italian dancers who had been responsible for the previous angst. However, he was impressed by their grace and delicacy of movement and went backstage to compliment the two lead performers, Teresa Casacci and Anna Binetti. The competing demands of gentlemanly conduct, courtesy towards ladies, respect for noble rank, repressed emotions and embittered jealousies between the women meant that every word and gesture from that point on had consequences.

Casanova's is the only account we have, and he writes that as he was about to enter Casacci's dressing-room he saw Branicki arrive accompanied by an officer of his regiment, Biszewski. Casanova withdrew in accordance with Polish etiquette which, he explains, differed in this from manners in Italy where courtesy would have decreed that the first-comer had priority. In the corridor he was confronted by Branicki who looked him up and down 'as tailors do', and asked him what he was up to with the lady. Did he love her? Casanova replied that he did, but this may have been a misunderstanding, since in the previous sentence he had written that he was only there to compliment her on her performance and on the enthusiastic response from the royal party. Branicki retorted that he too loved her and since he was not in the habit of tolerating rivals he wished Casanova to cede her to him. Casanova's reply was that he had had no inkling of this 'taste' of Branicki's but he continued, 'jovially' he says, that he would be pleased to cede her to a 'fine knight' like the count.

There is no indication that Signora Casacci's views were taken into account. The two gentlemen had a minor squabble over her, but until that point no real harm had been done. Casanova turned to move off, but Branicki then transgressed. The two had been speaking in French, and Branicki used a word of such vulgarity that Casanova considered it appropriate to leave it untranslated in his reports of the encounter. He quotes Branicki as saying, 'A poltroon who gives way, when he has given way *f**t le camp*.' Casanova explains to Italian readers that the words means 'deserts the field', but adds that the term used is vile and indicates an attitude of superiority towards someone of a lower order. He further interpreted the words as implying not only contempt but a threat of physical violence but, having been educated to act with moderation, he resisted 'the strong temptation' to kill the man on the spot, limiting himself to placing his hand on the hilt of his sword, which was in itself a kind of challenge. As he moved off he heard Branicki exclaim behind him: 'Just as well the Venetian poltroon is off. I was going to tell him to *f***re* himself.' Once again Casanova conceals the actual word in the more delicate French, but the vulgar language was not in Casanova's eyes the central offence, which was the reference to his native place, Venice. Casanova insists that if Branicki had not added the epithet 'Venetian' to the term poltroon, however crass that word may have been in itself, he might well have let the insult pass, but 'there is not a man who can pardon a word which slanders his nation.' He could not allow this insult to pass unanswered, so he shouted, 'a cowardly Venetian will this very moment dispatch a brave Pole to another world.' National offence had been piled on top of personal disrespect, so the codes of the day required some form of reaction. He waited more than half an hour at the theatre door for Branicki to come out and settle the whole business with a few blows, but it was dark, it was snowing and it was cold so he called his carriage and went to the palace of the Prince Palatine of Russia where he was expected for a game of cards and dinner. Wars have been fought, invasions averted, battles won or lost, men killed or spared for less.

Nonetheless, the words uttered constituted a deeply offensive provocation for a man who put store by his honour, as all gentlemen of all European nations did. The matter, being now governed by a ritual and a code as unquestionable and unappealable as a religious rite, required to be settled.

'A mere bagatelle'

This may have been the eighteenth century of the Christian calendar, this may have been the Age of the Enlightenment, this may have been a time when established nostrums were being questioned in Paris, London, Koenigsberg and Milan, this may have been civilized Europe and these may have been two men who represented both the continent's traditional Christian beliefs and its new learning, but they were still in thrall to a culture and set of beliefs which in part drew on older cultures and only in part questioned them. Satisfaction, a curious word but one laden with sinister connotations, would be required, but in what form should the demand for it be delivered? The king was expected at the prince's palace, and Casanova hoped to seek guidance from His Majesty, but the monarch sent word that he was detained elsewhere. Casanova was restive that evening and was reproached by his host for coming late and also for being incapable of concentrating on the card game when he did arrive. Other guests came along and began excitedly recounting the incident at the theatre and offered Casanova the mock consolation of telling him that Branicki had been drunk, but these words only heightened his agitation. When the guests were seated, the whispered conversation at the far end of the table left him confused and fearful that his honour was being questioned. After the meal, the Prince Palatine drew him aside and made him relate all that occurred, something Casanova was glad to do because he wished to seek authoritative advice on the dictates of honourable conduct. The prince's counsel was gnomic and deeply unhelpful. He declined to come down on one side or the other but intoned, 'It is right for the honest man when faced with such a dilemma to do much or to do nothing at all.' The prince then retired. The oracle at Delphi could not have been more enigmatic.

Casanova was confused and sent for his coat and carriage, returned home, took the medicine prescribed some three weeks previously for an ailment he does not name, wrote some letters to Italy since the post was due to leave the following day and sat awake to ponder the words spoken to him by the prince: 'to do much or to do nothing at all.' His course of action, his decision whether or not to challenge Branicki was not to be based on an emotional spasm, on injured pride or a desire for revenge, much less on feelings of antipathy or personal aversion, but the decision would determine what manner of man he was in his own eyes as well as in the view of society. His next step needed to be taken in a moral framework, so in his midnight meditations he turned to Plato, Christian teachers and Rousseau. Plato seemed at first sight to offer support for doing nothing. In *Gorgias*, he had written that the essence of true heroism consisted in not injuring anyone and in accepting with equanimity damage done to oneself. In his own translation of Plato's words, Casanova introduces the crucial word 'honour' and quotes Plato as saying that there is less dishonour in enduring injury than in inflicting it. It was clear to him that this approach was in keeping with Christian doctrine which he also considered, and he reproaches himself for turning first to the pagan philosopher and only secondly to religious authority. The combination of the two might seem conclusive but they were only one side of a dialectic, the other represented by unnamed, secular 'philosophers of court'. It is significant that he gives these figures the dignity of being 'philosophers', of equal dignity to the Greek thinkers and the traditional theologians, and not merely courtiers or gossips. The very choice of the term 'philosophers of court' suggests that his instinct was to weigh the argument in their favour. They held that honour should have the upper hand, and that honour should be defended by military means. The consequence was that while if he followed Plato, Casanova would also establish himself as a good Christian, he would at the same time and by the same act be 'dishonoured and despised, not to say driven from the court and from noble assemblies with contempt'.

What a dilemma for a gentleman of Casanova's stamp and ambition! But it expressed a sharply felt problem for many men over the succeeding century, torn between Biblical commandments and the edicts of the honour code. It was of no help to him to realize that in England a man who has uttered an offensive word may be summonsed to court and if he fails to prove his case, the offender and not the victim is ruined, for that is not the situation elsewhere. Still prevaricating, he turned to Cicero who helped him see in a different context the enigmatic judgment of the Prince Palatine. In Casanova's interpretation, Cicero believed that in general a mediator should know what a man who seeks his counsel wants, but these Ciceronian words had to be set against those of Rousseau, whom Casanova had met, and who conveniently believed that the real criminal is not the one who kills but the one who had in the first place compelled him to kill.

As the night wore on Casanova was - if his account is reliable - left in an intellectual, moral and social quandary. He had had recourse to a remarkable gallery of renowned thinkers in the western tradition, and if his hesitation has few resonances today, his wariness is an expression of a dilemma which faced men of culture in those and later times when they found themselves reflecting on duelling, or even considering 'calling out' a miscreant and requiring him to attend the field of honour. However alien the choice seems to later generations, for Casanova and many others two sets of valid demands stood in opposition: the Ten Commandments which included the precept Thou Shalt not Kill, and the contemporary expectations of a gentleman's behaviour and standing. He found himself in the situation of St Augustine when he prayed for purity, 'but not yet', even if Casanova expressed the second pressure on him in material rather than ethical terms. Philosophy was an abstract pastime, he concluded, while he aspired to ease, comfort, luxury and the respect of the ruling classes. He regretted the 'damned pride' which governed human affairs, but concluded that while philosophy might deplore 'the malignity of human nature', the fact was 'those who wished to adhere to its maxims would be constrained to live anywhere but at court'. And he knew where he aspired to live. The implicit philosophy/court choice offers a significant glance into Casanova's private world, and helps clarify the mentality of many other professing Christians who took part in duels. He was no crude hypocrite and certainly no atheist but when faced with a clash between the sacred and the profane, he preferred the profane. He knew he ought to be motivated by transcendent considerations but, like Macbeth, he found himself prepared to 'jump the life to come'. A sybarite attracted by luxury and power, he had no doubt where he wished to spend his days.

The pamphlet *Il duello* is in part a narrative of unfolding events but also an apologia for actions which Casanova could never be certain were wholly justifiable. He complimented himself on his moderation in not behaving like a 'barbaric man' who upon receiving an offence would immediately strike out, perhaps killing his adversary but not exposing himself to any risk. This point was of primary importance in the ethical framework of the gentleman. The moderate, civilized man restrains such impulses, stands back, takes stock and acts in conformity with the rational standards of the code of honour, and in this context that implies that he must issue a life-or-death challenge, one where two men will meet on an equal footing. Casanova's mind was made up. If there was no nobility in felling an adversary who had not been alerted, there was a decency in giving due notice and running risks oneself. That was the nature of the honour code and the *code duello*, and no other writer before or after so clearly spelled out its paradoxes, contradictions and dilemmas. He drafted a *cartello* for Branicki, but cautiously couched it in terms which, he believed, reduced his risk of legal consequences in a land where duelling was outlawed and punishable by death. The tone was courteous but accusatory. Branicki was guilty of an offence which gave Casanova grounds for concluding that his adversary hated him and wished to see him expelled from the earth. Casanova was happy to accommodate him in this wish, and so requested Branicki to accompany him to some spot where the law did not prohibit duelling. His concluding words were: 'I would not make this proposal, Monseigneur, had I not formed some idea of your generosity.'

Branicki replied within half an hour in similarly dignified tones, accepting the challenge and inviting his rival to state when he would have the honour of meeting him. The 'laconic nobility' of this reply impressed Casanova and set him reflecting on Branicki's state of mind and his presumed manly qualities. Was Branicki afraid that he in his turn might appear cowardly to Casanova? Was he worried that the challenger underestimated him, and was scoffing at him? But then perhaps the fact of issuing the challenge suggested to Branicki that Casanova was endowed with real courage, meaning that Branicki had a 'religious duty' to offer satisfaction. How flexible is the concept of religion! Both men were convinced that they were duty-bound to comply not only with the other's demands but also with the requirements of religion and honour, even if these obligations were subject to a delicacy of interpretation which would not have been out of place in a medieval monk's cell.

After due consideration, Casanova replied that he would present himself the following morning at Branicki's residence. He received a further communication to the effect that a delay of even one day was unconscionable and that Branicki wished Casanova to come immediately to choose weapons and venue. This was a deviation from standard practice, which would normally have left time for both sides to appoint a second and to put their affairs in order. In consequence, Casanova demurred and insisted that the meeting should take place the following day. He said he had some material to send to the king, a last will and testament to prepare, and, grotesquely for a man possibly facing his last day on earth, some medicines to take. As to the arms, he preferred the sword.

He had taken to his bed when to his astonishment Count Branicki turned up in person. Casanova reproduces what he claims to be the dialogue between the two men, and while his Memoirs make it clear that he was gifted with remarkable powers of memory, there must be a question over how much of the exchange was recalled and how much invented. The dialogue is a verbal *pas de deux*, conducted with a theatrical sharpness of wit worthy of Beaumarchais. Courtesy is maintained, as laid down by the protocols of honour and the etiquette of mutual gentlemanly respect. There are no outbursts of rage, no loss of self-control, no overt contempt much less enmity between the two. The words are calm and reflective, as though each was afraid of deviating from courtly standards. Branicki wonders if Casanova was jeering at him with his initial letter, drawing the hurt response: 'How could you think such a thing! I have the greatest respect for your person.' He pointed out that Italy had taught 'skill and civil manners' to Poland, and that he held Branicki in such esteem that he would travel one hundred leagues on foot to meet him. Branicki affected a lordly disdain for life and death, since 'a duel is a mere bagatelle'. As to timing, they came to an accommodation, with Casanova giving way and agreeing to meet the following afternoon, but continued to differ over weapons. Casanova claimed right of choice, which was questionable, and preferred the sword, but Branicki objected on the grounds that he did not know Casanova, who might be a master swordsman. When he made no headway he changed tack and appealed to Casanova to give way 'as a favour to a friend'. Casanova was briefly lost for words, and regarded this as a low blow. He objected to pistols on the seemingly odd ground that they were 'too dangerous' and added that with swords one or the other might desist after drawing first blood, an option not available given the unreliability of pistols. Behind the discussion between the two men lay a centuries-old, learned debate over the admissibility in duelling of that vile modern device, the gun, and over whether a duel worthy of the name need necessarily to be fought to the death. Casanova again yielded and since he was equipped only with dress pistols, Branicki promised to provide the appropriate duelling pistols. He then offered his hand, and assured Casanova that after the duel they would be 'good friends'. The count agreed to pick up Casanova in his carriage the following day so that they could travel together to the appointed place.

Casanova decided that a sumptuous meal with a bottle of Burgundy was in order, and he called on two young knights of his acquaintance to share his food and drink. A reconstruction of the conversation would task the imagination of a dramatist, but it is reasonable to believe that Casanova was in a relaxed mood. He was later shocked to discover that Branicki used the time to attend Mass and make his confession.

The appointed place was the estate of the Baron von Brühl in Wola, a village outside Warsaw, the historical site of the election of kings during the days of the Polish-Lithuanian Commonwealth. It was believed to be outside the legal jurisdiction of Warsaw, meaning that the victor would not be liable to the legal penalties for duelling. The king's adjutant-general had been brought along under false pretences, but he did his duty in inviting the two men to find a reconciliation. He was overruled and the two stood face to face 'ten geometric paces' apart. Casanova invited his adversary to fire first, but he dallied a few seconds, which meant that both fired simultaneously, each wounding the other. Casanova's wound to his left hand was not life-threatening, but Branicki fell to the ground. The bullet had entered his rib cage, but missed his vital organs. Casanova ran to his assistance, but two of Branicki's henchmen, including Biszewski, in defiance of all the rules of chivalry, ran towards him with their sabres drawn and would have cut him down had not Branicki himself intervened with the shout which Casanova quotes in French, *'canaille, respectez ce cavalier'* (villains, respect this knight). Those words, uttered in such extreme circumstances, express the deepest essence of the code of honour and of the gentleman. Respect was Casanova's due, even if he had left his opponent at death's door. Posterity can only watch in amazement.

Branicki, as would happen after many other duels, showed concern for the man who had wounded him and advised him to flee, since he could not vouch for the conduct of his followers. Casanova records that he kissed Branicki on the forehead and fled, stopping a passing sledge and paying the driver to take him to the city, where he found refuge in a Franciscan friary. There the nobility of Poland, who had no high opinion of Branicki, flocked to visit him, but the danger had not passed. The king sent a message pardoning Casanova for participating in a duel and so rescinding for him the crime he had committed under Polish law, but not everyone behaved with due restraint or gentlemanly dignity. According to Casanova, there was an outcry and a state of general anarchy in Warsaw. It had been bruited abroad that Casanova had killed Branicki, so soldiers of his regiment were now prowling the streets searching for the killer of their commander. Meanwhile Biszewski went on a rampage and, being convinced that the unfortunate Tomatis was hiding Casanova, went to his residence to demand that he be handed over to him. Tomatis pleaded ignorance, but Biszewski disbelieved him, drew out a pistol, shot at his head but missed. He turned his attention to a Count Moscynski who made an attempt to pacify him, but who was slashed from the forehead to the lower lip for his pains. Biszewski then pointed his gun at another aristocratic bystander, taking him hostage until he reached his horse. It has often been written that the underpinnings of civilization are slender and weak, and that each generation is equidistant from the jungle. The codes of the duel may be observed with finesse and polish, but they are a step towards barbarity, liable to unleash animal forces.

The two protagonists themselves continued to behave with knightly decorum, sending messengers each day to enquire after the other's health. Casanova's main task continued to be justifying his conduct in his own eyes in the light of his, genuine if highly adaptable, Christian conscience, and he dedicates a few perplexing, abstruse pages in *Il duello* to this issue. He was puzzled when he found out that Branicki had gone to Mass and made his confession before setting off with the duelling pistols, and wondered how, since he was about to take part in an exercise which could have ended in an act of murder, he could have received valid absolution from a priest. He was baffled by Branicki's conscience as well as by the priest's willingness to give absolution for what could only have been a 'falsely obtained confession' since there was no possibility of the necessary 'firm purpose of amendment'. Later observers will be equally confused by Casanova's own state of mind and his attempts to reconcile the practice of duelling with the Christian ethic and the dictates of the Church which excommunicated anyone guilty of duelling.

It is clear, though, that if Casanova was perplexed in the abstract, he suffered no pangs of guilt and certainly entertained no doubts over his own purity of soul. He expressed his belief in his own guiltlessness in a contorted prayer he had made before the duel begging God not to allow him to be killed instantly before he had time to repent for what he was doing, since immediate death without repentance would have seen him condemned to hell for all eternity. He was conscious that this prayer was 'absurd and contradictory' since he had every intention of going through with the act for which he needed forgiveness, but he made the prayer nonetheless.

However, as he delved more deeply post factum into his mind and conscience, he began to have second thoughts about the nature of the act he had committed, and to wonder whether it did in fact constitute a duel. He was fortunate to find a Jesuit at his most Jesuitical to confirm him in his belief in his own sinlessness. His opening gambit in his dialogue with the priest, in the face of evidence and common sense, was that he had not fought a duel at all. Of course the two men met on the field of honour, had fired at each other, had received wounds, but Casanova insisted that he had acted in self-defence, and that self-defence made his actions justifiable and placed them in a different category from a duel. 'I was attacked and I defended myself,' he stated, and so he declined to accept the sacrament of confession since there had been no duel and hence no sin. The Jesuit was left in a dilemma as the absolution could only be administered to someone who goes through the verbal act of confessing, but together they came up with a compromise formula. Casanova agreed to the formula of words: 'If it was a duel, I beg for your absolution, and I beg for nothing from you if it was not.' This satisfied both parties. Casanova added that 'the Jesuits are admirable at finding subterfuges to suit any occasion.' As was Casanova himself.

His health was still a cause for concern and medical opinion was that he would require to have his hand amputated, but he indignantly refused and to the amazement of all the danger of gangrene was averted. He actually went to visit Branicki whose wounds were more severe, and the two chatted amiably. Casanova was lionized in Warsaw for two months and dined at the best tables. He was gratified to find that the case had been reported in the press all over Europe, even commanding some columns in the *London Public Advertiser*. Regrettably from his own point of view, he then made the mistake of going off to the provinces on an extended tour, and when he returned, he found that the climate had changed as a result, he believed, of malicious gossip and the circulation of anonymous letters. He found all doors closed to him, including that of Branicki, although the two remained on good terms. The king ordered him to leave Poland within a week, which he did but only after collecting sufficient funds to discharge the debts he had accumulated during his sojourn in Poland. He concluded his own account of his duel and of those days in Poland by declaring that nothing he had done or written could bring into doubt 'the dutiful reflections of a Christian man'.

1 Giacomo Casanova, *Il duello*, first edition, 1780; edition used, Genoa: ECIG, 1991; *The Duel*, translated by J.G. Nichols, with Foreword by Tim Parks, London: Hesperus Press, 1990. Casanova gave another account of the event in his *Histoire de ma vie*, vol. 10, chapter 6, Paris: Librairie Plon, 1961. A translation of the relevant section is given in *The Duel*, pp. 67-108. The translations from *Il duello* are mine, unless otherwise indicated.
2 hn Masters, *Casanova*, London: Michael Joseph, 1969, p. 227. 'The Leads' was the name given to the prison contained close to the Doge's Palace.
3 J. Rives Childs, *Casanova, A New Perspective,* London: Constable, 1989.
4 *Ibid*, p. 104.
5 Quoted by Nichols, *op. cit.*, p. 67.

2

Birth of a Tradition

Single Combat, Joust and Tournament

The word 'duel' is a combination of two Latin terms, *duo* and *bellum*, making a duel an act of warfare involving only two adversaries. In the modern age, the word first appeared in Italian as *duello*, and was used in that Italianate form throughout Europe after the Renaissance when Europe was in thrall to Italian habits of mind and social customs. The origins of the duel are complex, and the nature of single combat, as well as the motivations of the combatants, has varied down the centuries in accordance with society's prevailing beliefs. The western mind and imagination are a tangled residue of overlapping moral, cultural, political and religious elements from which at different points in history one strand may be pulled to give intellectual support for habits, practices and developments which are otherwise bereft of sense or justification. Men, individually or in tribal groups, have from the earliest times faced each other in struggles over resources, women, land or food, but only as civilization progressed did they feel the need for some ethos to make this conduct take on the elaborate trappings of civility. In some writings in the late Middle Ages and in many treatises in the Renaissance, that ethos took the form of a cult of honour, as will be discussed in a later chapter.

Males have always been spurred by competitiveness or self-assertion and prone to blow their bugle and to war over gold or reputation, or over matters whose importance was visible only to the participants. Some distinction was made in every creed between ritual combat and respect for the martial virtues on the one hand, and precipitate brawls or mere hooliganism on the other. The distinction lay in the respect of the former for recognized rules as against the lack of restraint and self-control of the latter, and this is true of the boxer or wrestler as much as of the samurai, the duellist or the jousting knight. The brawl was for hoi polloi, who were moved by lower instincts, unlike the samurai, the knight or the gentleman, who respected honour and the martial virtues. This self-serving hierarchy of values was often undermined in practice and is open to criticism in principle, but it was an article of faith of the gentlemen we wish to discuss here.

The duel was unknown in ancient Greece and Rome, although ingenious efforts were made to find precedents in the Bible or in Greco-Roman mythology, the twin sources of the western tradition. When William Caxton drew up his list of those he regarded as fit for the pantheon of heroes, three were from ancient history - Hector, Alexander the Great and Julius Caesar - three from the Old Testament - Joshua, David and Judas Maccabeus - and three from medieval sources - King Arthur, Charlemagne and Godfrey of Bouillon. All played a part in the foundation mythology of the duel. Combat between gladiators in amphitheatres around the Roman Empire belonged to a different mental and political world, and will not feature here. There were two episodes recorded in the Old Testament which could plausibly be presented as duels, but they were open to different interpretations. The first was the dispute between Cain and his brother Abel, ending with the primal act of fratricide. While it may have been more an act of homicide than of duelling, defenders of the *code duello* seized on the fact that in issuing his challenge Cain used words remarkably similar to the standard formula employed by duellists. The translation from the Greek, if not the Hebrew, reads, 'Let us go to the field', a formula easily made equivalent to the challenge to meet on the field of honour. Enthusiastic exegetes made much of the fact that after Cain had slain his brother, and in spite of the fact that he lied to God about the killing, God showed himself remarkably indulgent. Cain was made a 'fugitive and wanderer' on earth but had inscribed on his forehead what was known as the 'mark of Cain', which was not a curse but God's order that no man should touch Cain. Thus the killer himself would not pay for his crime, if it was a crime.

The encounter between David and Goliath was the event most frequently cited by champions of the duel when asked to provide moral, or at least Biblical, backing for single combat. David represented his own people in a struggle with the overbearing neighbours, the Philistines, and with the two armies facing each other, the giant Goliath came forward to jeer at the Israelites over their failure to name a champion to face him man to man. Saul, as recorded in the Book of Samuel, declined the challenge, thus showing himself to be cowardly and, it is implied, inadequate both as king and as a man. The boy David came forward and offered to accept the challenge, even refusing to wear the armour Saul offered him. He took up his sling, picked five pebbles from a stream and with the first shot struck Goliath on the forehead, bringing him down. David then rushed forward to decapitate his opponent. The outcome was of particular value to defenders of the medieval 'judicial duel' since the victory of the weaker party was viewed as an instance of divine intervention in history on the side of right and justice. It provided an overwhelming, if also convenient, refutation of the argument that the victor in any duel was likely to be the more militarily experienced or physically stronger party. God had shown himself willing to stand alongside the weaker party and ensure his triumph.

The epics of Homer and Virgil gave ample, vivid accounts not only of battles but of single combat between heroes. Before the siege of Troy was properly underway, Menelaus challenged Paris to a single combat and the initially fearful Paris was shamed by Hector into accepting. In the ensuing duel Menelaus knocked him to the ground, but paused before delivering the final blow, a hesitation which allowed Aphrodite, who was still in debt to Paris for selecting her ahead of Athena and Hera as the most beautiful of the goddesses, to snatch Paris and carry him off to safety inside the city walls. Paris was thus not the ideal hero, but the clash between the two dramatizes the confrontation between glory and cowardice. This duel was also a fight over a woman, and there would be many such in subsequent history. Menelaus had the dignity of a hero, but Paris was a more ambiguous figure, a lover who was also somewhat effeminate, and an example to be shunned.

There were better models, like Hector, who slew Protesilaus on the plains of Troy, then killed Patroclus and finally, heedless of the loving pleas of Andromache, his wife, went out to face the Greek hero of heroes, Achilles. This encounter ended badly for him, in part because Achilles had the advantage of the divine assistance of Athena, who had the power to make herself invisible and was thus enabled during the duel to pass back to Achilles spears he had hurled but which had fallen short of the target. The triumph of Achilles was thus almost inevitable, but he too deviated worryingly from the code of the duel, firstly in his failure to accept equality of odds and secondly in his refusal to act honourably and accept the dying Hector's plea that traditional funeral rites be celebrated over his body. He dragged Hector's corpse arounds the walls of Troy, the final act of contempt and humiliation. The duel of Aeneas and Diomedes in the *Aeneid* was frequently quoted, even here too if each had the backing of a goddess, a feature of life not easily replicated. Artists from Renaissance to Victorian times depicted all these figures as stirring models of men who showed their mettle against individual adversaries.

The struggle between Menelaus and Paris had another ramification which was cited on several occasions in history. The two leaders met face to face before the armies clashed and had Paris been slain, the Trojan War might have been averted. Livy records such an event in pseudo-history, when Rome was still ruled by a king and war loomed between the city and Alba

Longa. Centuries later the French painter David depicted the historical moment in his grand painting, the *Oath of the Horatii*. The monarchs agreed that pitched battle between the two armies would leave both cities fatally weakened, and reached the compromise that two sets of triplets, the Roman Horatii and the Curatii from Alba Longa, would meet to settle the dispute. All three Curatii were wounded but two of the Roman brothers were killed. The survivor feigned flight and was pursued by the three men, but they ran at different speeds and so caught up with him at different times. He slaughtered them one by one, averting war and setting Rome on the path to imperial greatness. Plutarch records a similar event which has greater historical authenticity. Mark Antony, admittedly when he was aware he was losing the civil war with Octavian, challenged his adversary to single combat to resolve the matter without further loss of Roman life. Octavian declined the offer, telling Mark Antony that there were other ways by which he could die if that was his choice.

Age of the Joust

The medieval period was reassessed or re-imagined in 1919 by Johan Huizinga in his classic work, *The Waning of the Middle Ages*. He explained the title of his opening chapter, 'The Violent Tenor of Life', by writing that 'so violent and motley was life that it bore the mixed smell of blood and roses. The men of that time always oscillate between ... cruelty and tenderness, between hatred and goodness, always running to extremes.'[1] This judgment has a romantic flavour, and throughout his work Huizinga gives the impression that in the medieval period, even in the twilight phase which he takes as his subject, violence was in the air, whether in some strictly ritualized form or in more intemperate outbursts. Our concern is not with random brawls but only with certain standardized forms of combat, which in those Middle Ages meant above all the tournament and the joust, contests which were celebrated and justified by the mores of the age and which, by having precise protocols at their heart mark a definite stage in the development of the duel.

The joust, or proto-duel as it will be convenient to designate it, takes on two principal and distinct forms: the chivalric and the judicial, the latter including both trial by ordeal and trial by combat. The judicial duel was conceived as a means of attaining justice and righting a supposed or genuine wrong. The omnipresence and universal beneficence of God were unquestioned verities for the medieval mind, and so, in spite of evidence of the contrary, it was the most basic of all assumptions that God, as he had shown in the case of David and Goliath, could not stand by and allow malice to triumph in a combat. God's judgment could be ascertained by trial by combat but also by trial by ordeal, where ordeals included dipping a hand in boiling water, clutching a red-hot iron or walking over burning coals but showing no sign of harm. If God failed to intervene to work a miracle on behalf of an accused person, his guilt was taken as established. It was also possible for an accused person to request trial by combat either by undertaking the combat in person or by appointing a champion to undertake the struggle on their behalf. This kind of combat was unavoidable when the accused person was female.

The knightly joust was a later innovation, conceived as sport, and its appeal rested on the opportunity it gave to display manliness, to enhance individual prestige and, above all, to demonstrate the possession of honour. It can be seen as a precursor of the gentleman's duel of honour. During the period discussed by Huizinga, tournaments which featured knightly jousts became public festivals of aristocratic sport. They enjoyed legal status and were, at least most of the time, encouraged by royalty. The lower orders were barred from participating but were enthusiastic spectators, as were ladies, whether as queen for the day or as occupants of special pavilions lining the closed field. There is evidence of the lower clergy attending and giving their blessing to individual knights at arms, but it has to be added that there were condemnations issued by ecclesiastical hierarchies at different times in different countries, and even bans forbidding tournaments proclaimed by the Church and by some sovereigns concerned at the number of knightly casualties and fearful of the diversion of energy from the central martial interests of the age, the Crusades above all. These ecclesiastical or political vetoes had a short life span and were commonly disregarded even when supposedly in force.

In its earliest incarnation, the tournament, which seems to have emerged in a recognizable form sometime between the late eleventh and the early twelfth century, was a kind of mini-battle involving great detachments of knights, at times running into the hundreds, often arbitrarily allocated on arrival to one side or the other. The image of the knight errant was not pure legend, and there are accounts of young noblemen travelling considerable distances, even across national boundaries, to attend and participate in tournaments. The origins of the word tournament are disputed, but it may well be associated with the French verb *tourner*, to turn, the motion required of mounted knights in a defined space when they reached one boundary and turned their horses back to charge at the opposing squadron and engage in the melee, another term dating from that period. The melee was a free-for-all which by its nature could not be controlled, although there were attempts to define the type of weapon whose use was permitted.

The tournament embodies something of the confusion of ideals and practice, and of the push to extremes Huizinga speaks of.[2] At its heart lay a celebration of manliness in the form of ritualized violence ennobled by grand pageantry. The display of heraldry, the train of squires and pages, the lushly decorated aristocratic pavilions, the punctilious preparation of the lists on the designated field, the election of the Queen of Beauty and Love, the parade of the knights in armour, some ostentatiously displaying some token of his lady's esteem, all as a prelude to the final clash of arms must have been a colourful, stirring spectacle and was well worthy of the narration and celebration it received in the poetry of the day. Contemporary chronicles record some unexpected outcomes. In the reign of James IV of Scotland a 'Moorish lass' who had been captured on board a Portuguese privateer and brought as a prisoner to the royal court had the honour of being made lady of 'the tournament of the black knight'. She was won by the king himself after his success in jousts.[3]

There were several well-documented occasions in the Middle Ages when monarchs issued a challenge to their enemy counterparts to settle disputes. King Louis VI of France, irreverently known as Louis the Fat, challenged Henry I of England to single combat on a bridge over a stream with the armies lined up on either side, but Henry declined. Sicily had been in a state of permanent turmoil ever since the death of Frederick II in 1250. The House of Anjou eventually took power but the Sicilians rebelled against their French overlords in the Sicilian Vespers, which led to the war of succession between Charles of Anjou and Peter III of Aragon, causing Peter in 1283 to challenge his rival to meet him in single combat in Bordeaux, with one hundred soldiers on either side. Terms were agreed and Edward I of England was invited to adjudicate, but he refused. The two kings turned up on different days and both claimed victory. Lordship in Sicily was settled on more conventional battlefields. In 1340, in the early days of the Hundred Years War, Edward III made a similar offer to Philip VI to fight either 'body to body' or with a force of one hundred on either side, but again the combat did not take place. Later in the same war, Richard II, a more astute ruler than Shakespeare's depiction of him has transmitted to history, challenged his French counterpart, Charles VI, to a duel which would decide under God their competing claims to the French and English thrones. This challenge too was declined, but like the others, while there was a state issue at stake, it has the savour of a judicial duel rather than a trial of strength. Both parties were convinced of the justice of their cause and anticipated the support of the deity.

A tournament could include several jousts, which involved mounted knights charging at each other on either side of a tilt. To minimize the risk of bodily harm, 'arms of courtesy' were sometimes introduced, or else the heads of the spears were removed and swords blunted, but participants often incurred serious injury. Fatalities were common as excitement rose in the heat of battle. No doubt the tournament allowed for an outlet for aggressiveness in periods of relative peace, but certainly it was an activity for peace-time. In its heyday the tournament was a means by which aristocratic men could win glory, enhance their prestige, confirm their valour and above all increase honour, and it was of its essence a form of sport or entertainment. In this it differed from the judicial duel.

As it evolved, the joust came to constitute the central act of the tournament, and was fought for honour alone. It was a means of building a reputation, winning spurs, establishing a celebrity position in society, but it was also sport, muscular fun, courtly enjoyment. Although free men, knights in a joust had about them something of the gladiator, while for spectators the pleasure they derived must have been similar to what the Roman public experienced while attending the Colosseum, or Spaniards a *corrida*. An effete, perhaps phoney, appreciation

A nineteenth-century representation of a medieval tournament (Wikimedia Commons)

of technical expertise savoured at a safe distance from events where the highest of all risks are being taken has always provided violent voyeurism with balm for the conscience. The tournament was an arena for grand ceremonial and the event could last several days. After the opening celebration of mass, the younger knights were given the opportunity to parade in their finery before tilting at each other. The more experienced and famous knights entered the lists later. During the joust itself competitors had at their disposal more than one lance to permit several charges at the opponent if the first lance was broken.

The two opponents had to be of equal rank, and fairly matched in all other respects, a ruling which had curious consequences. In 1390, the Scottish knight Sir William of Dalyell, who had lost an eye at the Battle of Otterburn, attended with several other Scottish knights a grand tournament in London arranged by Richard II. The event was on a scale befitting royal patronage, with the queen seated in a specially constructed summer castle. The main event was a joust between Sir David de Lindsay and Sir John de Wells, and the fact that the chroniclers were Scots may account for the fact that they give prominence to accounts of a 'spiteful' rumour among the English lords that Sir David cheated by tying himself to his saddle. When he heard this, Lindsay leaped from his horse, bowed to the queen and, although dressed in full armour, sprang back onto his horse. In the resumed tilting he brought Wells down, and since this was a duel to the death, he would have been entitled to kill his defenceless opponent. However, Lindsay helped Wells to his feet and escorted him to the queen's throne.[4]

Meanwhile Dalyell became embroiled in a dispute with one Sir Peris Corteney, which ended up with a challenge being issued and accepted. Corteney had been parading around with a falcon embroidered on his surcoat with a scroll in his beak threatening death to anyone who disrespected him. Dalyell had a surcoat speedily made with a magpie whose words were a threat to peck the nose of anyone who came near him. This exchange was deemed of sufficient gravity to require satisfaction by armed duel. There was a problem of parity under the laws of chivalry, however, and the wily Dalyell appealed to the king to have one of Corteney's eyes gouged out to render the two champions equal. The demand was not as absurd as it may now appear. Two centuries later, in his authoritative work *Of Honour and Honourable Quarrels*, Vincentio Saviolo debated the question of whether one knight might have his leg or arm bound if he was facing an opponent with a disability of that sort, and extended his reflections to the rights of a one-eyed knight. He did not reach any firm conclusion. King Richard dismissed Dalyell's claim, but agreed the duel should be abandoned and remarked that Dalyell had demonstrated the superior wit of the Scots.[5]

Chivalry

The governing code in these events was chivalry, a short-hand term for a legion of medieval ideals and for contemporary hypotheses, surmises, approximations, conjectures, contentions and interpretations. This is not to say that the age of chivalry was always dead, or that its code was always false and fictitious, but it is to admit that the hierarchy of values and virtues which lay at its heart were visionary and utopian and in consequence rarely attained. It is easy to launch accusations of hypocrisy against medieval Christian knights when confronted with their behaviour during the Crusades and elsewhere, but war puts humanity in extreme conditions, and the attempt to impose humane standards in warfare has challenged law-makers from the Middle Ages to the Geneva Convention. Chivalry was a pan-European ideal, and among its many precepts and principles, which applied to a range of manners and standards across a wide spectrum of life, were those governing behaviour towards ladies, conduct in war, treatment of enemies as well as of opponents in jousting. The two most authoritative manifestos, or discussions of chivalry, were produced by John of Salisbury in one section of his *Policraticus* (c1159) and Ramon Llull with his *Llibre de l'orde de cavalleria* (c1275/6), written in Catalan.[6] Both men saw chivalry as laying down a code of decent conduct in society as well as on the field of battle, and both saw chivalry as having its origins in Christian belief. Llull decreed that an aspiring knight should spend the night before his initiation in prayer in a chapel. The knight was required to display three characteristics: to be a defender of the Church and the faith, a loyal servant of the established hierarchy, and a protector of the weak, such as widows, orphans and the elderly. Llull differed from John on the one crucial point that while Llull saw no incompatibility between the knightly, Christian ideals and participation in sporting tournaments, John saw the popularity of such events as a symptom of decadence.[7] Both agreed that at the core of the chivalric code there should lie a notion of honour, an ideal which would be refined and would inform European, predominantly male, aspirations over the coming centuries.

The spectacle of two champions demonstrating their prowess against each other beguiled the medieval mind and appealed to readers and to the spectators who gathered at tournaments. The clashes narrated in the eleventh-century Carolingian romance *La Chanson de Roland* are complex and enriched with that indulgence in hyperbole, grandiloquence and grandiosity of deed and narration which are the marks of the genre. The names of Roland and Oliver (or Olivier) have entered the language of several European countries as an instance of perfectly balanced, competing forces, each with right on his side. In the epic, it is recorded that Charlemagne was outraged at an act of disrespect shown him by Count Gerard, and set out at the head of an army to teach him manners by storming his castle at Vienne. After months, or possibly years - there is some uncertainty on the chronology - of unsuccessful siege warfare, the rival leaders decide that single combat between two champions is the most efficient means of resolving the issue. Roland, the nephew of Charlemagne, is selected to engage Oliver, a representative of Count Gerard. Love, sex and Romeo-and-Juliet gallantry are added to the mix, as Alda, the beautiful sister of Oliver, and Roland fall in love with each other across the lines. The two knights meet on an island, a frequently chosen venue for duels imaginary and real, but after a period of five hours - or five days in some accounts - of jousting with lances, breaking shields, fighting with swords, even exchanging blows, the two decide that neither man would ever prevail and call an honourable truce, each one expressing respect and comradeship for the other. They remain close friends for the rest of their days, as happened not infrequently in the history of the duel as well as in fiction. Alda and Roland are wed, while Roland and Oliver fight together against the Saracen and die together at the battle of Roncesvalles.

This rout of the Franks and the death of the two heroes at Roncesvalles were the cause of a quite different duel between Pinabel and Thierry which occupies the concluding sections of the *Chanson*. The former was a friend of Ganelon, who along with Judas, Brutus and Alcibiades became one of Europe's great traitor figures. On his return to his palace with the bodies of those who had fallen in battle, Charlemagne summoned a court to decide who was guilty of the act of treachery which left his army exposed. Ganelon accepted his responsibility but pleaded in his own defence that he was motivated not by treacherous feeling but by a desire for revenge since Roland had offended him. This singular defence carried some weight and the nobles were unsure whether he deserved death. A joust was obviously the only way to settle the dispute and Pinabel offered to defend Ganelon against any accusers. Thierry of Anjou, although the youngest of the knights, accepted the challenge to prove Ganelon's guilt. Pinabel was defeated and killed in the first clash of the lances, meaning that Ganelon's guilt was established. He was condemned to be executed not with knightly dignity but being pulled apart by four horses. His torments did not end there for Dante placed him in the freezing lake in the lowest circle of hell, suffering the punishments reserved for the treacherous.

The duels in Chrétien de Troyes' later *Yvain, the Knight of the Lion* combine some of the characteristics of judicial trial with the newer knightly trial of prowess. Yvain leaves home for an agreed period of one year to allow him to seek adventures as knight errant, but overstays his licensed time, and even suffers a period of madness. He comes across a lion under attack by a dragon, intervenes on the lion's side and cuts the dragon in two, thereby winning the devotion of the lion who follows him back to his castle. During his absence Lunete, his wife's maid, has been accused of adultery by three men and condemned to be burned at the stake, unless some champion can be found to defend her good name. Fortunately Yvain makes his return in time to offer his services and vanquishes all three opponents, who suffer the fate they have demanded for the maiden. In spite of the not inconsiderable advantage of the assistance of Yvain's pet lion, Chrétien explicitly concludes that the outcome shows the operation of divine justice.

The issue is muddier in another of Chrétien's romances, *Lancelot*. Guinevere, the wife of King Arthur, and Lancelot are among the most celebrated adulterers in history but Lancelot goes to great lengths to defend her undeserved reputation for purity of mind and body. She is accused of adultery by Sir Meliagaunt, who has seen blood on her sheets, and there is indeed blood there but it is that of the governor of the castle who was being treated for an injury. This excuse is not credited, but Lancelot knows it is true because he himself has been the occupant of Guinevere's bed on the night in question. Meliagaunt doggedly pursues the case, which means that he and Lancelot have to confront each other, which ends with Lancelot splitting his opponent's head in two. There are later difficulties created by Lancelot and Guinevere's long-standing affair. A group of righteous knights force their way into the royal bedroom to find the pair *in flagrante*, but Lancelot manages to fight his way out, leaving Guinevere to face the music. She is condemned to the stake, but her gallant knight return to fight on her behalf and rescue her. Alfred Lord Tennyson authored *Idylls of the King*, a cycle of poems on the Arthurian knights of the round table, but while he was at ease in describing the death of Arthur or the feats of Galahad, whose 'good blade carves the casks of men' and whose 'tough lance thrusteth sure', he had to bowdlerize his portrayal of Lancelot and Guinevere for a Victorian audience.

Dante Gabriel Rossetti, *Sir Launcelot in the Queen's Chamber*, 1857, Birmingham Museum and Art Gallery (Wikimedia Commons)

A quite different tale of a more heroic King Arthur is recounted by Geoffrey of Monmouth, which has the king, having pacified all Britain, set his eyes on Gaul, still part of the Roman Empire and governed by Frollo. Arthur routed the Gallic forces and pursued his foe all the way back to Paris where, in an echo of the Horatii, he issued a challenge to Frollo to meet him personally on an island in the Seine. There Frollo was defeated and killed, and on the spot of his triumph Arthur founded the church which became Notre Dame. There is, admittedly, some dry-as-dust dispute among architectural historians over the accuracy of this poetic account of the foundation of the cathedral, but Geoffrey gave the people what they wanted, always a guarantee of success in fiction.

1 Johan Huizinga, *The Waning of the Middle Ages*, London: Penguin, 1968, p. 25.
2 David Crouch, *Tournament*, London: Hambledon and London, 2003, p. 3.
3 Jennifer Melville, www.nts.org.uk/stories/africans-at-the-court-of-james-iv
4 George Neilson, *Trial by Combat* (first edition 1890), Clark, NJ: The Lawbook Exchange, 2009, p. 235.
5 Documents on Dalyell family, Motherwell Heritage Centre; Neilson, *op. cit.*, pp. 232-7.
6 John of Salisbury, edited by Cary J. Nederman, *Policratus*, Cambridge: Cambridge University Press, 1990; Ramon Llull, edited by Marina Gustà, *Llibre de l'orde de cavalleria*, Barcelona: Edicions 62.
7 Llull, *op. cit.*, pp. 21-2.

3

THE COURTIER AND THE KNIGHT THE RENAISSANCE

In his classic study, *The Civilization of the Renaissance in Italy*, Jacob Burckhardt did more than any previous writer to establish the Renaissance as a precise, self-contained period in European history with a distinct culture and philosophy of life. He chose to focus not on the great artists of the age but on the 'development of the individual' at a time when 'man became a spiritual individual and recognized himself as such', unlike previous ages when 'man was conscious of himself only as a member of a race, people, party, family, or corporation.'[1] This new man, this model human being, devoted time and study to questions of individual perfectibility and refinement, and to the traits of mind, character and conduct which marked the courtier, the forerunner of the gentleman, and differentiated him from lesser fellow beings. Ideas developed in Italy were of international interest at this time when all Europe looked there for inspiration not only in the arts but also in questions of manners and mores, especially as regards the conduct of the gentleman. In his introduction to the *Fairie Queen* (1590), Edmund Spencer stated that 'the general end [...] of all the book is to fashion a gentleman or noble person in virtuous and gentle discipline.' Italy was the finishing school for those who wished to acquire a grounding in notions of honour, culture and civilized living.

Burckhardt's work has had its critics, some of whom have questioned the very idea of a Renaissance as a disparate period and have suggested with varying levels of vitriol that the author should have looked fore and aft, should have taken a more nuanced view of the break between the medieval and Renaissance ages and given greater weight to a continuity of outlook, culture and philosophy embraced by figures on either side of the divide. Burckhardt's historical survey in fact opens in the early fourteenth century, earlier than the already imprecise date when the developments taken as typical of the Renaissance are normally assumed to have appeared. There is in any case no doubt that humanist thinkers themselves looked with some disdain on the preceding age, whose art Vasari termed Gothic or Byzantine, and always dismissed as crude. It was the humanist thinkers in the fifteenth century who coined the definition 'Middle Ages' to denote what they considered the arid, dark period between the glorious years of classical culture and its rebirth, or Renaissance, in the Quattrocento.

Italy's great artistic and cultural innovations and achievements in the period Burckhardt studied were developed not only in such cities as Florence or Rome but also in the country's many smaller courts and palaces, such as Urbino, Ferrara or Mantua. The political division of Italy with its proliferation of small statelets each with its own ruling family - something deplored as a weakness by Machiavelli when the country was threatened by foreign invaders - provided a multiplicity of forums for the patronage of artists and writers. Their polished debates and dialogues on art, manners and mores, on fashion and style, on politics, philosophy and notions of beauty set the tone for Europe in the fifteenth and sixteenth centuries. They also established new standards and a code of secular ethics, based above all on a sophisticated, reformed notion of honour.

The new ideals were elaborated in many tracts, treatises and primers, the most significant of which were *The Courtier* (1528) by Baldassare Castiglione and *Galateo* (1558) by Giovanni Della Casa,[2] which together laid the groundwork for a new civilization and the development of a wholly new style of civility. The prime aim of such works was to offer precepts on the social behaviour and individual qualities required of the men and women who frequented the courts of Italy, but they became the principal authority for the new culture of individual civility, courtesy, sophistication, gentility and taste. Although the writers did not neglect the role of women, and did not demote them to a wholly subservient position as is lazily believed, attention was focused firstly on the male and his rights and responsibilities.

Castiglione was a courtier in Urbino in the retinue of Federico da Montefeltro, himself a refined humanist, renowned soldier and *condottiere*, an elegant euphemism for mercenary. The new culture was not democratic but was aimed at a new elite, whose members were not permitted to be laggardly. Castiglione elaborated the ideals to be practised by the courtier, predecessor of the gentleman, a term that would only come into vogue in other countries in later centuries. The courtier was called on to master an impressive range of skills and achievements, and to be if not quite a universal man, at least an all-round master of many arts and skills. He was expected to have a good command of languages, show wit and learning but avoid scurrility, be well versed in letters, painting and sculpture, aim for the golden mean in all things, be a good dancer and sportsman where sport meant largely hunting, and above all display in all things grace and a quality Castiglione named *sprezzatura*, a term which defies wholly accurate translation but indicates a studied nonchalance. The new man was not permitted to be effete or precious, since he was required to have an advanced mastery of the arts of swordsmanship and warfare, and to be skilled in the more physical arts of wrestling, fencing and jousting, attributes which might be needed to serve his prince if the state were under attack, but also to defend himself and his honour. The question of the duel was a consequence of this need. Centuries later, Casanova would display these attributes in their highest form as he rode to his duel in Warsaw.

Della Casa was of like mind. In the opening chapter of *Galateo* a comparison is made between 'good manners' on the one hand, and 'heroic virtues' on the other, so his ideal man should possess a combination of civility and courage. In addition, the aspiring gentleman is told to make himself respected in the private sphere by showing mature judgement and by his demeanour in everyday actions. Deportment, posture, speech, gesture and elegance were hallmarks of elegant conduct. The gentleman should not fail to honour others when it is merited, but should avoid excessive adulation, should become the object of admiration but must avoid gossip or spreading scandal. There are some eccentricities in Della Casa's advice. The gentleman must refrain 'as far as possible from making noises which grate upon the ear, such as grinding or sucking teeth, making things squeak', and should 'take care not to sing, especially solo, if the voice is discordant or tuneless'. There were, in short, few occasions when a man could afford to drop his guard, and the necessary attributes included not only social skills but a mastery of martial qualities.

These attitudes are apparent not only in the treatises but in contemporary poetry, in lyrics and also in the epics, or mock epics, which celebrate knightly prowess and chivalric themes. Even if poetic duels are, generally, fought to the last blood, fantasy enlivens the adventures and tempers violent realism. Giants, monsters, female warriors, magicians, witches, flying horses, enchanted wells, flights to the moon, swords with magic powers, men protected by spells, superhuman knights capable of slicing opponents in two with one mighty blow are part of the drama. An undercurrent of sardonic mockery is noticeable, but it is not such as to totally undermine codes of chivalry, as the archpriest of raillery, Cervantes, would do. Some overlap between the medieval and the Renaissance poetics is undeniable, not least in the fact that the principal epic poets, Luigi Pulci (1432-84), Matteo Mario Boiardo (1441-96) and Ludovico Ariosto (1474-1553) paid homage to the France of Charlemagne and Roland in their narratives. Roland's name was Italianized to Orlando and many of the old tales were retold, even if there was a new emphasis on the power of love alongside the display of valour. At the same time, greater emphasis is placed on the role of the individual knight, so that narratives of the clash of great armies, of battles and warfare between Christian knights and Infidels are interspersed with episodes of single combat, of jousts and duels. It has been estimated that there are seventy such in Boiardo's *Orlando Innamorato* and thirty in Ariosto's *Orlando Furioso*, and it has even been proposed that 'the duel is the fundamental event in the plot of the chivalric romance as such.'[3] The prominence given to single combat at this decisive moment in cultural history helped pave the way for the duel in its later, fully developed form.

Even when on opposing sides, the knights and heroes in their view of themselves and of each other are imbued with the new code of civility and honour. *Orlando Innamorato* (Orlando in Love), written between 1483 and 1495, opens at the court of Charlemagne as a knightly tournament is underway, disrupted by the arrival of the fabulously beautiful Angelica, daughter of the King of Cathay. The fact that she is Saracen causes no upset. The valiant Frankish knights are left dumbstruck by her beauty, none more so than the two protagonists of the fable, Orlando and Rinaldo. Orlando wastes no time in advancing his suit, but Angelica counters by laying down her conditions. All claimants to her hand must engage her brother Argalia in single combat: if victorious he will win her hand, but if defeated he will be made her prisoner. Fair play was an unknown concept, and Argalia avails himself of the assistance of magic weapons, a force whose possible use worried contestants in actual judicial combats. He is successful in the first joust, but when his enchanted devices are stolen, he is pursued from the field and killed by his fellow Saracen knight, Ferrau. Angelica flees, pursued by several knights, including Orlando and Rinaldo who have previously been brothers in arms but are now rivals in love. Angelica stops in a forest to drink of a well which happens to be enchanted and whose water makes anyone who drinks of it fall in love with the next person they see, who in her case is none other than Rinaldo. As luck would have it, he has slaked his thirst in a fountain of hate, meaning that he has come to detest Angelica, who is now in love with him. After various twists and turns involving the magician Malagigi, who at Angelica's request seizes Rinaldo and takes him to his enchanted island, Orlando comes back on the scene and meets Rinaldo, who attempts to persuade him to return to Paris to help the beleaguered Charlemagne. The two cannot come to an agreement and engage on a new duel.

The poem was unfinished, and the themes and plots are taken up by Ariosto, who is also credited with coining the term 'humanism' to denote the new culture. His *Orlando Furioso* (The Madness of Orlando) of 1516 has the same cast of characters as Boiardo, and the same succession of jousts and single combats but with a more pronounced undercurrent of irony. It has often been noted that irony is a device for having it both ways, allowing the reader to indulge both in the straightforward delight of the stories and in the conviction of superiority over all this nonsense. Ariosto certainly faced both ways over questions of chivalry, both mocking it and exploiting its dramatic potential. Although both on the Christian side, Orlando and Rinaldo spend as much time fighting with each other over Angelica as they do warring with the enemy. They travel far but are diverted by calls to defend ladies previously unknown to them but to whom, as an act of chivalry, they offer their services as champions.

An illustration by Gustave Doré for a nineteenth-century edition of *Orlando Furioso* (Wikimedia Commons)

The most celebrated and instructive of these episodes is set in the 'Caledonian forest' where Rinaldo lands after a journey through many lands. He enquires of monks at a nearby abbey if there is some virtuous act to which he could lend his sword, and they recount the misfortunes of Ginevra, daughter of the King of Scotland, previously engaged to Ariodante but allegedly guilty of sexual impropriety with one Polinesso, Duke of Albany. Under the 'impious and severe law' of Scotland, any woman found guilty of such misconduct is condemned to die at the stake unless a champion can be found to defend her, while no punishment of any kind will be visited on the man involved. There was a lively debate in the Renaissance over the position of women, and Ariosto was very much a proto-feminist. Outraged at this injustice, Rinaldo sets off to champion her cause, but is distracted by the screams of another woman who is being assaulted by a man. He goes to her assistance, an incident which allows Ariosto to inveigh against man's inhumanity to woman and to wonder if anywhere in the animal kingdom such brutal conduct of male against female is ever to be found. The woman, named Dalinda, informs Rinaldo of the backstory: she was deeply in love with Polinesso, but he lusted after the chaste Ginevra. He persuaded Dalinda to aid him in a dire plot which will see him tell Ariodante that his beloved Ginevra has been unfaithful and invite him to stand under the balcony in the royal palace where he can witness a repetition of this adulterous scene. In fact, the couple on the balcony are Polinesso and Dalinda, who has been duped by Polinesso into disguising as Ginevra. In despair, Ariodante attempts to drown himself.

His brother, Lurcanio, demands that Ginevra be put to death, but Rinaldo arrives in the nick of time to denounce Polinesso as a liar and to issue a challenge to a joust. An Unknown Knight also arrives on the scene, but it is Rinaldo who fights the duel, overcomes Polinesso and makes him confess. Justice is done by this duel, as was supposedly the case with the medieval trial by combat. It then transpires that the Unknown Knight is none other than Ariodante, who has not died, so all is resolved. This episode was borrowed by Shakespeare for *Much Ado about*

Nothing, and provided the libretto for an opera by Handel. The duel and the joust had lost none of its appeal for a refined Renaissance public.

Duels feature in *Gerusalemme Liberata* (Jerusalem Delivered, 1581) by Torquato Tasso, who broke free of French models to set his work at the time of the First Crusade, although he felt no great obligation to historical fact. His epic features episodes of romance, acts of individual heroism, sweeps of fantasy, journeys into space, grand battles, duels and jousts between Christians and the equally chivalrous Saracens, as well as between male and female knights. The official hero of the work is Goffredo, leader of the Christian army, but the real protagonists are Rinaldo, all fire and passion, and Tancredi, brave, introspective but impulsive. It is they who will enter the fray against the Saracens, and will confront them and each other in struggles over the faith but also in disputes of passionate or unrequited love.

Our concern is not with the overall plot, although we will pause to note the respect the poet affords the Muslim soldiers and the prominent part played by female warriors. There is a series of set-piece battles, skirmishes and duels throughout the poem, and these allow Tasso to display in equal measure a respect for honourable conduct and for the virtue of courtesy which Castiglione had identified as the essential attributes of the new man. Love and bravery are poignantly intertwined in the tale of Tancredi and Clorinda, the beautiful and courageous female Saracen warrior. Tancredi falls in love with her, but her sortie in armour means she is not recognized by her devotee when he engages her in a duel. After toppling her from her horse, he dismounts, removes her visor and discovers the woman he loves on the point of dying. He takes the remaining time to administer the sacrament of baptism, meaning that she becomes Christian and eligible to be admitted into heaven, where he hopes they will one day be reunited.

As a result of this event, Tancredi develops a hatred for the Saracen leader, Argante, whom he blames for the misunderstandings which led to the death of Clorinda. The crusaders had taken Jerusalem, but Argante refuses to surrender. Tancredi orders his followers not to touch Argante, since he himself wishes the satisfaction of taking his life. The description of the eventual duel is free of all mocking irony, and indeed Tasso deliberately draws on the great single combats of the *Iliad* and the *Aeneid*. After charges and counter-charges, thrusts and parries, Tancredi finally has his adversary at his mercy, but has the generosity and clemency to offer to spare him, an offer contemptuously rejected, since the Saracen, an honourable man, prefers death to being made the object of pity. These epics were popular works, in any sense of the term. Tasso's epic was written in the period of the Counter-Reformation, and the poet actually handed his work to the Inquisitors for their approval, which they gave.

It is worth noting that when in the reign of James VI & I Francis Bacon wrote attacking the duel, he made explicit reference to two Renaissance romances as bearing part of the responsibility for spreading the practice in England. When prosecuting Lord Sanquhar in 1612 for the murder of a fencing master in London, Bacon declared:

> I must tell you plainly that I conceive you to have sucked those affections of duelling in malice rather out of Italy, and outlandish manners, where you have conversed, than out of any part of this island, of England and Scotland.[4]

The tones, emphases and style with which these treatises and these epics are imbued will vary over the centuries but the underlying values, attitudes and outlook have an undeniable constancy. The same union of the drives which Freud named *Eros* and *Thanatos* was also at work, but they were subsumed into a concept of manliness, itself suitably transposed into a quasi-ethical code which imposed duties. Duellists, whether Christian or Saracen knights or bourgeois gentlemen, were expected to be motivated by high ideals, to be selfless and capable of altruistic admiration of the adversary. Both sides were expected to display sincerity, respect, truthfulness and fairness, and indeed some of the more excitable defenders of duelling made the intending duellist sound like a candidate for holy orders. Overt hatred was not decorous, respect for an adversary the appropriate stance but quarter not given or expected. It is unnecessary to say that most duellists fell short of this ideal, although Alexander Hamilton in the note to his wife written the night before his duel with Aaron Burr, came close. The essence of the infringed code was the elusive concept of honour, and a man had to be ready to face risk and perils if he was to maintain a sense of self-respect. Cowardliness was the ultimate sneer, whether on the fields of Troy, the valley of Roncesvalles or later in the Bois de Boulogne or Hyde Park. The ethics first appeared in the Renaissance and would underwrite conduct for centuries to come.

Fair Play

There was one irritant which came to the fore in the fifteenth century to torment Ariosto and which would return in different forms in subsequent ages. What constituted fair play? The term belongs to later ages, but the dilemma was felt from the outset and was never really resolved. In a duel, an honest and honourable man should face his peer, openly, frankly and on an equal footing, but new weaponry was likely to undermine ancient ways and ideals, giving one side an unsporting advantage. Contemporary chronicles record the dismay of King Desiderius when at the siege of Pavia in 773 he saw Charlemagne's infantry wearing suits of iron armour, carrying iron lances and shields, and his cavalry equipped with iron stirrups. This the king felt to be unsporting. Petrarch and later Cervantes bemoaned the introduction of cannons and gunpowder artillery as an offence against manly or knightly chivalry. Chroniclers and poets on the French side in the Hundred Years War lamented the power of archery which left the French infantry and cavalry exposed, unfairly they believed, to the undoubted superiority of English bowmen.

The basic objection was to the anonymity of these devices, and this inchoate feeling became a howl of outrage all over Europe when Jacques de Lalaing was killed by a stray cannon ball at the siege of Ghent in 1453 when he was only thirty-two.[5] Lalaing was regarded as the flower of chivalry and had fought in

Jacques de Lalaing Fighting Jean Pitois at the Passage of Arms of the Fountain of Tears, about 1530–40, J. Paul Getty Museum, courtesy the Getty's Open Content Program.

tournaments in France, England, Scotland, Portugal and Italy, vanquishing his foe, often requiring the president of the event to intervene to put an end to the combat. His awed biographer described him as strong and virtuous, as well as having the 'name of a knight but the courage of a king'. There was a perceived injustice in seeing such an outstanding man taken down by an artilleryman of the lower orders.[6]

By the eighteenth century, this issue came down to a choice between the pistol and the sword, and while the consensus was that the challenged party had the right of choice, that did not altogether remove the suspicion that there was something unmanly about the pistol. The real duel, it was implied, was two men at sword's length from each other. That had been was an issue in the Casanova-Branicki duel. Casanova, in an excess of deferential courtesy, waived his privilege, and Branicki chose the pistol because he had no knowledge of how skilled a swordsman his opponent was. Fairness was an indispensable point of the emerging code.

In the fifteenth century, the problem was the development of long-distance firearms and cannons. Ariosto was appalled. His hero Orlando expressed his dismay by bravely tossing a 'thunder-piece' into the depths of the sea but this gesture was futile because it was raised by 'vile craftsmanship' and its mechanism investigated to allow 'France, Italy and other lands' to learn the 'cruel skill' of manufacturing firearms. Ariosto did not call for an end to the arms' race but lamented the death of chivalry, if not the end of civilization as it was known. The poet is unsparing in his denunciation, forecasting the onset of mere savagery:

> O hideous invention! By what means
> Did you gain access to the human heart?
> Because of you all glory's long fled long since;
> No honour now attaches to the art
> Of soldiering; all valour is pretence;
> Not Good but Evil seems the better part;
> Gone is all courage, chivalry is gone,
> In combat once the only paragon.
>
> [...] This is the worst device, in all the years
> Of the inventiveness of humankind,
> Which e'er imagined was by human mind.[7]

Chivalry, honour and the concept of man-to-man fairness clashed, it appeared, with technology. Not that it mattered to those in other countries who were inebriated by Italian ideas of culture and civility. The gilded youth of Britain and other countries made their way to Italy to be instructed in the new styles of life. The first generations studied at its universities while later generations embarked on the Grand Tour to pick up culture by being present at a *conversazione* in its salons. Not all returned with the necessary polish, and some did not return at all. James Crichton (1560-82), known as the Admirable Crichton on account of his prodigious intellectual attainments, was one of the first Britons to travel to Italy to pursue his studies and to improve his social polish. Born probably in Perthshire, he attended St Andrews University and reputedly knew twelve languages as well as being an accomplished musician, swordsman and orator. Presumably deciding that home universities had little to offer him, he left first for Paris but found the French professors equally inadequate, and so moved to Italy, doing a tour of the most renowned seats of learning before ending up in Mantua. The admittedly not totally reliable accounts make him the incarnation of the new man idealized in contemporary Italian treatises, but he seemingly fell foul of Vincenzo Gonzaga, son and heir of the ruling family and ended up fighting a duel with him. Whatever the circumstances, he was killed and is buried in the church of San Simone.

Crichton's death pointed to the distaff side of the portrait of civic virtue. Duelling was coming onto the agenda for a man whose status, sense of self, standing in company or honour were demeaned. The courtier was not called on to be a saint or to give evidence of piety, and the newly sovereign individual had to see to his own reputation. To accept humbly and meekly an insult was to allow one's honour and standing in society to be diminished, perhaps irreparably so. The preservation and defence of honour was now a private matter, making some new form of reprisal necessary, but the nature of honour had still to be settled.

1 Jacob Burckhardt, *The Civilization of the Renaissance in Italy*, London: New English Library, 1960, pp. 121-2. (First edition, 1860)

2 Baldassare Castiglione, translated by George Bull, *The Book of the Courtier*, London: Penguin, 1967; Giovanni Della Casa, translated by R.S. Coffin, *Galateo*, London: Penguin, 1958.

3 Giuseppe Monorchio, *Lo specchio del cavaliere*, Ottawa: Biblioteca di Quaderni d'Italianistica, 1998, p. 8.

4 Quoted in Stephen Banks, *A Polite Exchange of Bullets: The Duel and the English Gentleman*, 1750-1850, Woodbridge: Boydell Press, 2010, p. 5. The Sanquhar case is discussed in chapter. 8 of this work.

5 Chiara Frugoni, *Inventions of the Middle Ages*, London: The Folio Society, 2007, pp. 128-38.

6 Margaret Wade Labarge, *Medieval Travellers: The Rich and the Restless*, London: Hamish Hamilton, 1982, pp. 173-6.

7 Ariosto, translated by Barbara Reynolds, *Orlando Furioso*, London: Penguin, 1975, canto XI.

4

THE PURSUIT AND DEFENCE OF HONOUR

One of the most poignant love poems in English is surely 'To Lucasta, Going to the Wars', by Richard Lovelace (1617-57). An adherent of the royalist cause, Lovelace fought against Cromwell and the Puritans in the English Civil War and spent time in prison for his troubles. The poem ends with the wistful, romantic couplet:

> I could not love thee, Dear, so much,
> Lov'd I not Honour more.

The sentiments are delicately expressed so it may be unseemly to reduce them to a schema, but the poem dramatizes a deeply felt struggle between an emotional longing and an intellectual-moral belief. Both are imperatives, but the pull of honour makes prior demands, so the poet would not be a full man, or gentleman, if he failed to defer to its requirements. This is not misogyny, nor does it demean women or exaggerate the force of emotions in men. In this poem Lovelace gives expression to a hierarchy of values newly arrived in England from Italy. He would be worthless to himself and to the woman he loves if he did not place honour, or Honour, in a higher sphere.

All belief systems strain credulity among non-adherents, but for believers they dictate behaviour. The clash between Lovelace's sentiments and twenty-first-century materialism, cynicism, nihilism or hedonism is now so complete that the earlier code invites derision. The present chapter uses Lovelace's outlook as a starting point to examine the pursuit, display and conservation of honour, the main component in the ethos of duelling, and thus to analyse the collective, cultural legacy passed on to men of later centuries who viewed recourse to the duel as normal. Italy will play a substantial role in this discussion. 'It is commonly agreed that Italy led the world, not only in the new learning, but also in the arts and all the polite accomplishments of civilisation,'[1] writes R.S. Pine-Coffin, although he could have added that in the same period Italy also led the way in the development of the darker arts, sometimes unintentionally, as when its focus on honour prepared the way for duelling. Machiavelli was a contemporary of Castiglione, and he beguiled Elizabethan dramatists. Markku Peltonen corrects any imbalance when he writes that

> despite medieval precedents, the duel of honour was essentially a Renaissance creation... From the very beginning the duel of honour was an integral part of the new Renaissance ideology of courtesy and civility. It was created in the new court culture, where the prime emphasis was placed on sophisticated manners and where the courtiers and gentlemen were compelled to control and suppress their emotions.[2]

Measure and self-control were essential to any man who wished to gain and retain a reputation for honourable conduct, and meekness was no virtue.

The code of honour itself requires reconstruction to make it comprehensible today. Its absence in modern life intrigued the nineteenth-century Italian poet, Giacomo Leopardi, who wrote in his notebooks:

> One of the significant aspects of any consideration of the code of honour is how completely it has disappeared, how totally the grip of a way of thought and action which once determined exchanges between human beings, particularly males, has vanished. It might be worthwhile spending a few moments to think of the

power of cultural forces as such, how completely they determine the behaviour not only of abstract belief but of supposedly free styles of behaviour.

Leopardi's reflections on the disintegration of the code are acute, as is his wider questioning of the enigma of changing modes of thought and consequent styles of conduct which the individual deludes himself he has freely chosen. Culture can be an expression of personal and community conscience as well as of consciousness, acting not only to enrich an inner world, but also as an invisible vigilante overseeing seemingly discretionary actions. In no sphere is Francis Bacon's aphorism more valid: 'Truth is the daughter of time, not of authority.' The modern ridicule of honour is as much a function of our times as was deference to it in centuries past. Lovelace's lines were not dictated by any spirit of irony, for the code of honour was a duty which demanded and deserved allegiance, and had to be weighed against competing emotional or moral costs.

For centuries, this code was a dominating feature of European male life and culture but its nature and the obligations its observance imposed were already in the Renaissance the subject of ardent debate. Writers probed into the characteristics of mind and heart, into the class implications, and limitations of caste as they applied to those who aspired to possess and display honour. It has always been an elusive concept, never entirely absent in European cultural history, sometimes given primacy and at others relegated to a more modest position in a portfolio of values. It had been claimed and protected by the heroes of antiquity and referred to by Plato, Cicero and other Greek and Roman writers, but while it was not created *ex nihilo* by humanists it was probed in their philosophical writings more deeply and polemically. The Renaissance is, rightly, seen as a revival of classical culture, but Italian humanist authors operated in a Christian framework and Honour came to occupy that prime place in the hierarchy of values that St Paul once attributed to charity. There was more than a nuance of difference between the two but they were not incompatible. Honour only lost its central position with, approximately, the age of Disenchantment ushered in by the Second World War.

The number of works penned during the Renaissance on the subject is astonishing. That tireless critic and historian Francesco Espramer estimated that some one hundred treatises were produced in those years,[3] all struggling to find a satisfactory definition. As a prelude to discussion of honour, the focus was on the dignity of man, most powerfully expressed in the treatise by Pico della Mirandola with that title. The universally accepted notion was of the excellence of humankind, plainly with gradations according to birth, intellect and education, but it was common ground that human beings as such were endowed with a dignity which put them just below the angels but above the beasts, as the cliché had it. Honour was the offspring of dignity, and was to prove the most long-lasting and most decisive part of the nascent formation of gentlemanly codes. It had both interior and exterior connotations. It was in some ways an ethical quality, but when the need arose it had to be defended by means whose ethical status was uncertain in a Christian framework. It was related to, but not entirely synonymous with, glory, respect, celebrity, dignity, prestige and honesty, all qualities intrinsic to the redefined ideals of courtesy and civility. Honour was essentially a matter of a self-esteem, but was bolstered by the consideration of others, and so required public recognition. As Franco Cardini puts it, 'Honour is an expression of a personal quality recognised at a community but not at a societal level, this latter being by definition that in which the majesty of the law is exercised.'[4] Reputation rested on the possession of honour. For the high-minded in all countries, honour entailed the chivalric willingness to defend the weak and downtrodden, although this precept became secondary and remained more honoured in the breach. There was, unlike medieval knighthood, no initiation rite, and no right of succession. It was an elite quality assigned to, or seized by, a select band. Any idea of universal human rights was far off.

Moderation and the golden mean were important. In its heyday, honour was inseparable from military valour, but by the late sixteenth century we find Montaigne distinguishing between the honour belonging to the nobility of the sword and that claimed by the nobility of the robe, the latter made up of the professions, the magistracy and the like. The view of himself as honourable, and the acceptance of that assessment by his peers, gave a man membership of a select band of brothers, but these could on an instant, after a perceived slight, be transformed into antagonists. The problem was that honour could be lost and a man tumble into shame, perhaps brought about by his own pusillanimity or degeneracy, or else by slights, insults and insinuations uttered by others. The loss of honour was a humiliation in itself, *ipso facto* causing a lowering of a man's standing which required him to react, but there was the rub. Honour is a moral, or at least para-moral, concept but it had often to be defended by means which clashed with Christian ethics and civil law. Without some understanding of honour, the subsequent frequency of the duel over succeeding centuries would be simply incomprehensible.

Questions of honour and the duel were then intertwined. Could and should honour, once lost, be recovered? By what means? These dilemmas brought into play the morality, justification and even necessity of the duel, a particularly thorny issue for ecclesiastic authorities. Peltonen writes:

> From the very beginning the duel of honour was an integral part of the new Renaissance ideology of courtesy and civility. It was created in the new court culture, where the prime emphasis was placed on sophisticated manners and where the courtiers and gentlemen were compelled to control and suppress their emotions.[5]

In the High Renaissance, the medieval judicial duel was a distant memory, and the knightly joust in most countries a relic disdained by courtiers who had other, more elevated, means of entertainment, even if they were still required, by Baldassare Castiglione above all, to acquire the ability to take up arms for their prince and patron. The joust survived in ceremonial form in England, where Queen Elizabeth's annual Accession Day was an occasion for celebrations of a distinctly medieval character, and there were other special occasions, such as her visits to the Earl of Leicester's pleasance at Kenilworth, when she relished the spectacle of the joust. She was a keen spectator, as was noticed by observers from France when jousts were made part of her lavish reception of the Duke of Alençon, an envoy bearing the proposal of marriage from his king.[6] Such occasions were now an exception, however, and chivalry no longer commanded the attention of all the authors of treatises, preoccupied as they were by subtler questions.

Renaissance Treatises and Tracts

There was an outpouring of treatises, dialogues and tracts on honour and on duelling, sometimes in the same work but also in separate writings, by humanist thinkers in the Renaissance. One of the most influential was by the jurist Andrea Alciati (1492-1550), author of a Latin work, *De singulari certamine liber* (On Single Combat), published in 1544 together with a lengthy commentary by Mariano Sozzini (1482-1556).[7] Alciati enjoyed international fame in his day. He moved to France when he decided that Italy had exhausted its intellectual energy, but thereafter commuted between the two countries to take up various academic positions. He became friends, or was in correspondence, with such prominent figures of the time as Erasmus, Montaigne, Cardinal Bembo and Giorgio Vasari. His work on duelling draws on his knowledge of classical history and Roman jurisprudence, but his insights and judgments also bring a contemporary humanist questioning, not medieval dogmatism, to bear.

He seems to presume that discussions on honour have already taken place, leaving him at liberty to offer his own moral vision linked to a manual of behaviour for duellists. The contradiction is that, like virtually all writers on this subject, he is officially opposed to the practice, and expatiates on the origins of the word before restating the bans on duelling in civil law and papal edict. Having established that point, he oscillates over the question of whether the need to defend honour might constitute a valid exception, giving expression to the possibility of alternative codes which will over the coming centuries torment theorists and provide a self-vindication for duellists. He notes that while the duel is forbidden by law and morality, it is tolerated and even encouraged by custom, a word which can be taken as synonymous with culture. 'So many laws, so many judges, so many established edicts in the public sphere that each may almost go his own way,' he sighs in Chapter XVI.

There are discussions of other, more technical difficulties - can a man who loses a duel issue a second challenge, what to do when antagonists are of unequal rank, when can a champion be appointed, and which side can choose the weapons - and yet he repeatedly returns to the fundamental question of moral acceptability. Drawing on his knowledge of Greek culture, he notes that on the one hand the victor in a competition or combat returned home to be greeted with song and celebration, while on the other Diogenes the Cynic objected to this facile triumphalism by asking whether the winner in, for example, the Pancratium games, had faced opponents who were stronger, equal or more moronic. Diogenes' cynical reply was that since the winner had bested his antagonist, the loser had obviously not been stronger or even equal, leaving only the option that he had been more moronic, so where was the glory in such ignoble a prize? In his comments, Sozzini also hesitated over the acceptability of the duel, and relates an anecdote concerning one Cesare Fregoso who, having been insulted in 1537 by Cagnino, retorted that he would reply only 'with weapons in his hand'. Was that a worthy response, Sozzini wonders? From there, he proceeds to an examination of the Biblical and papal authorities but at some point in the book's history this analysis irritated some nameless reader who scribbled in the margin of the copy I read - *duellum non sit prohibitissum*, let the duel not be wholly prohibited. It was not.

Five years later, the Venetian Girolamo Muzio (1496-1576), a courtier-poet, produced a handbook simply entitled *Il duello* and some twenty years further on a treatise *Il gentilhuomo* (The Gentleman), the two being inextricably linked. His approach, like Alciati's, was a mixture of religious precept and philosophical analysis, supported by copious references to Aristotle and Plato.[8] The human being, a self-determining and self-governing agent, was endowed with rights but subject to moral constraints, and as regards the duel Muzio found himself, like predecessors and successors, struggling between opposing convictions. In the first book of *Il duello*, he devotes several chapters to the different kinds of lies which can legitimately lead to a duel - lies certain, conditional, general, spectral, stupid and then an unlabelled, milder category which does not entail recourse to arms. Since the accusation of lying is an unforgivable offence against honour, he also gives advice on how to compose a *cartello*, the note containing the challenge. (Sir Walter Raleigh's poem 'The Lie' contains the couplet: ... to give the lie / deserves no more than stabbing.)[9]

The second book addresses the duties of seconds, a subject with which all subsequent writers would return, and also with the management of the actual field. The sixteenth century was not yet the age where the duel was a purely private contest to be fought in a remote spot. It still retained aspects of the joust and was contested in public, so duellists were obliged to turn to some lord to request him to set up a field where the fight, normally with swords but no longer on horseback, could take place. The third chapter examines other awkward questions, such as the entitlement of illegitimate sons to take part in duels, the possibility of engaging champions and also the nature of the appropriate 'satisfaction'. The question of the essence of honour is left in the background, but he concludes his treatise with the significant words: 'we have stated that the institution of the duel has not been established with gaining honour as its purpose: but we have treated this matter in accordance with the laws of honour.' In other words, in this new age, unlike in the medieval period, the duel was not to be fought merely to gain enhanced status or prestige as a warrior, but there were regulations in honour which governed its conduct.

Giovanni Battista Possevino (1520-49) ranged more widely and deeply in his posthumously published *Dialogo dell'honore* (Dialogue on Honour, 1553). The subtitle declares that the work will deal with 'the duel, nobility and all ranks in which conflicts of honour might occur'.[10] The text quickly established itself as an essential exposition of the new courtly culture, and was distinguished by its integration of contemporary ideas with more traditional notions of chivalry. Aristotle is the first reference and with that authority Possevino is able to assert that honour is a reward for virtue, before going off on the first of many subtle, or baffling and redundant, distinctions, in this case between those who are compelled to be good and those who choose to be so. The first category can claim little merit, both speakers agree, since the essential component of virtue is freedom of choice. Doing good under compulsion carries no ethical merit. Other moral questions prove more bothersome. Is there a difference between choice and judgment?, he asks, and his dissection of this dilemma leads Possevino back to Aristotle and the separation of the rational soul from the sensitive soul but we will not follow him into that confusing labyrinth. The author emerges from it to show concern over the situation of a private soldier who is a good man by choice and thus merits being viewed as honourable, but is subject to a captain who is a scoundrel. Could the soldier challenge his superior officer? This question is only posed to be slapped down, because rank counts, and any other answer could lead to an ordinary subject being entitled to challenge a king or an emperor, which is plainly unthinkable. The issue of caste would be debated in succeeding centuries, and the consensus was quickly reached that a gentleman could not issue or receive a challenge from someone of a lower class, although he was entitled to administer a punitive whipping.

In Book V the two debaters face the central issue of the duel 'as an instrument and a means suitable for re-acquiring lost honour'. Possevino repeats that the duel is immoral and should be avoided, but his expression of these views is deeply ambiguous. He initially takes a lofty, almost abstract approach, like churchmen discussing the just war. Of course, such thinkers asserted, war was evil, of course war was to be avoided, of course the rational human being would do all in his power to ward off war, but if all else failed, if a nation were faced with a powerful and threatening enemy, then war could be viewed as just. Erasmus was one of the few to challenge the very idea of a 'just war'. With the duel, the first principle for Possevino is that honour is the supreme good, the most valued possession of the individual man, the quality which he has the right and duty to defend, so if the offence is of sufficient gravity, if other means of seeking a remedy have met with a refusal, a duel is morally justifiable. Oddly, Possevino seems to prefer the immediacy of the duel to cumbersome legal wranglings when indisputable wrongs have been endured. If the offence is regarded as grievous by wont and custom, and if the preservation or restoration of honour is the purpose of the duel, then the duel can go ahead. On the grounds which would later be termed *realpolitik*, he advocates showing honour to men who are 'strong and just', because strong men are needed in times of war and just men in times of peace.

Possevino was later accused of plagiarism, a charge from which he was defended by his brother, Antonio, and was the object of polemical counter-arguments from the disputatious Annibale Romei (c1523-90), author of works on such subjects as chess. He dedicated the third book of his *Discorsi* (1585) to a range of topics, including honour.[11] He trained his sights on Possevino, but agreed that while 'honour was the most precious of all the eternal gifts', it was of two types, either 'innate and imperfect' or 'acquired and perfect'. The second was by far preferable, since some of those born into what was viewed as honour tended not to give proof of being so endowed. His work restates old chivalric standards, and he writes that honour is acquired by works of charity, but still holds that it is more likely to be acquired by those of good breeding. In Book Four, *On the Iniquity of Duelling*, he regrets that not enough has been written about it - which is far from true - and that this lack has allowed many misapprehensions to gain currency. His statement that the duel is 'a combat between two peers, caused by honour, at whose conclusion the defeated falls into infamy and the victor remains in possession of his honour', is as clear a definition as ever given, even if he proceeds to say that this view of the outcome is based on an erroneous view of honour, which is not the opposite of infamy, but is associated with charity. In any case, he adds, duelling is a thing of the past, having been condemned by the papacy and Christian princes. His work was a strong as a philippic but weak as prophecy.

The most widely quoted and probably most influential of all such treatises, certainly in Britain, was written in English by Vincentio Saviolo (d.1598/9), an immigrant from Padua who established a fencing school in London where he introduced a new style employing the sword in one hand and the dagger in the other. In 1595, he published a manual with the unambiguous title *Vincentio Saviolo, his Practise. In two Bookes. The first intreating of the use of the Rapier and Dagger. The Second of Honor and honorable Quarrels.*[12] The early sections proved to be of value to Elizabethan dramatists who made use of Saviolo's jargon and teaching on the *code duello* in plays where the style of dress and the weapons carried or worn by the characters showed Italian influence:

> The days of the swashbucklers drawn from the serving men classes were over; all eyes were shifting to the rapier-trained gentleman. The fashion came from Italy and swept all before it. When Shakespeare wrote *Romeo and Juliet*, he gave the servants swords and bucklers to fight with and armed the gentlemen with rapiers.[13]

As was normal, Saviolo adopts a tone of hypocritical regret over the habit and frequency of duelling, laments the degeneracy of the present and hankers after the greater courtesy and magnanimity of mind of ages past. Where Rousseau would write that man was born free but is everywhere in chains, Saviolo proclaims that men were born 'naked', that is, without the claws or sharp teeth other animals are endowed with and so created for peaceful ways, but everywhere around him he sees men too readily driven to violence over matters which do not merit such extremes. There are those whose swaggering pride in their own strength or prowess leads them to believe they may 'lawfully offer outrage and injury to any man ... as though they were heirs of Mars and more invincible than Achilles.' Others, carried away by 'choler or wine', demand satisfaction for injuries which could be settled by other means, such as by the civil law which had been established by 'wise rulers'. He gives instances of various impolite excesses, such as staring too boldly in the face of strangers, an annoyance which would still occasion challenges in the nineteenth century, as well as more recognizable provocations like spreading malicious rumour.

He writes that there are cases such as 'murder committed by treachery, or rape' which can only be met by the duel, and as he proceeds it becomes clear that no matter how strenuously he has urged moderation, his assumption is that the single

Woodcut illustration from *Vincentio Saviolo, his Practise* (Academy of Historical Martial Arts)

combat is now part of life. Since he had set up a school of fencing, it was plainly in his interests to issue warnings against the omnipresence of violence, for example footpads who might leap out on the innocent passer-by and who thus represent the same danger as an armed knight on a battlefield. In a section *Of Honor and honorable Quarrels* he proposes that there are two kinds of injury, by word or deed, and both can be remedied by a fulsome apology, but this is not always forthcoming. Of all the forms of verbal insult, giving the lie is the most gross, since it involves undermining the standing of an individual, branding him as untrustworthy, treacherous and thus dishonourable, a judgment which will never be disputed in subsequent history. Saviolo descends into sophistry to sub-distinguish the 'manner and diversity' of lies, here borrowing shamelessly from Possevino, but while there may be some uncertainty over who is the challenger and who the defendant, Saviolo believes that the man who has given the lie to another is *ipso facto* the challenger because he has impugned honour. The offended party has thus the privilege of choosing weapons and place of duel. The basic principle he proposes, in an echo of Lovelace, is that 'in an honourable person, his honour ought to be preferred above his life.' Formerly gallows were set up near the place of combat and the vanquished was immediately hanged, but Saviolo considers this to be no deterrent since, as he declares in ringing rhetoric, defeat already means the loss of honour, 'for love whereof there is no noble mind that will not spend his blood.'[14]

Decades later, Berlingero Gessi junior (1613-71), a native of Bologna and a member of the senate of that city, produced *La Spada di Honore* (The Sword of Honour, 1671), subtitled *Observations on Chivalric Ethics* and published posthumously. He explicitly combined honour and the sword in the very title, and a deep ambiguity permeates his writing and thinking as he struggles to reconcile two conflicting positions, the right to defend injured honour and the condemnation of armed combat. Gessi regards all forms of duel practised in earlier times, specifically the judicial duel, as mere superstitious primitivism which men of his time, who have attained more mature understanding, are right to shun. The sword is 'certainly not a means of uncovering a hidden truth but rather a senseless judge [...] it is neither a proper nor necessary instrument for acquiring or recovering honour.' Laws and evidence are the appropriate means for establishing justice, since it is false to assert that 'God favours in a duel the innocent or the truthful. The judgments of God are impenetrable.' Gessi permits himself to write vigorously about duels in Homer and Virgil, but while the deeds of classical heroes and the precepts of classical philosophers are of value in other fields, they are not for him an example to be followed in this case. He aligns himself with the standard thinking of his age in linking the defence of honour and the duel, but then diverges when he remembers he should be a tenacious, uncompromising opponent of the armed duel in every form. His opposition to duelling was expanded in a later work, *Lo Scettro Pacifico* (1676, soon after translated as *Monks and The Peaceful Sceptre*), and in an introduction to an edited version of an edict of Louis XIV against duelling.

His first premise is the beauty of honour, 'the distinguishing mark, the gem which honourable men carry in their breasts, the character imprinted in their hearts as evidence that they are enrolled in respected and decorous company'. The honourable were an elite band, and honour itself was 'supreme among human values'. This being asserted, he sets himself off in dizzying, intellectual circles to justify his assertion that 'chivalry can be said to be the most noble honour in the world, and the honour of nobles can be said to be the most necessary and natural of chivalry', only to realize that this elegant coupling of honour and chivalry creates difficulties for him in his rejection of the duel itself. He continues circling round the subject, declaring that 'this word honour carries various meanings: sometimes taken as the beauty and ornament of things; sometimes dignity, responsibility or rank upheld; for the female sex, it is honesty and modesty; at times it can be a person's virtue or merit'; at other times it can define the nobility and antiquity of a dynasty; at others again the reputation or good name of a person; and finally the reverence and observance shown by external appearances. Like many subsequent analysts, he made the distinction between a lady's honour, which consisted of 'acting chastely and modestly', and that of the knight which lay in 'behaving with justice and valour'.

Honour could be lost but he struggled to identify remedies available and justifiable for the knight or courtier whose honour had been impugned. With one part of his mind he maintained his antipathy to duelling and strove to uphold the commandment against killing, quoting papal edicts condemning the practice, but at the same time he was plainly troubled by his failure to identify acceptable redress for a man in society who finds himself demeaned or his honour mocked. Gessi admits that 'some say' - and the decision to disclaim authorship and attribute the belief to others is significant - that 'chivalric justice consists in the reasonable equity with which one regulates one's self-love or opposes the pride of someone who aims to offend it; to defend it or defend himself a knight will take up the sword.' He puts in italics a crucial passage where he weighs the claims of power and those of justice. '*Honour must receive the strength of the zealous sword to fight back against injuries when necessary,*' but the level of necessity has to be set on the scales of justice to allow the injured party to assess 'the nature of the offence and the intentions of the offender, not less than adequate satisfaction for the offence itself'. He warns against over-hasty or excessive reaction, and thunders against times past 'when the duel was permitted', and underlines that even in that more barbaric age 'as in other arenas, so in this this bloody tribunal, exceptions could be found', and reparation made in other ways. His confusion reflects the uncertainties of the time.

The debate extended across Europe and Robert Ashley, in *Of Honour* (1600), followed Italian footsteps in writing that Honour was a good in itself, indeed 'a moderate desire of Honour is not only very convenient but (is) also above all other good things (virtue only excepted which it normally accompanieth.)'[15] He worried about the impact of ambition on the pursuit of honour, since ambition is a 'base-minded activity', so his important chapter on eligibility, that is, the question of 'who was capable of Honour and who was not', suggests that honour is only in the grasp of those who have no need to strive. Its attainment is beyond the grasp of the common run of humanity, leaving the practice and defence of Honour as the preserve of the nobility. So far so good, but who was noble? The day of the gentleman had not yet dawned, and the age of the citizen was well in the future, so the debate focused on the courtier, the *habitué* of the court, a figure who had a recognized place in the social hierarchy. The fact that honour could only be attained by an elite did not exclude knights, ministers, servants of the rulers, artists, leisured attenders at courts, refined spirits who participated in discussions on the arts and philosophy. Agricultural workers were definitely off-limits, as were inn-keepers, coach drivers, manual workers and the like. Ashley's treatise differs from the contemporary Italian works only in the fact that he offers no treatment of the duel, but other English writers did. Writing in 1660, the Marquis of Dorchester noted that 'duellists were engaged in the fight to demonstrate their sense of honour rather than to achieve a definite result.'[16]

The reverse side of the code of honour was the fear of disgrace or humiliation for failing to comply with expectations. This hidden force was only given a name in the twentieth century when the American anthropologist Ruth Benedict, writing on Japan coined the terms 'guilt culture' and 'shame culture' to denote a fear of seeming inadequate in the public eye.[17] A later critic, E.R. Dodds, applied this notion to his study of Greek culture and the conduct of heroes such as Achilles and Ajax.[18] Shame culture emphasized not the pursuit of honour or glory in themselves but the power of the fear of not conforming, of not living up to socially sanctioned standards. A code of honour which was explicit, conscious and private was balanced and, paradoxically, reinforced by a need for public esteem and fears of public contempt for falling short.

Both sides are present in Shakespeare. The claims of honour were loudly made in *Richard II*, where Thomas Mowbray declares;

> Mine honour is my life: both grow in one
> Take honour from me, and my life is done.

In *Troilus and Cressida*, Hector is equally forthright:

> Mine Honour keeps the weather of my fate.
> Life every man holds dear; but the dear man
> Holds honour far more precious-dear than life.[19]

The opposing view could be expressed only by those on the fringes of society, whom Saviolo would have judged in any case incapable of honourable conduct. *Henry IV, Part 1* was by general consent written in the mid to late 1590s, a period which, even if its energy was largely expended in Italy, can be regarded as the high point of the English Renaissance. The contrast between Hotspur, who incarnates military valour and chivalric honour, and Prince Hal, who is initially devoid of such qualities but comes to aspire to the same status, is central. However, Falstaff pours scorn on all such grandiloquent notions, above all in his celebrated speech ridiculing the very concept when called to order before the Battle of Shrewsbury.

> ... well tis no matter; honour pricks on me. Yea, but how
> if honour prick me off when I come on? How then? Can
> honour set-to a leg? No. Or an arm? No. Or take away the
> grief of a wound? No. Honour hath no skill in surgery,
> then? No. What is honour? A word. What is in that word
> 'honour'? Air. A trim reckoning! Who hath it? He that
> died o' Wednesday. Doth he feel it? No. Doth he hear it?
> No. 'Tis insensible then. Yea, to the dead. But will it live
> with the living? No. Why? Detraction will not suffer it.
> Therefore I'll none of it. Honour is a mere scutcheon:
> and so ends my catechism.

His 'catechism' was a contradiction of the catalogue of valour and virtue expected of the soldier and the aristocrat, but Falstaff was no aristocrat. As a member of lower orders, honour was

Sir John Falstaff's grand manœuvre, at the Battle of Shrewsbury!

Illustration from *The Life of Sir John Falstaff* by George Cruikshank
(Gutenberg)

not associated with men of his stamp. The same could be said
of the infantrymen and peasants who appear in the theatre of
the actor-author Ruzante (1496-1542), especially in *Parlamento
de Ruzante* (The Veteran, ?1529), the account of a soldier who
runs from the battlefield and who on returning to Venice finds
he has lost home and wife, and honour. Both writers were aware
of standing at a point where the old world of chivalry was dying
and a new world was being born.

1 R.S. Pine-Coffin, introduction to Giovanni Della Casa, *Galateo*,
   London: Penguin, 1958, p. 15.
2 Markku Peltonen, *The Duel in Early Modern England: Civility,
   Politeness and Honour*, Cambridge: Cambridge University Press,
   2003, p. 5.
3 Francesco Espramer, *La biblioteca di Don Ferrante: duello e onore
   nella cultura del Cinquecento*, Rome: Bulzoni, 1982.
4 Franco Cardini, *Onore*, Bologna: Il Mulino, 2016, p. 98.
5 Peltonen, *op. cit.*, p. 5.

6 James Shapiro, *1599: A Year in the Life of William Shakespeare*, London: HarperCollins, 2006, p. 279; Carolly Erickson, *The First Elizabeth*, London: Macmillan, 1983, p. 324.
7 Alciati, *De Singulari Certamine*, Venice: 1544; with additional section by Mariano Sozzini. Translations from Latin mine.
8 Girolamo Muzio, *Il duello*, Venice: 1550. Accessed https://archive.org/details/ilduellodelmutio00muzi/page/n5/mode/2up, 25 June 2020.
9 Sir Walter Raleigh, consulted at https://www.poetryfoundation.org/poems/50019/the-lie-56d22cb6afd43
10 Giovanni Possevino, *Dialogo dell'honore*, Venice: 1565. Accessed https://archive.org/details/bub_gb_N4_aHDUEvh8C/page/n17/mode/2up, 25 June 2020/
11 *Discorsi del Conte Annibale Romei, divisi in Cinque Giornate*, Venice: 1585. Accessed https://archive.org/details/bub_gb_WB2L1w8U5IcC 25 June 2020
12 Vincentio Saviolo, *His Practise* (1595), in *A Gentleman's Guide to Duelling*, edited by Jared Kirby, London: Frontline Books, 2013.
13 Ruth Goodman, *How to Behave Badly in Renaissance Britain*, London: Michael O'Mara Books, 2018, p. 179.
14 Saviolo, *op. cit.*, pp. 110 & 137.
15 Robert Ashley, *Of Honour*, edited by Virgil B. Heltzel, San Marino CA: The Huntington Library, 1947, pp. 24 & 48.
16 Peltonen, *op. cit.*, p. 2.
17 Ruth Benedict, *The Chrysanthemum and the Sword*, Boston MA: Houghton and Mifflin, 1946.
18 E.R. Dodds, *The Greeks and the Irrational*, Berkeley CA: University of California Press, 1951.
19 William Shakespeare, *Richard II*, Act 1, scene 1; *Troilus and Cressida*, Act 5, scene 3.

5

THE LAW, THE DUEL AND THE BRAWL

King James VI & I, the first monarch of Great Britain, had always abominated duelling. His reign, both in Scotland and then in Britain, is in regard to the duel a transitional age, when the culture, practices and vocabulary of chivalry were not quite dead but the gentleman's code had not quite established itself. Like Queen Elizabeth before him, the king attended tournaments and jousting. While both abhorred the senselessness of duelling which deprived them of some valued aides, duels became increasingly frequent in the last decades of the sixteenth century and the early decades of the seventeenth. The practice already enjoyed the ambiguous status it was to maintain over succeeding centuries of being forbidden by law but tacitly sanctioned by society. The vague, inchoate view was frequently heard that the duel was essentially foreign, specifically Italian, and not quite English or British. A new word, Italianate, was coined for this new culture and the new man who embodied it. It was not a compliment. The word was exported back to Italy in the couplet - *Inglese Italianato / diavolo incarnato*, which could be given a rhyming translation - Englishman Italianate / Devil Incarnate. The Italianate Englishman was simultaneously foppish, effeminate, affected and phoney, but also subtle, underhand, sly, Machiavellian and prone to violence. He was likely to be instigator or receptor of challenges. Interestingly, the Scottish Earl of Gowrie, who gave his name to a mysterious conspiracy in Perth in 1600 against King James, was dubbed in certain quarters as 'romantic and Italianate'.[1]

Another sign of the transitional nature of the age concerned the duel itself. The word was in common use, but the definition of what constituted a duel and its distinction from an impromptu brawl or fracas was not as sharp as it would later become. The protocols of the duel, crucially those governing the appointments of seconds and the etiquette of exchanging cartels and postponing the meeting until time and place had been agreed, were not at this time in place, and would only be drawn up in written form in 1777. The risk of an argument degenerating into a fight, especially after drink had been taken, was heightened by the fact that gentlemen wore swords almost as a fashion item, and so had deadly weapons to hand. Pistols were not in use in duels at this time.

The number of duels of which there remains some reliable record rose steadily. Lawrence Stone established that there were only five recorded in the 1580s but around twenty in the succeeding decade, and that numbers continued to rise thereafter in the seventeenth century.[2] These figures refer only to duels of which there is some mention, and plainly there must have been many more of which no trace is extant. The archives of the Star Chamber record some 200 cases during the reign of James.[3] The reasons for this rise are anything but clear but several writers at the time put it down to the dissemination and acceptance of those beguiling but pestilential notions of honour, civility and courtesy newly imported from Italy which carried with them the need to defend them in person. The influential courtier Henry Howard, Earl of Northampton, viewed the new cult of honour as a passing vogue, but also held that it was an important factor in the cult of duelling. Northampton was a shrewd observer and his belief that even self-destructive habits can be dictated by something as trivial as a fashion is worth consideration, even if there were other factors in play. Yet by no means all the duels were motivated by questions of honour. Some, however designated, seem like straightforward hooliganism, while alcohol was frequently a factor.

James first gave voice to his repugnance for duelling in a remarkable document he drew up in 1598 in Edinburgh, before his accession to the English throne. This work, a treatise on the challenges and responsibilities of kingly government, bears the title *Basilikon Doron*, Greek for 'royal gift', and was addressed to 'Henry My Dearest Son and Natural Successor'.[4] When it was later published in England it was interpreted as a defence of royal absolutism and of the divine right of kings, but it was initially a private work, intended for Henry's eyes only. In it, James denounces the crimes which he held to be most heinous in themselves and most damaging for the stability of the State. The full list runs: 'witchcraft, wilful murder, incest (especially within the degrees of consanguinity), sodomy, poisoning and false coin'. He declines to discuss warfare in any depth since 'that art is already treated by many', although he does offer guidance on the just war and tells his son, who died young and never became king, not to consult on this question 'necromancers or false prophets'. He countenances the revival of jousting which was underway in the Elizabethan age, but is forthright on that form of private warfare which is the duel.

> Neither commit your quarrell to bee tried by a Duell: for beside that generally all Duell appeareth to bee unlawful, committing the quarrell, as it were, to a lot; whereof there is no warrant in the Scripture, since the abrogating of the olde Lawe: it is specially moste un- lawfull in the person of a King; who being a publicke person hath no power therefore to dispose of himselfe, in respect, that to his preseruation or fall, the safetie or wracke of the whole common-weale is necessarily coupled, as the body is to the head.

This was his first, somewhat cursory, statement on duelling and with it he rejects the practice itself on two grounds: firstly, that following the abrogation by Jesus Christ of the Mosaic Law of the Old Testament, duelling has no basis in Sacred Scripture, the authority to which he refers all throughout this work; and secondly, that the outcome is determined by the chance (lot) of superior strength and technique, not by justice. There is an additional veto on duelling for the person of a royal ruler, a specific obligation which is undoubtedly a reference to the fate of Henri II, who had been killed in a joust in Paris in 1559, an incident which had ramifications for Scottish history and for the Stuart dynasty. Henri had called a tournament to celebrate the ending of the wars with the Hapsburgs and decided to participate in person, choosing as his opponent in a joust Gabriel Montgomery, an officer in the Royal Scottish Guard. A splinter from a lance entered the king's eye and he died three days later. Henri had supervised the education in the French court of Mary Queen of Scots, James' mother, whose first husband was François II, son of Henri. Louis XIII banned all duelling in France, and James imposed the same law in his kingdoms, but both met resistance.

James VI of Scotland became James I of England in 1603 and was accompanied to London by a group of courtiers and aristocrats, not all men of unblemished reputation or selfless devotion to the king's rule. In his *Tales of a Grandfather*, an

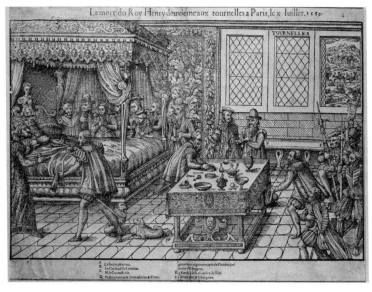

A contemporary woodcut of Henri II's death (Wellcome Images)

account of Scottish history, Sir Walter Scott was unsparing in his condemnation of many in that clique. 'Each individual Scotsman expected to secure some part of the good things with which England was supposed to be endowed... James was shocked at the greediness and importunity of his fellow countrymen.' Nonetheless, James, as was to be expected of a man pitched into a foreign environment, came to rely on them and to show favour to some. Scott was a scrupulous chronicler and commentator and pointed out that 'the benefits which he conferred on people who had supported him in England irked the English who considered everything given to the Scots as conferred at their expense.' Resentment against outsiders for taking 'our' jobs and impoverishing 'us' has been levelled at immigrants in all ages and all classes, and was aggravated in that age by traditional antagonism between Scotland and England. It is hard to quibble with Scott's final observation that since the two countries had only recently been enemies it was beyond the king's ability 'to prevent bloody and desperate quarrels between his countrymen and his new subjects'.[5]

The patience of the king was tried by the frequency of duelling among men of his court who were close to him and indispensable for the smooth running of the State. Several such 'bloody and desperate' duels pitched Scots against English noblemen. Writing in 1613, John Chamberlain gives as an example 'a proper young fellow who served Sir Francis Bacon [and who] was arraigned at the King's Court for killing a Scot and being found guilty of manslaughter was burnt in the hand.'[6] Other cases came under James' direct purview. Lord Herbert of Cherbury, neo-Platonist thinker, MP and *habitué* of the court, was given preferment by James early in his reign. In December 1609, we find him challenging a Scottish usher to a duel in Hyde Park. The servant's name may have been Jacques Buchan, but he was certainly Scottish, and his offence was to have snatched a ribbon from the hair of Mary Middlemore, a woman whose striking beauty made her the unattainable but much desired subject of sonnets. She was also Maid of Honour in the suite of Queen Anne of Denmark, wife of King James. Herbert was quite properly outraged at this act of insubordination and discourtesy, and slapped the man on the spot. The matter might have ended there, but the fashion of the age and the more or less established dictates of honour meant that, philosopher or not, he felt obliged to follow this spontaneous reaction with an official challenge. The one incongruity was the incompatibility of rank. A gentleman was permitted to challenge only an equal, and the two men were unquestionably of different classes. Such a duel would not have been permitted in a later age when it was established that a thorough horsewhipping was the appropriate means of dealing with an inferior, but it may also be that Herbert's philosophical meditations allowed him to view all class-based prescriptions with disdain. There is no knowing how the affair would have ended, or what loss to philosophy might have ensued, because the Privy Council intervened to forbid the match.

Another duel in 1609 between Sir James Stewart and Sir George Wharton was a more serious matter and more distressing to the monarch. The two men belonged to the aristocracies of their respective countries. Sir James, the son of the Earl of Blantyre, received his education along with the future king at the hands of the stern humanist scholar, George Buchanan. His father was an influential figure in Scottish royal circles and held such offices as Lord High Treasurer of Scotland, although the vagaries of power play meant that he also spent some time in prison. Sir James married Dorothy Hastings, daughter of the Earl of Huntingdon, and a Maid of Honour at the court of Queen Elizabeth and later of Anne of Denmark. One recurring item in her correspondence with her royal mistress was a request for a grant or a salary to preserve the honour of Scotland by enabling her husband to pay off his debts. The king did make a grant in his favour from the royal purse, and while it is only surmise that the debts may have been incurred by gambling, it seems that the dispute between him and Wharton started as a row over a game of cards before escalating into bitter words and an exchange of blows. Wharton was a knight, a member of the Order of the Bath, a courtier who is reported to have had no particular occupation except hunting and playing cards. He was plainly a quarrelsome individual, and there are accounts of various duels, the first over a woman when he was only twenty. Later he got into a quarrel with the Earl of Pembroke over accusations of cheating at cards, the same allegation which brought him and Sir James Stewart to face each other. Wharton issued the challenge to Stewart in bitter words:

> Your misconstruing of my message gives me cause to think you extreme vainglorious, a humour which the valiant detests. And whereas you unjustly said I durst not meet you in the field to fight with you, you shall find that you are much mistaken; for I will fight with you with what weapon you shall appoint, and meet you where you will, being content to give you this advantage, not valuing the worst you can do.[7]

The braggadocio of the language, the insults based on manliness, the defiance in the name of valour are classic chivalric expressions of wounded pride and offended honour. Stewart's reply implies that Wharton's second when delivering the message made an attempt to restore peace, but if so all such attempts were repulsed. Stewart wrote:

> And now you have to acknowledge no other speeches than you charged me with, which is, that I said you durst not meet me in the field to fight. True it is, your barbarous and uncivil insolence in such a place, and before such a company (for whose respect I am only sorry for what I then did or said), made me do and say that which I will now make good. Wherein, since you find yourself behind, I am ready to do you all the right you can expect.

The words 'meet me in the field to fight' may well be a reference to the challenge issued by Cain to Abel. Stewart's language is in any case somewhat contorted, but the two men were determined to fight and went to some lengths to avoid legal bans.[8] All that remained was to choose weapons, time and place. Stewart continued:

> I have sent you the length of my rapier, which I will use with a dagger, and so meet you at the farther end of Islington (as I understand nearer to you than me), at three of the clock in the afternoon; which things I scorn to take as advantages, but as my due, and which I have made indifferent.

The use of the rapier and short sword was obvious proof of Vincentio Saviolo's influence, and both plainly used them to good effect since both died in the confrontation. The king was reported to be distraught and ordered that they be buried in the one grave in Islington, where they still lie. Their deaths were commemorated in *A Lamentable Ballad of a Combat Lately Fought, near London, between Sir James Steward, and Sir George Wharton, Knights*, a lengthy, mournful piece which has strange echoes of the Border Ballads. The opening stanzas run:

> It grieves my heart to tell the woe
> that did near *London* late befal,
> On *Martlemas*-eve, O woe is me,
> I grieve the chance and ever shall,
>
> Of two right gallant Gentlemen
> who very rashly fell at words,
> But to their quarrel could not fall,
> Till they both fell by their keen swords

The ending of the duel is recounted in suitably pious terms:

> Our English Knight was the first that fell
> the *Scotch* Knight fell immediately,
> Who cryed both to Jesus Christ,
> Receive our souls, O Lord, we dye.

The scansion may be faulted by a perfectionist, of whom there were many in that age, but the final stanzas are a call for loyalty to the king and queen and an expression of the patriotic hope that '*Britain* still may live in one / in perfect love and unity.'

The case of Robert Crichton, the Scottish Lord Sanquhar, took a different turn. Sanquhar had already incurred the king's displeasure in Scotland in 1596 when he challenged Patrick Stewart, Earl of Orkney, a notorious roisterer who was later executed for treason. James got wind of the matter and ordered them to desist. Sanquhar was in the entourage which came south with the king, and on arrival he enrolled at a fencing school in London, not Saviolo's but a rival establishment run by John Turner. There were obviously no holds barred in the training sessions, and in one particularly energetic bout he lost an eye. The instructor's apologies were accepted at the time, but some years later on a visit to the court of Henri IV of France, whom he knew from a previous diplomatic mission, Sanquhar was asked by the king about his lost eye. He explained the circumstances, and according to all accounts the king asked if the man responsible for this disfigurement was still alive. The question cut Sanquhar to the quick. He took it as a slight on his own status and honour and on his return to London laid a trap for Turner and had him shot during a drinking session with some of his men. King James was enraged and issued a proclamation offering a reward for the capture of Sanquhar dead or alive. He surrendered, hoping for a royal pardon, but the king was implacable. The chief prosecutor at his trial was Francis Bacon, who argued that Sanquhar's Scottish background was irrelevant and that his murderous behaviour was the result of his exposure to the new Italianate culture and ideas of honour. Although Bacon used the occasion to denounce duelling, Sanquhar's conduct was not that expected of a gentleman-duellist. Turner was not killed in a man-to-man encounter and had no chance to defend himself. Sanquhar was hanged on 29 June 1612 in Westminster Palace yard.

There was more blood to be shed before that perfect unity the balladeer sought could be attained. James was probably more distressed or enraged by the duel in 1613 between Edward Sackville, later Earl of Dorset, and the Scottish Lord Bruce of Kinloss than by any other combat. The two men had been close friends but they fell out calamitously over Venetia Stanley, another lady whose beauty was celebrated in poetry. It was said that as their relationship came under strain, Bruce slapped Sackville on the face, an unpardonable offence against individual dignity and honour. A challenge was inevitable and to avoid legal barriers, they chose to move to the continent. The two kept in touch over arrangements, and in the first instance Lord Bruce was prevented from making the crossing by bad weather at Dover, giving the king time to intervene, more or less telling them to behave. They pretended to comply, but in fact Bruce used the time to receive lessons in fencing.

The challenge was repeated and the preliminaries conducted with the delicacy which normally accompanies preparations for a christening or wedding. However, the exchanges between them, while punctuated at a distance by the rattle of sabres, suggest that while they conformed to the knightly rituals and idiom, they were also restrained by a human, all too human, reluctance to actually engage. The messages they exchanged demonstrate that, unlike the Stewart-Wharton case, they still felt at this stage the persistent urges of the old Adam. The instinctive will to live was in conflict with the swashbuckling language. In the negotiated agreement, the two accepted that were one of the parties to slip or fall, the combat should cease, and that if one sword were to break, the opponent would not take advantage of that mishap but they would either be reconciled there and then or else would stop and make a completely fresh start on equal terms. Discussions over the length, breadth and weight of the swords went back and forth. Sackville gallantly sent his to Bruce for comparison, but the latter raised the stakes by choosing a sturdier one. They turned to an independent arbiter, but Bruce gave way and accepted a sword of the dimensions Sackville wished. His acceptance was accompanied by the swaggering words, 'a little of Earl of Dorset's blood would not serve his turn.' The fight was to be to the death. Mutual friends protested that such intentions were unnecessary given the honour, nobility and rank of the two men, and that the fight to first blood ought to be sufficient to meet the case, but the die was cast. A piece of land in Flanders was purchased for the sole purpose of hosting the duel.

The two rode together to the appointed place, not side by side or exchanging small talk as later gentlemen would do, but one behind the other. A novelist would seize the opportunity to delve into the minds of the men to recreate their reflections and hopes, their fears and regrets, their memories and aspirations, their thoughts of family and friends, but we in a changed culture can only look and wonder. They dismounted on what was reported to be marshy ground, and set to work. Saviolo had warned that no quarter was to be shown or expected even when former friends met, and the two may well have read his words because the fighting was savage, even if interspersed with moments of truce. Sackville left his own detailed account, a narrative of thrusts and parries, of wounds and blows given and received, of each being wrestled to the ground as they fought for 'the greatest and dearest prizes we could ever expect trial for, honour and life'. The two, life and honour, are inseparably linked. Sackville received a wound to the body and lost a finger, and in a pause in the fighting, he recalls that the two even considered calling a halt, but 'when amity was dead, confidence could not live', so the talking ceased and the swordplay resumed.

Sackville gained the upper hand and with his dagger at Bruce's throat offered him the option of life or of at least yielding his sword, but Bruce declined both offers, a choice Sackville considered brave. He then aimed at Bruce's heart, and passed his sword through his body. Bruce shouted out, 'Oh I am slain,' but still had the strength or doggedness to attempt a counterattack. Again Sackville offered to spare his life, but again Bruce refused. Sackville was impressed, but desisted on hearing the surgeon's appeal to be allowed to intervene since Bruce was on the point of death. He wished it to be known that he did not renew his demand to take Bruce's sword 'counting it inhuman to rob a dead man, for so I held him to be'. The demands of chivalry were fully respected, as is also shown by one final gesture from Bruce. Against all the protocols, Bruce's surgeon charged Sackville with drawn sword, and although Sackville warded off 'those base hands', the surgeon was reproved by Bruce's last words, 'Rascal, hold thy hand.'

The case was widely reported and caused a sensation in Jacobean England. Bruce was buried near the field, but his heart was removed and interred in Culross Abbey in Fife, which had been erected by his father. The casket was recovered in the Victorian age. As a footnote, the lady married another man, one Sir Kenelm Digby, and presumably lived happily ever after. As did Sackville. He was readmitted into society and prospered, holding several public offices, thereby demonstrating that participating in a duel and killing an adversary would not lead to social ostracism. In later life, he became at various times an MP, a member of the company which founded the state of Virginia, twice ambassador to France, governor of the Bermuda Islands Company and officer on the royalist side in the Civil

War. Incredibly, he was also one of the men Francis Bacon, who abhorred duelling, turned to when in 1625 he was drawing up a brief for the prosecution in a court case based on a duel arising from a point of honour.[9]

'A common custom'

There was no let-up in the frequency of duels. John Chamberlain, whose correspondence provides valuable insights into life of Jacobean England, gives a vivid account of the dimensions of the phenomenon. He refers first to the Sackville-Bruce duel, and then continues in an excited, gossipy vein to chronicle other duels threatened, upcoming or foiled:

> Here is speech likewise that the Lord Norris and Sir Peregrine Willoughby are gone forth on the same purpose, and that the Lord Chandos and the Lord Hay are upon the same terms. There was a quarrel kindling 'twixt the earls of Rutland Montgomery, but it was quickly quenched by the King, being begun and ended in his presence. But there is more danger 'twixt the earl of Rutland and the Lord Davers, though I heard yesterday that it was already, or on the point of compounding. But that which most men listen after is what will fall out 'twixt the earl of Essex and Master Henry Howard, who is challenged and called to account for certain disgraceful speeches of him. They are both gotten over, the earl from Milford haven, the other from Harwich, with each of them two seconds.[10]

The Earl of Essex in question was the son of the man whom Elizabeth loved in her own way but who later fell into disgrace when he overstepped the mark by bursting into her bed chamber. He was beheaded for treason, causing the family to be stripped of the title until it was restored by King James. The second earl became a close friend of Prince Henry Stuart, the heir apparent. When he married Frances Howard, his future seemed assured, since the Howards were Earls of Sussex and her father had been nominated Lord Chamberlain by King James. However, all did not go well between the couple and the marriage was annulled in 1613 on the grounds of non-consummation. The 'disgraceful speeches' which Chamberlain mentioned referred to taunts and jibes made at Essex's expense by Frances' brother Henry over his impotence and inadequate virility. No man, lord or vassal, could ignore such jibes and Essex issued the inevitable challenge.

Neither seems to have had much inclination to fight, and the negotiations between the seconds dragged on. Once again, both seem to have been caught between the need to display chivalric manliness and a straightforward *timor mortis*. In addition, both men aspired to promotion at court and knew of the king's distaste for duelling. Essex blew hot and cold, indicating that he would content himself with some lesser form of satisfaction, but Howard demurred. An appointed day was set but it came and went with nothing much occurring, so a new time and place was fixed, once again in Flanders. In September 1613, the two men made the crossing separately, accompanied by their loyal seconds. Nothing now stood in the way of the duel, except the indecision, hesitance or downright fear of the parties involved. A message was received forbidding the duel, ostensibly from the king, but possibly a forgery from some acquaintance who was either appalled at the prospect of the duel or simply exasperated at the un-knightly vacillation. The sigh of relief at the receipt of the communication might have been heard across the water. The king took the matter in hand and imposed a settlement without blood being shed.

This event, following the Essex-Howard affair, spurred King James into further action. There was a feeling, and not only in royal circles, that things were getting out of hand, and that duelling especially among the aristocracy was becoming too easily the automatic recourse even in petty arguments. The king banned all writing on the subject so as to deny the practice what a modern prime minister would term the oxygen of publicity. In 1613 he issued his *Proclamation prohibiting the publishing of reports or writing on duels*, complaining, among other things, that duels had become 'a common custom'.[11] To help strengthen the law, King James turned to Francis Bacon, whom in 1613 he appointed attorney general, with a request that he turn his considerable energies as lawyer and philosopher to extirpating the practice. Bacon was glad to oblige and together they launched what has come to be known as the Jacobean Anti-Duelling Campaign.[12]

Francis Bacon by Pourbus the Younger, 1617
(Wikimedia Commons)

The accession of King James had led to an improvement in Bacon's fortunes, although it was at best intermittent. He was knighted in 1603, and given the post of attorney general in 1613 before becoming lord chancellor in 1618, although that did not stop him being subsequently impeached and briefly imprisoned three years later.

He may have been willing to sacrifice friendship and principle on occasion, but on duelling he saw eye to eye with the king. The blood that was flowing was blue blood, and the law was not strong enough, or was not imposed with sufficient vigour to staunch its flow. In his *Essays or Counsels*, which went through three editions in his lifetime, Bacon included an essay *On Revenge* where he gave a famous definition which was held up by subsequent generations of critics as a model of pithy clarity. 'Revenge is a kind of wild justice; which the more man's nature runs to, the more ought law to weed it out. For as for the first wrong, it doth but offend the law; but the revenge of that wrong putteth the law out of office.'[13] Nothing in Bacon's subsequent legal career suggests that he believed revenge to be any kind of justice, however wild, and he certainly believed that the wildness had to be checked. Nor did he hold any truck with notions of honour as justifying a man in seeking reparation on his own behalf. Bacon's aim was to uphold the law and defend the State, not only against external enemies but against internal agents who were, however unintentionally, undermining its very foundation.

The revenge-law antithesis, where revenge is personal action and law a community endeavour, sets the parameters and establishes the standards by which the duel, or revenge, is to be judged inadmissible. He emphasized his point by asserting in the essay that 'vindictive persons live the life of witches; who, as they are mischievous, so end they infortunate (sic).' Making duellists equivalent to witches was a particularly telling blow when King James was on the throne. In Scotland he had issued a tract on the subject, and it is probable that Bacon was appealing to that obsession of his royal master's, as was Shakespeare when in *Macbeth* he introduced witches as motivators of regicide. Those who sought private vengeance were akin to witches, but like witches they would come to an unfortunate end.

Bacon reinforced, subtly but powerfully, his notion of the centrality of law in another essay with the title *Honour and Reputation*, in which he deepened the cultural attack on the spurious Italianate notions of honour he had adumbrated in the prosecution of Lord Sanquhar. He advocated a different, more traditional, view of honour. 'The winning of honour is but the revealing of a man's virtue and worth without disadvantage,' he wrote. Honour was not a quality to be asserted or defended by sword, since true human honour was a moral quality. Bacon's attack on the cult of the duel was thus twofold, philosophical and jurisprudential. The approach he advocated was based on a radical rejection of the whole texture of Renaissance theories which shaped received ideas in aristocratic circles of what constituted honourable and rational behaviour. His fear was that this voguish outlook would became part of the normal way of life, secure and shielded by quotidian common sense and thus beyond all questioning. Bacon's aim was to construct a counter-culture to the code of honour itself, the wellspring of the malaise which was exercising him and his royal master. However, he was not naive enough to believe that merely printing proclamations or publishing essays was sufficient to end this 'present mischief'. He was a forthright proponent of repressive measures, and was dismayed at the inconsistency with which in London as much as Paris statutory punishments were nullified by the issuing of royal pardons. Since the majority of duels were fought by aristocrats who by instinct aspired to royal favour, he proposed as one possible punishment perpetual exclusion from the royal court, but he realized that stronger measures were needed. He favoured hauling miscreants not to ordinary courts but to the Star Chamber, which met in secret and was more amenable to political manipulation.

There he prosecuted a case himself in January 1614 against two lowly subjects, Thomas Bellingham and Brice Christmas who were arrested at Dover on their way to fight their duel abroad. His case for the prosecution has become known as known as *Bacon's charge touching duels*,[14] and in it he reiterated his charge that the duel was, among other things, a challenge to the state and the rule of law, the usurpation of the rights of the law by individuals and the privileging of private action over community policy. He still preferred to employ the term 'revenge' rather than justice, and his objection was that 'duelling extorted revenge out of the magistrate's hand', thus making 'private men to be law-givers to themselves'. Bacon anticipated by several centuries the argument advanced by Max Weber of the State's claim to 'the monopoly of violence'. The rule of law is weakened, Bacon believed, and the king's (or the State's) exclusive entitlement to the use of force is nullified if subjects insist on duelling. He dismissed the prior claim of individual honour, and insisted that the only legitimate way to right a wrong was in a court of law, but that law had to be consistently applied. Centuries before the idea became common currency in criminology, Bacon was of the view that the certainty of detection and punishment rather than the severity of penalty was the real deterrent. His target was not the leniency of judge or jury, although that would become a problem in later years, but inconsistency in applying penal policy.

Duelling was not stamped out by Bacon's laws and later in the century Samuel Pepys, in an entry for 18 August 1662, provided an incredulous and incredible account of the warlike behaviour of certain peers of the realm, notably that of 'my Lord Bellassis', over his 'ridiculous falling-out at my Lord of Oxford's house'. A group had gathered for a social occasion, but the entertainment was followed by 'high words and some blows, and the pulling off of periwigs', and degenerated so far that 'my Lord Monk took away some of their swords and sent for soldiers to guard the house till the fray was ended.' Pepys was scandalized and added the indignant comment that 'to such a degree of madness the nobility of this age is come!' This story jolted his memory and made him recall a more serious event when Mr Jermyn and Colonel Giles Rawlins engaged in a joint duel against Captain Thomas Howard and an unknown man. The result was that Rawlins was killed and Jermyn 'mortally wounded'. One aspect of that affair which puzzled Pepys was that Howard had twice sent challenges which were refused but a third produced an agreement to meet, in Pall Mall. Pepys was baffled by the fact that Howard declined 'to the last to tell Jermyn what the quarrel was; nor does any body know.' Pepys reported that the Court was in a turmoil over the news, and he himself hoped that it would 'cause some good laws against it'. Good laws remained an aspiration, but they were often ignored when passed.

Later commentators believed that Lady Shrewsbury had been responsible for that duel, but the nature of the misdemeanour committed by or against her has been lost, and her alleged involvement may result from a confusion with her role in a 1668 duel between her cuckolded husband and the Duke of Buckingham. Pepys had strong views on that lady, and in an entry for 17 January 1668 he roundly dismissed her ladyship as 'a whore, (who) is at this time, and hath for a great while been, a whore to the Duke of Buckingham. And so her husband challenged him.' The seconds at that time were expected to participate in the fighting, so one of Shrewsbury's seconds was badly injured while Buckingham's second, Sir John Jenkins, was killed. The unfortunate Shrewsbury himself was also wounded and died two months later. Lady Shrewsbury did not mourn him and was rumoured to have observed the duel in disguise as a page boy, and to have gone off with Buckingham afterwards to spend the night with him while he was still dressed in a blood-stained shirt. Pepys shook his head sadly at the spectacle, and wondered if the event would 'make the world think that the King hath good councillors about him, when the Duke of Buckingham, the greatest man about him, is a fellow of no more sobriety than to fight about a whore.' The killers of Jenkins received a royal pardon, a policy Bacon had raged against. Pepys too remained steadfast in his disapproval of all duels and judged their frequency 'a kind of emblem of the general complexion of the whole kingdom'. He himself was not the most faithful of spouses, but was discreet and so evaded challenges. Hypocrisy is always the best policy.

Monday 29 July 1667 was a busy day for him, even by his normal standards. He spent the morning discussing the second Anglo-Dutch war, which was going badly, before making for Westminster Hall in preparation for hearing the king address Parliament. He was disturbed by the sight of a Quaker running about naked shouting 'Repent, repent', and decided to forego listening to the king because of the overcrowding. In the event, the royal speech was an anti-climax and caused much murmuring among the assembled lords and parliamentarians. In spite of all this activity, Pepys was still sufficiently motivated to record at length an account of another duel involving Thomas Porter, a playwright of some renown at the time, and Sir Henry Bellasis, a military officer. Pepys wrote that 'it is worth remembering the silliness of the quarrell', and found it especially piquant that the two men were 'the greatest friends in the world' and had dined together with every sign of conviviality. They had drunk deeply, and Bellasis' voice rose in volume as he grew increasingly excited, causing some bystanders to wonder if they were quarrelling. He rebuffed them with presumably drunken bluster that 'I never quarrell, but I strike; take that as a rule of mine.' The playwright seemingly took this personally and retorted, 'strike! I would I could see the man in England that durst give me a blow.' Bellasis did not explain himself but instead did what he held he had been invited to do: 'give him a box of the eare.' The matter was now beyond all remedy. As Porter made his exit he met no less a man than John Dryden, whom Pepys helpfully identifies as 'the poet'. Porter apprised him of the situation, but there is no evidence of Dryden attempting to intervene. He was asked by Porter to allow his boy to 'bring him notice of which way Bellasis goes', and it would appear that the boy did as he was requested. Porter hired a coach, made for the coffee house where a perhaps calmer Bellasis was seated, and called on him to come out. Pepys continues:

> ... both drew: Tom Porter asked him whether he was ready? The other answering he was, they fell to fight, some of their acquaintance by. They wounded one another, and Bellassis so much that it is feared he will die; and finding himself severely wounded, he called to Tom Porter, and kissed him, and bade him shift for himself; 'for,' says he, 'Tom thou hast hurt me; but I will make shift to stand upon my legs till thou mayest withdraw, and the world not take notice of you, for I would not have thee troubled for what thou hast done.' And whether he did fly or no I cannot tell: but Tom Porter showed Bellassis that he was wounded too.

Pepys commented: 'And this is a fine example; and Bellassis a Parliament-man too, and both of them most extraordinary friends.' He was not impressed by the closing display of solidarity and friendship, but in his diary Pepys passed seamlessly on to report the gossip that 'the Archbishop of Canterbury do keep a wench, and that he is as very a wencher as can be.' Bellasis himself was badly wounded in a later duel in 1691 with Colonel Richard Leveson, but survived and his career as soldier and politician suffered no harm. It could be added that Porter had had previous experience of duelling and had killed a man in 1655, for which he was tried for murder, convicted of manslaughter and sentenced to be burned in the hand.

Although regarded at the time as a duel, the encounter between Bellasis and Porter was more of a drunken brawl. They had failed to respect any gentlemanly etiquette over arrangements on time and place, but it was not this deviation which scandalized Pepys. It was the fact that the ready recourse to weapons demonstrated the 'general complexion' of the manners which made duelling unremarkable. Of the three duels Pepys discusses only the Shrewsbury-Buckingham duel was fought over an identifiable cause, adultery, but as the terrain was delicate, false steps were easily taken and the *Zeitgeist* favoured a facile recourse to arms over even trivial disputes. Shrewsbury's son John would also die in a duel with the Duke of Grafton, illegitimate son of Charles II, for having upset the duke by his intemperate language.

The Glorious Revolution which forced the Stuarts into exile and brought the Dutch House of Orange to the throne changed little as regards duelling, which remained illegal, although this was undermined by the willingness of King William to issue pardons, as his Stuart predecessors had done. All the indecisions in official and unofficial circles over duelling came to the fore in an encounter in 1694 which saw John Law kill his opponent Edward 'Beau' Wilson. At the time Wilson, an elegant dandy whose opulent lifestyle dazzled London society but left it bewildered as to the source of his wealth, was the better known of the two. John Law had come down from Edinburgh and was living in modest lodgings with a Mrs Lawrence, who may have been his landlady or his lover, or conceivably both. Wilson's sister moved into the same premises, and her presence and subsequent decision to leave in high dudgeon caused friction which brought Wilson into the picture, but the reasons for this burgeoning hostility are unclear. The two men had an unfriendly correspondence but it may have been by chance that they met in a tavern. Whatever transpired, Law left on foot, and

Wilson and a Captain Wightman took a carriage. The two parties met in Bloomsbury Square, and the subsequent trials had to decide whether this was a pre-ordained appointment or a casual mishap. Wilson immediately drew his sword, Law did likewise and with his first blow stabbed Wilson in the abdomen, killing him on the spot. Law did not flee and waited to be arrested.

He was initially accused of manslaughter, but this was raised to a murder charge as enquiries continued, meaning that Law faced capital punishment. If the two men had arranged in the tavern to meet later, that would justify the capital charge, for which the penalty was death by hanging. If on the other hand, the fight had been a sudden flare-up, the lesser charge was appropriate. Legal proceedings dragged on, with Law first acquitted but then re-arrested when Wilson's family appealed. The event had aroused little interest in its first stages, but risked becoming an affair of state between England and Scotland. It was also raised with the king. After months in captivity, Law eventually escaped.

In his biography, James Buchan writes that 'the duel was the capital event in John Law's life ... had he stayed in London, Law might have been just another financial pamphleteer.'[15] His life took a different turn and he became one of the most prominent figures of his age. His wanderings took him to different countries, before he fetched up in France, which was almost bankrupt after Louis XIV's wars. He set up in 1716 the General Private Bank, which assumed responsibility for the country's national debt. He developed the use of paper money, a revolutionary move for which he was mocked by Voltaire among others, but has since seen him celebrated as 'the man who invented modern finance'.[16] He might even have been 'the richest man who ever lived'.[17] However, he was also responsible for the Mississippi Bubble, the name given to the project which caused widespread disruption when the speculating Mississippi Company collapsed, an event which some historians view as a contributory cause of the French Revolution.

Law had to flee and made his way to Venice, where he is buried in the church of San Moisè. There is a plaque marking his tomb on the floor near the doorway, and tourists walk over it without looking down at the inscription, but his survival in his duel changed the course of European history.

1 Andrew Lang, *The Gowrie Conspiracy*, London: Longman, Green & Co, 1909, p. 23.
2 Lawrence Stone, *The Crisis of the Aristocracy*, Oxford: Oxford University Press, 1965, p. 245.
3 Markku Peltonen, *The Duel in Early Modern England: Civility, Politeness and Honour*, Cambridge: Cambridge University Press, 2003, p. 81.
4 Antonia Fraser, *King James*, London: Book Club Associates, 1974, p. 69.
5 Walter Scott, *Tales of a Grandfather, Being Stories Taken from Scottish History*, 3 vols., Glasgow: Gowans & Gray, 1923, vol. 2, pp. 26-8.
6 Lisa Jardine & Alan Stewart, *Hostage to Fortune*, London: Victor Gollancz, 1998, p. 342.
7 Andrew Steinmetz, *The Romance of Duelling in All Times and Countries*, London: Chapman & Hall, 1868, vol. 1, p.170.
8 Peltonen, *op. cit.*, p. 76.
9 *Ibid*, p. 145.
10 John Chamberlain, *The Letters of John Chamberlain*, edited by E.N. McClure, Philadelphia PA: American Philosophical Society, 1939, p. 35.
11 Peltonen, *op. cit.*, p. 92.
12 Markku Peltonen, 'The Jacobean Anti-Duelling Campaign', in *The Historical Journal*, Cambridge, March 2001.
13 Francis Bacon, *Essays*, London: The Folio Society, 2002, p. 14.
14 Jardine & Stewart, *op. cit.* pp. 341-2.
15 James Buchan, *John Law: A Scottish Adventurer of the Eighteenth Century*, London: MacLehose Press, 2018, p. 46.
16 Janet Gleeson, *Millionaire: The Philanderer, Gambler and Duelist Who Invented Modern Finance*, New York: Simon & Schuster, 2000.
17 Edward Chancellor, 'The Man Who Invented Money', *New York Review of Books*, 18 April 2019.

6

THE AGE OF LIGHT
GENTLEMANLY DEBATE

It is conventional to think of the eighteenth century as the gilded age of literary salons when Enlightenment thinkers challenged dogma and superstition, when political beliefs in absolutism and divine rights gave way to notions of the social contract, when the scientific revolution made experimentation and observation the basis of knowledge and when the early stirrings of the industrial revolution laid the groundwork for a growth of prosperity, at least for some. The *habitués* of salons and coffee shops believed that they were living in an Age of Improvement, a judgement broadly and flatteringly confirmed by posterity. This century of the *lumières*, as French historians have dubbed it, has also been called, only semi-ironically, the golden age of the duel, when the code of honour was being polished, or calcified, in France and Britain into the code of the gentleman. Both honour and the duel were subject to critical examination by essayists and philosophers, but whereas the earlier Renaissance humanists perceived a necessary compatibility between these notions, many thinkers and men of letters of this age were exercised either by the flaws in the concepts themselves or by what they perceived as a clash between them.

It is thought that during the reign of George III (1760-1820), there were 172 known duels in England alone, resulting in sixty-nine recorded fatalities.[1] In all probability, the actual number was much higher, since it was rarely in the interests of the combatants to publicize the matter. Many of the combatants were either born in the palaces and mansions of the aristocracy, or else attained high office in politics or the army, but all regarded participation in a duel in whatever capacity as a natural part of their social standing, like attending a ball or riding with hounds. André Malraux once wrote that Europe has produced only two models of male life, the British gentleman and the Spanish *caballero*, and for both unwritten precepts had the force of the Ten Commandments, indeed in certain circumstances they superseded divine law. It is significant that some contemporary philosophers, even if not specifically referring to the duel, were drawn to comment on the habit of human beings to seek the safety of conformity. Adam Smith, analysing human nature, which he viewed as eternal and universal, wrote that 'self-deceit, this fatal weakness of mankind, is the source of half the disorders of human life'. Even more shrewdly, he pointed out in the same work that self-deceit was inevitable, 'so partial are the views of mankind with regard to the propriety of their own conduct, both at the time of action and after it; and so difficult is it for them to view it in the light in which any indifferent spectator would consider it.'[2] His contemporary David Hume wrote of the 'contagion of fashion', and judged 'habit' to be a guide of life and basis of conduct, while Rousseau believed that for most of humanity customs provided a moral code.

There were continued, if futile, efforts in different countries to outlaw duelling. The anecdote was often recounted of how in the seventeenth century the great Gustavus Adolphus of Sweden had treated two officers who came to request an exemption from the ban on duelling. The king, to their surprise, consented and fixed a time and place. To their greater surprise, he turned up at the appointed time with a detachment of soldiers and told the two to fight to the death, but informed them that the soldiers would then march onto the field and execute the victorious duellist on the spot. The ardour of the two men cooled. In Poland in 1712, King Augustus made duelling illegal. Catherine the Great issued a similar edict in Russia but in both nations duelling was quietly condoned. Ten years later in Vienna, Emperor Joseph II expressed his contempt for a count and a captain who requested leave to fight a duel: 'I will not suffer duelling in my army ... I am resolved that this barbarous custom, worthy only of the times of Tamerlane and Bajazet, and which has so often thrown families into mourning, shall be repressed and punished, should it even cost me half of my officers to effect it.'

Men of *honour*

Such drastic measures were not the British way. In his *Review of the Affairs of France* (1704), Daniel Defoe devoted a few pages to the subject, noting complacently, and inaccurately, that duelling had never been as common in England as it had on the other side of the Channel. He was uncomfortable with the very idea of the duel and was scathing about the culture of honour, so he praised French kings for outlawing duelling altogether and was enthusiastic about the Court of Honour established as an alternative means of resolving conflicts. A court of this sort would be proposed many times, from Malta in the days of the Knights of St John to the Southern States of the US in the nineteenth century.

The main forums for discussion were the journals which are such a characteristic of eighteenth-century literary life, and the duel could not fail to attract the attention, mainly satirical, of the essayists who contemplated the morals and mores of the age, as did Richard Steele and Joseph Addison. Already at the outset of his career Steele authored in 1701 *The Christian Hero*, a high-minded tract which criticized in the light of Anglican teaching the behaviour of his male contemporaries, and included the duel among his targets. He and Addison founded *The Tatler* in 1709 as a vehicle for their own, broadly Whiggish, ideas. It lasted only two years but was quickly resurrected as *The Spectator*, which in its original incarnation remained in business until 1714. The two collaborated very fully, jointly signing articles in both journals as 'Isaac Bickerstaff', a *nom de plume* invented by Jonathan Swift but adopted by them. Bickerstaff preferred the light-hearted approach to lambast fashionable notions of honour, as in an essay entitled *Duello*:

> As things stand, I shall put up no more affronts; and I shall be so far from taking ill words, that I will not take ill looks. I therefore warn all hot young fellows not to look hereafter more terrible than their neighbours: for if they stare at me with their hats cocked higher than other people, I will not bear it. Nay, I give warning to all people in general to look kindly at me, for I will bear no frowns, even from ladies; and if any woman pretends to look scornfully at me, I shall demand satisfaction of the next of kin of the masculine gender.

In the ninth edition of *The Spectator*, Addison's satire opened with a description of what he termed 'Hum-Drum and Mum Clubs', focusing, on one which had been established in the days of Charles II.

> I mean the club of duellists, in which none was to be admitted that had not fought his man. The president of it was said to have killed half a dozen in single combat; and as for the other members they took their seats according to the number of their slain. There was likewise a side-table for such as had only drawn blood, and shown a laudable ambition of taking the first opportunity to qualify themselves for the first table. This club, which consisted only of men of *honour*, did not continue long, most of the members being put to the sword, or hanged, a little after the institution.

Steele features as soldier and essayist in Thackeray's historical novel, *Henry Esmond*, where he assists Esmond, then a young recruit in the Life Guards, to make his first steps in the world of publishing. More unexpectedly, there is also a reference in that novel to a duel fought by Steele, and this is no invention. Steele discovered that it was one thing to state an abstract principle in print but quite another to act on it in life when he found himself drawn into an argument between officers in the Coldstream Guards. There were paradoxes within paradoxes in this odd affair. After taking umbrage at certain remarks, one officer was on the point of issuing a challenge to another but was dissuaded when Steele's arguments were brought to his attention. It may be one of a very few occasions when literature actually altered life, but alas! not for long. Other officers were less convinced and spread the word that Steele's views undermined the very concept of honour and constituted a denial of the offended gentleman's right to seek redress. They were not mistaken in their interpretation but Steele then found himself arraigned in absentia, judged guilty of unacceptable behaviour, duly challenged and thus left in a quandary. On the one hand he was opposed to duelling but on the other he recognized, and was obviously bound by, the demands on his own honour. He tried to mend the affair, but to no avail. A duel had to be fought. Steele had some competence in swordsmanship, and chose the sword as the weapon for his encounter, believing that with some fancy footwork and skilled parries he could avoid sustaining or doing any injury. In this respect he failed since he inflicted on his opponent a wound of such seriousness that he was not expected to survive. In fact he made a good recovery, his honour, if not his health, intact. Whether Steele's honour was equally secure is a more complex matter.

In *The Tatler* in 1711, Steele contributed a more serious report on an actual case between Sir Cholmondeley Dering and Richard Thornhill. The two gentlemen were imbibing together in an inn but the conversation took an ugly turn, and led to an unseemly brawl in which Dering knocked out some of Thornhill's teeth. Teeth are expendable but honour is not, so the latter issued a challenge. They agreed on the use of pistols and Sir Cholmondeley lost his life, which seems a heavy exchange for a few molars. Thornhill was duly charged with murder but, as was common, was convicted only of the lesser crime of manslaughter on the grounds of provocation. Normally that would have been the end of the matter, but the case returned to the news two months later when Thornhill was stabbed to death by two men who shouted 'Remember Sir Cholmondeley Dering.'[3] Both Steele and Jonathan Swift made reference to the case in purely factual terms, although Swift did dignify the dead man as 'Poor Sir Cholmondeley'.[4]

Debates in France over the punctilios of honour proceeded according to a different logic, but they did not produce any greater level of consistency. Jean-Jacques Rousseau displays something of the uncertain confusion of the time. He had a deep distaste for duelling, writing that it was not 'an institution of honour but a horrible and barbarous custom which a courageous man despises and a good man abhors.' Unlike Voltaire, he himself never prepared to fight a duel, but his views are complex. In his *Letter to D'Alembert on Theatre*, he is critical of French attempts to ban duelling by law since the legal approach assumes 'a shocking opposition between honour and the law, for even the law cannot oblige anyone to dishonour himself.'[5] The core concept of honour was not subjected to scrutiny. The more traditional dilemma was over an incompatibility between religious morals and the *code duello*, but in the Enlightenment framework Rousseau would not be the only writer to posit a purely secular clash which upheld the right to duel in the name of honour, whatever the law laid down.

There were various unexpected events involving unlikely figures, none more so than the occurrences involving Voltaire, the mocking satirist of modish customs and beliefs. In 1726, the Chevalier de Rohan-Chabot, an aristo of impeccable pedigree, had a verbal altercation with the philosopher. The exact words are disputed, but it is beyond doubt that the chevalier made some disparaging remarks about Voltaire, who replied with a trenchant witticism to the effect that while his name would be remembered with honour on account of his genuine achievements, the name and the honour of Rohan-Chabot would be forgotten since had achieved nothing. The sally was judged demeaning and upset the chevalier's delicate sense of self-worth. Instead of following the gentlemanly path of issuing a challenge on his own behalf, he hired some thugs to assault Voltaire. He may, of course, have decided that such was the gulf in rank between the two that it was beneath him to dignify a commoner with a duel. The dispute, however, then took a surprising turn for after the assault Voltaire decided that he had been offended and that in consequence a duel was the only appropriate riposte. Being unskilled in swordsmanship, he engaged a tutor to give him lessons. The image of Voltaire sword in one hand, heeding advice on posture and footwork, while practising feints, parries and thrusts is one of the more incongruous images in the entire history of duelling, or philosophy.

There is no way of knowing what level of proficiency he reached because word of his intentions reached the ears of the Rohan family who had Voltaire arrested and confined in the Bastille. It is hard not to be grateful for this move and to conclude that, however gruelling life was in prison, it was better for the history of western culture to have Voltaire safely enclosed there rather than standing on the field of honour facing a man of undoubtedly greater expertise in swordsmanship. He negotiated his release in exchange for a promise to go into exile in England, where he spent two years and wrote several works, including the celebrated *English Letters*. Several times thereafter, he returned to the question of duelling, dismissing it as an absurdity practised only by the aristocracy.

The days of aristocratic *hauteur* were, however, numbered. The last decades of the eighteenth century in France, well before the tumbrils of the Revolution began to roll through the streets, can be seen, at least in retrospect, as a troubled and transitional age. Although none suspected it in 1774 when Louis XVI was crowned, the coronation and the king's own inadequacy ushered in one of Europe's 'twilight ages', to revert to the vocabulary of Huizinga. Glittering and unshakeable as the *ancien régime* seemed at the time of the ceremony, the succeeding years represented the last season of feudal rights and the *douceur de vivre* they guaranteed for the privileged, for this was also the age of the *philosophes* and of the rising bourgeoisie, a class which was still excluded from power. The philosophy they expounded was subversive in every sphere, not only in politics, as was recognized by Thomas Carlyle, no admirer of the new trends, who asked polemically in his classic work, *The French Revolution*, whether there was anything to be said in favour of 'those decadent ages in which no Ideal either grows or blossoms? When Belief and Loyalty have passed away, and only the cant and false echo of them remains?'[6] His sour words targeted the Enlightenment thought of the great *Encyclopédistes*, but the old nostrums were being subjected to refined mockery not only in the salons of Paris but also in circles frequented by a new generation of the nobility.

Benedetta Craveri has identified such a group, named by her *The Last Libertines*, who came to maturity in that epoch and who exemplify that doubt and loss of self-confidence which commonly precede a shift in power. She quotes the Comte de Ségur writing towards the end of his life that 'we mocked the old customs, the feudal pride of our fathers and the solemnity of their ways,' even if he adds the significant rider, 'so as to continue to enjoy all our old privileges'.[7] The lives of these men and women straddled the monarchy, the Revolution, the Napoleonic empire and the Restoration and some sided with the revolutionaries in the early stage of that process, but all concluded later that their mockery contributed to the suppression of those old privileges.

It was again Carlyle who drew attention to the limitations in this age of questioning as regards honour and the duel. 'Nay, one virtue they (the nobles) are still required to have (for mortal man cannot live without a conscience): the virtue of perfect readiness to fight duels.' It may be remarked that Carlyle, for all his worship of heroes, was no admirer of duelling. He wrote in the same work: 'Of duels we have sometimes spoken: how, in all parts of France, innumerable duels were fought; and argumentative men and messmates, flinging down the wine-cup and weapons of reason and repartee, met in the measured field; to part bleeding; or perhaps *not* to part, but to fall mutually skewered through with iron, their wrath and life alike ending, - and die as fools die.'

The new culture took some time to crystallize, and longer to be transferred into action, particularly over such well-established beliefs as honour and duelling, so while scorn was expressed in the abstract over the custom of duelling, some of new thinkers and revolutionary leaders still took part in duels. Carlyle regarded Mirabeau as a champion of anti-duelling and records that he tossed aside the many cartels he received with a 'stereotype formula: Monsieur, you are put upon my List; but I warn you that it is long, and I grant no preferences.' This is a picturesque utterance, redolent of aristocratic disdain, but not the whole truth. Mirabeau, the conscience of the Revolution in its first days and the man whose untimely death may have changed its very course, attacked the practice in theory but had fought several duels in his youth, while during the Revolution he engaged in a duel with swords with Victor de Fay (later Marquis de La Tour-Maubourg) from which he emerged badly wounded. For a time, honour was still esteemed and duelling continued, even as the patrician culture which generated them was collapsing and as the writings of the *philosophes* circulated.

A French duel featuring smallsword and sabre, Pierre Jacques François Girard, 1740.

France and Britain eyed each other warily. Tobias Smollett was a cosmopolitan who was well informed on French affairs, but as regards the duel he himself took contorted thinking to a new level of schizophrenia. Few novelists have so gloried in the dramatic potential of the duel in their fiction, and none have been so forthright in their condemnation of it in life. His heroes show high-minded intolerance of any slight on their honour or manhood and are prompt to issue challenges when these qualities are called into question, so his novels are enlivened by multiple duels, described in heroic detail. However, faced with actual duelling in society he had no truck with any tormented self-questioning or subtle moralistic distinctions over rights conferred by law or justified by wont and custom. Smollett's most mature thoughts on the subject occupy Letter 19 of his *Travels Through France and Italy*, first published in 1766 but modified until his death five years later. He had a miserable time on his travels with villainous continental inns and the appalling fare they served, but found the energy to provide vigorous descriptions and denunciation of various ludicrous, pathetic or unusually brutal duels. He never lacked the will to offer his forthright advice on how to suppress the evil once and for all.

I will make bold to propose a remedy to this gigantic evil, which seems to gain ground every day: let a court be instituted for taking cognisance of all breaches of honour, with power to punish by fine, pillory, sentence of infamy, outlawry, and exile, by virtue of an act of parliament made for this purpose; and all persons insulted shall have recourse to this tribunal; let every man who seeks personal reparation with sword, pistol, or other instrument of death be declared infamous, and banished the kingdom ... if any man is killed in a duel, let his body be hanged on a public gibbet, for a certain time, and then given to the surgeons; let his antagonist be hanged as a murderer, and dissected also; and some mark of infamy be set on the memory of both.[8]

In Italy, Cesare Beccaria, a member of the Milanese nobility
and a writer deeply versed in Enlightenment thought, subjected
the bases of civil and criminal law to critical examination in *On
Crimes and Punishments* (1776), the founding work of criminology.
In the two chapters devoted to honour and duelling, the author
calls attention to the contrast between civil laws and 'the
laws of what is called "honour", where pride of place is given
to opinion'. He rued the fact that many learned disquisitions
had been devoted to the definition of honour but 'without
any fixed and stable idea being associated with it'. A rigorous
thinker, Beccaria followed the political thought of Hobbes and
Rousseau in employing the myth of a primitive state of nature
in his discussion of the growth of the body politic, but adding
the original stance that humanity emerged from that primal
condition in order to prevent the despotism of one man over
others. He further held that in society there lay an area beyond
the rule of law, that is, the rule of law, the realm of opinion,
or reputation, and in this realm the real standard of exchange
was honour. 'Very many men are ready to stake their lives on
this *honour*,' he wrote, but such individuals are found only in
the upper echelons of society, since 'the need for the esteem of
others is less common among the humble classes.'[9]

If Beccaria the philosopher believed he had found an
explanation and even a justification of the phenomenon of the
duel, Beccaria the moralist continued to disapprove, but he was
unsure of what measures could be taken to outlaw it. It was
observable, he wrote, that 'attempts to put a stop to this custom
by decrees of death against those who engage in duels have
been in vain, for it is founded on something which some men
fear more than death,' that is, the loss of honour. Beccaria was
now in a state of perplexity, so he weakly recommended that
legislation should be enacted 'to punish the aggressor, that is,
the person whose action caused the duel'.

In the same decades in England, Dr Johnson tussled with
the same problems, and according to James Boswell, returned
to the question on more than one occasion. On 10 April 1772,
we find the two men at dinner at General Oglethorpe's in the

company of Oliver Goldsmith. It was Boswell who set the hare running that day by posing the question 'whether duelling was consistent with moral duty'. Oglethorpe, a bluff military man untroubled by abstract outpourings, replied that 'undoubtedly a man has a right to defend his honour'. Goldsmith turned to Boswell to ask 'what he would do if he were affronted', to which Boswell replied he would 'think it necessary to fight', a retort Goldsmith regarded as closing the argument. Not so Johnson, who stated that 'it does not follow that what a man would do is therefore right.' This reply prompted Boswell to raise the familiar moral question, 'whether duelling was contrary to the laws of Christianity'. Johnson expatiated on this point in what Boswell viewed as 'a masterly manner':

> Sir, as men become in a high degree refined, various causes of offence arise; which are considered to be of such importance, that life must be staked to atone for them, though in reality they are not so. A body that has received a very fine polish may be easily hurt. Before men arrive at this artificial refinement, if one tells his neighbour he lies, his neighbour tells him he lies; if one gives his neighbour a blow, his neighbour gives him a blow: but in a state of highly polished society, an affront is held to be a serious injury. It must therefore be resented, or rather a duel must be fought upon it; as men have agreed to banish from their society one who puts up with an affront without fighting a duel. Now, Sir, it is never unlawful to fight in self-defence. He, then, who fights a duel, does not fight from passion against his antagonist, but out of self-defence; to avert the stigma of the world, and to prevent himself from being driven out of society. I could wish there was not that superfluity of refinement; but while such notions prevail, no doubt a man may lawfully fight a duel.[10]

Few more eloquent statements of the complexities of the honour-duel fusion have been made than this spontaneous utterance by

Johnson. He personally deplored duelling and the 'superfluity of refinement' that offered its justification, but could not dismiss the import of honour in the affairs of an advanced society, and indeed believed that men of honour have dilemmas unknown to others.

More than a decade later, in 1783, Boswell returned to the subject, prompted on this occasion by the news that Lieutenant David Cunninghame, a nephew of his wife, had killed his antagonist in a duel and had been himself badly wounded. Boswell was a man of

Dr Johnson c. 1770 (National Library of Wales/ Wikimedia Commons).

delicate conscience, deeply Christian in his outlook, and may even have worried about the fate of the soul of his in-law. He hastened to Johnson's home to discuss the subject which plainly troubled him. A direct quote in Boswell's idiosyncratic style gives the flavour of the exchange.

JOHNSON. 'I do not see, Sir, that fighting is absolutely forbidden in Scripture; I see revenge forbidden, but not self-defence.' BOSWELL. 'The Quakers say it is; "Unto him that smiteth thee on one cheek, offer him also the other."' JOHNSON. 'But stay, Sir; the text is meant only to have the effect of moderating passion; it is plain that we are not to take it in a literal sense. We see this from the context, where there are other recommendations, which I warrant you the Quaker will not take literally; as, for instance, "From him that would borrow of thee, turn thou not away." Let a man whose credit is bad, come to a Quaker, and say, "Well, Sir, lend me a hundred pounds;" he'll find him as unwilling as any other man. No, Sir, a man may shoot the man who invades his character, as he may shoot him who attempts to break into his house. So in 1745, my friend, Tom Gumming, the Quaker, said, he would not fight, but he would drive an ammunition cart; and we know that the Quakers have sent flannel waistcoats to our soldiers, to enable them to fight better.' BOSWELL. 'When a man is the aggressor, and by ill-usage forced on a duel in which he is killed, have we not little ground to hope that he is gone into a state of happiness?' JOHNSON. 'Sir, we are not to judge determinately of the state in which a man leaves this life. He may in a moment have repented effectually, and it is possible may have been accepted by GOD.'

For all his reverence for Dr Johnson, Boswell was unconvinced and even baffled by this reply, which is indeed more than somewhat sophistical. He was plainly concerned that reproducing this passage might harm Johnson's reputation, so he added an explanatory, or exculpatory, footnote:

I think it necessary to caution my readers against concluding that in this or in any other conversation of Dr Johnson, they have his serious and deliberate opinion on the subject of duelling. In my *Journal of the Tour to the Hebrides*, it appears he made this frank confession; "Nobody at times, talks more laxly than I do;" and, ib., Sept. 19, 1773, "He fairly owned he could not explain the rationality of duelling." We may, therefore, infer, that he could not think that justifiable, which seems so inconsistent with the spirit of the Gospel.

In the after-dinner conversation on Skye referred to, Johnson moved from a discussion of the disappearance of prize-fighting, which he regretted since he believed that 'every art should be preserved, and the art of self-defence is surely important', onto the Highland use of the claymore which he considered an 'ill-advised weapon', which would be useless against the more flexible dirk, before returning to duelling. Boswell reports not the give and take of conversation but only Johnson's monologue:

> There is not a case in England where one or other of the combatants must die; if you have overcome your adversary by disarming him, that is sufficient, though you should not kill him; your honour, or the honour of your family is restored, as much as it can be by a duel. It is cowardly to force your antagonist to renew the combat when you know that you have the advantage of him by superior skill. You might as well go in and cut this throat while he is asleep in his bed. When a duel begins, it is supposed there may be equality; because it is not always skill that prevails. It depends as much on presence of mind, nay on accidents. The wind may be in a man's face. He may fall. Many such things may decide the superiority. A man is sufficiently punished by being called out and subjected to the risk that is in a duel.

This line of reasoning led him, under Boswell's coaxing, to confess that the rationality of duelling was beyond him, but he never did subject the idea of honour itself to examination. While bringing a high level of perspicacity and discernment to bear, Johnson approaches gingerly the complexities of a phenomenon which was firmly entrenched in society even if officially viewed with hostility by the Church and State. He relies on his famous, blunt common sense which in a different context led him to refute Berkeley's philosophical view that reality only existed when observed by giving a rock a firm kick. Duelling troubled him, but he could not bring himself to approve or condemn it outright. He adhered to a modified version of the honour code and held that a man's right to self-defence extended to the defence of his honour, but could not deny the inadequacy and even irrationality of such a course of action. Boswell ended up implying that when provoked or in the exuberance of conversation, Dr Johnson often expressed himself 'laxly', that is, giving vent to views weakly held and subject to the vagaries of conversation. In this, he resembled many of his contemporaries.

It was not only discussion that was lax. It was widely felt that the actual practice was unruly and anarchic. The need to introduce rules of acceptable conduct led to the drafting of a comprehensive code by a group of gentlemen meeting in Clonmel in Ireland in 1777. There were twenty-seven laws in total, covering the whole range of possibilities. The Clonmel outlined the nature of offences, distinguishing between those which could be erased by an apology and those for which no form of words could be adequate. It was that insults to a lady were more grievous than those to another man. The legislators left no room for doubt on choice of weapon, on behaviour at the actual encounter or on the duties of seconds, who were expected to make reasonable efforts to bring about a peaceful solution to any difficulty but who had to follow due procedures over loading pistols and timing of shots at the appointed time. There was a certain awkwardness over misfiring pistols, but it was agreed that this was simply bad luck and the opponent should have a free shot. These laws were meant to control Irish practice, but were adopted throughout the English-speaking world.

There were two influential, ponderous tomes published in the 1780s, both considering duelling and honour in the framework of political and moral philosophy: Rev William Paley's *The Principles of Moral and Political Philosophy* (1785) followed four years later by Jeremy Bentham's *Introduction to the Principles of Morals and Legislation*. Paley was unequivocal:

Duelling as a punishment is absurd; because it is an equal chance, whether the punishment fall upon the offender, or the person offended. Nor is it much better as a reparation: it being difficult to explain in what the *satisfaction* consists, or how it tends to undo the injury, or to afford a compensation for the damage already sustained.

He was equally scathing on the law of honour, since challenges are given 'without malice against an adversary ... or any other concern than to preserve a duellist's own reputation in the world.' Since, he writes, murder is forbidden, it follows that 'if unauthorised laws of honour be allowed to create exceptions to divine prohibitions, there is an end to all morality.' However, granted the 'insufficiency of the redress which the law of the land affords for those injuries which chiefly affect a man in his sensibility and reputation,' Paley proposes reforms to the law to allow for damage for such wrongs. For the army, he even recommends the revival of ancient Courts of Honour,[11] a proposal that would recur in all debates on this subject.

Bentham, the founder of Utilitarianism, found himself in a dilemma: being on the one hand convinced of the right to defend offended honour but on the other viewing duelling as an absurdity, he vacillated over condemning the duel outright. His hesitations were founded on his judgment of the inadequacy of current legislation in this sphere, so until the law could be made the natural forum for reparation, he found himself compelled, however reluctantly, to accept that duelling has its justification. 'Duelling entirely effaces a blot which an insult imprints upon the honour,' he wrote.[12] Recourse to the law would be preferable, but some of the legal remedies he advocated are eccentric. For instance, if a man insults a lady, he is to be dressed in woman's clothes and submit to be being ritually slapped by the offended female. No doubt he was convinced of the efficacy of ridicule and it is surely a matter of regret that this particular policy was never tested.

1 John Norris, *Pistols at Dawn: A History of Duelling*, Cheltenham, The History Press, 2009, p. 103.
2 Adam Smith, *The Theory of Moral Sentiments* (1759), Part III, Chapter IV, New York: MetaLibri, 2005, p. 207.
3 J.G. Millingen, *The History of Duelling*, vol. 1, London: Bentley, 1841, p.55
4 Jonathan Swift, *The Journal to Stella* (edited by George A. Aitken), Letter 22, London: Methuen, 1901; Richard Steele, *The Spectator*, 6 June 1771.
5 Mika Lavaque-Manty, 'Dueling for Equality: Masculine Honor and the Modern Politics of Dignity', *Political Theory*, December 2006, pp. 9-10.
6 Thomas Carlyle, *The French Revolution: A History*, London: Chapman & Hall, 1837, vol. 1, p.8.
7 Benedetta Craveri, translated by Aaron Kerner, *The Last Libertines*, New York: New York Review of Books, 2020, p.1.
8 Tobias Smollett, *Travels through France and Italy* (1766), edited by Frank Felsenstein, Oxford: Oxford World's Classics, 1999, p. 252.
9 Cesare Beccaria, translated by Richard Davies, *On Crime and Punishments*, Cambridge: Cambridge University Press, 1995, pp. 26-8.
10 I am grateful to Dr Gordon Turnbull, an unsurpassed expert on Boswell, for directing me to these conversations
11 William Paley, *The Principles of Moral and Political Philosophy*, Book III, Part II, Chapter 9, London: 1785
12 Jeremy Bentham, *An Introduction to the Principles of Morals and Legislation* (1780), edited by J.H. Burns and H.L.A. Hart), Oxford: Clarendon Press, 1999, p. 195.

7

THE AGE OF SCANDAL
UNGENTLEMANLY DEEDS

A less glorious side of eighteenth century life was identified by the novelist and historian T.H. White in his work, *The Age of Scandal*. He focused on the closing decades of the century but his judgments could be extended backwards to cast a less benign light on the age, especially on the upper echelons who viewed their lives as a model of refinement.[1] Social histories of the eighteenth century or biographies of its most prominent figures casually introduce facts which quite unconsciously demonstrate the ease with which men could, while strolling about in the most commonplace circumstances, be drawn into a banal argument which escalated into something worse. The sword was as much a standard feature of gentlemanly attire as the wig, and its ready availability facilitated brawling or duelling. To reduce the frequency of duelling, Richard 'Beau' Nash, Master of Ceremonies in Bath in the first half of the eighteenth century and the man credited with making the Georgian city the elegant social centre familiar from Jane Austen's novels, was compelled to issue a decree banning the wearing of swords in public. The House of Commons in 1711 debated half-heartedly an anti-duelling Bill, but it got nowhere until Parliament and the nation were galvanized by a particularly obnoxious duel.

The fourth Duke of Hamilton (1658-1712) played an important, possibly decisive, role in Scottish and British history for his part in the negotiations which led to the 1707 Act of

Union. He was undisputed leader of the anti-Union faction in Edinburgh, but on account of either pusillanimity or of bribery he failed to present himself for the decisive vote, which approved the measure. He was denied a place in the Scottish delegation to the House of Lords, but acquired a seat with his English title as Duke of Brandon. He was a Tory and a Jacobite, and his career underwent various vicissitudes under Queen Anne, but he appeared to have achieved the acceptance and success he craved when in 1712 he was appointed British Ambassador to France. He delayed his move to Paris, perhaps because of his efforts to settle his precarious financial situation. This latter part of his career intrigued W.M. Thackeray, who bent history to make him a character in *The History of Henry Esmond Esq*. In the novel he was a widower and, although much older, became engaged to the social climber, Beatrix Esmond, who was enamoured more of the position she could claim as his wife than of the unattractive man Thackeray portrays.

Charles Mohun, Fourth Baron Mohun of Okehampton (1675-1712), was a thorough scoundrel, or in the words of J.G. Millingen 'an unprincipled character, whose associates were in general as depraved and contemptible as himself'.[2] Duelling was a family tradition, and shortly after his birth his father died of wounds received in a duel. He himself fought more than one duel, including one in 1692 over a gambling debt with the Earl of Cassilis. Later that year, he took part in a plot to abduct an actress, Mrs Bracegirdle, for his friend General George Macartney. Her supposed lover was killed in the affair, but Mohun was acquitted in a trial in the House of Lords. He appeared in the same forum in 1697 charged with the murder of Richard Coote after a duel in Leicester Square, but was again acquitted, although on this occasion his co-accused, the Earl of Warwick, was convicted of manslaughter.[3] Mohun took his seat in the House of Lords, where he sat as a Whig. He and Hamilton were thus bitter political rivals, but that was not the only, or principal, cause of their enmity.

The wives of both men were members of the family of the Earl of Macclesfield, whose death in 1701 left the two men feuding over the rights of inheritance to his well-appointed estate. Women had very few legal entitlements, so it was their husbands who entered into the dispute, which they did with a will. The case dragged on for over a decade until eventually the two men were brought together in an attorney's office in November 1712. A crucial piece of evidence in favour of Mohun was provided by an old retainer, but his memory was failing and his testimony was dismissed by Hamilton as having 'neither truth nor justice to it'.[4] Mohun viewed this remark as offensive, as he was obliged to since his case risked falling apart. The negotiations foundered and challenges were issued.

The duel went ahead in Hyde Park. In Thackeray's depiction, the meeting was a mini-battle rather than a man-to-man duel, and the description is not inaccurate, as the seconds, Colonel John Hamilton, a relative on the duke's side, and General George Macartney, on Mohun's, were involved in the sword-fight. Both of the main antagonists received multiple wounds, from which

A contemporary depiction of the Mohun-Hamilton duel (Wikimedia Commons)

they died. It was alleged that the fatal blow to Hamilton was struck by Macartney, who did not wait to answer charges. He fled to the Netherlands, was tried in absentia and found guilty of manslaughter but later pardoned. Colonel Hamilton was arrested and put on trial but his defence of being unaware that the principals intended to fight was accepted, and he was convicted of the lesser crime of manslaughter..

Another account of the duel was provided by Jonathan Swift, a friend of Hamilton, who was not present during the actual fighting, but came on the scene shortly afterwards and attended Hamilton's death bed. In a letter to Mrs Dingley, he wrote:

This morning, at eight, my man brought me word that Duke Hamilton had fought with Lord Mohun, and had killed him, and was brought home wounded. I immediately sent him to the Duke's house to know if it was so, but the porter could hardly answer his inquiries, and a great rabble was about the house. In short, they fought at seven this morning. The dog Mohun was killed on the spot, but while the Duke was over him, Mohun shortened his sword, and stabbed him in the shoulder to the heart. The Duke was helped toward the lake-house, by the ring, in Hyde-park (where they fought), and died on the grass, before he could reach his house, and was brought home in his coach by eight, while the poor Duchess was asleep... Mohun gave the affront, and yet sent the challenge. I am infinitely concerned for the poor Duke, who was a frank, honest, and good natured man. They carried the poor Duchess to a lodging in the neighbourhood, where I have been with her two hours, and am just come away. I never saw so melancholy a scene, for indeed all reasons for real grief belong to her; nor is it possible for any one to be a greater loser in all regards - she has moved my very soul. The lodging was inconvenient, and they would have moved her to another, but I would not suffer it, because it had no

room backwards, and she must have been tortured with
the noise of the Grub-street screamers dinging her
husband's murder in her ears.[5]

The duel was a significant milestone. It was one of the last times
that swords were used and one of the final occasions when
seconds were called on to participate in the actual fighting.
Their role would be in future more circumscribed, but still vital.
Queen Anne condemned duelling at the opening of Parliament
the following year, and bills were introduced to outlaw the
practice, but they fell by the wayside of parliamentary procedure.
The fictional Beatrix Esmond is portrayed by Thackeray as
frustrated of her high hopes, but he also suggests that she
deserved nothing better.

Even in the aftermath, there was no unanimity in
the condemnation of duelling. *The Spectator* made some
disparaging references, causing Abel Boyer and John Oldmixon,
acquaintances of Macartney, to come to the defence of their
friend. Wit was not part of their armoury, but they counter-
attacked with leaden, fustian arguments. Boyer argued that
'as long as *Punctilios of Honour* are cherished and indulged as
the Distinguishing Character of a Gentleman' duelling would
continue, and Oldmixon added that it was 'the greatest honour'
to be invited to serve as second in an honourable duel.[6] Honour
and the sword were still as inseparable for some gentlemen as
beer and roast beef.

Unseemly brawls occurred on the doorstep of Parliament,
one involving the most unlikely of duellists, Horace Walpole
(1717-97) was the Fourth Earl of Orford, youngest son of Robert
Walpole, Britain's first prime minister. His correspondence,
assiduously collected by the man himself, chronicles the
fopperies and foibles of the society he moved in, and his
detached, patronizing, sardonic but captivating tone has
ensured that posterity views him as perpetually dressed in
velvet and brocade, a condescending smile permanently on his
lips and a glass in his hand as he stands on the sidelines of an
arena where the great events of his day were acted out. Yet the

image Walpole passed down to posterity could have been totally destroyed had the dice spun slightly differently one evening in 1743 when he found it necessary to cross swords with William Richard Chetwynd on the stairs leading out of Parliament. The provocation was severe. Defying protocols on parliamentary language, Chetwynd had said in the Chamber that Walpole 'deserved to be hanged'. The two men were observed exiting arm in arm, but the conversation grew heated and they pulled out the swords they routinely wore, as gentlemen did. Walpole had his man against a post preparatory to the final thrust when they were forced apart. This was more of a brawl of the sort Hogarth depicted among the lower orders. Chetwynd's blood could have been spilt and Walpole's image and outfit ruined. Probably the latter would have caused him greater distress.

Other men like John Wilkes, a multi-talented and unscrupulous character on the political scene, appear cut out to exemplify the contradictions of the respect and disrespect in which the code of honour was held. Elected to Parliament as a radical in 1757, he attained notoriety for his dissolute lifestyle. He was also a prolific journalist in scandal sheets, especially the *North Briton*, which he co-founded as a counterblast to *The Briton* which had been established by Tobias Smollett. These were confusing times, so while *The Briton* had been established by a Scottish writer, *The North Briton*, in spite of its title, was viewed as being anti-Scottish, and caused Wilkes to receive one challenge and one death threat, both from Scotsmen eager to defend the offended honour of their country, but he laughed both off. His duel in 1762 with Earl Talbot had its origin in a series of articles in the *North Briton*, which portrayed Talbot in unflattering terms. Articles were not signed and since Wilkes declined to confirm his authorship he was unable to apologize, leaving the duel as the only means of resolving the conflict. English gentlemanly demeanour was upheld by the radical and the aristocrat alike, so Wilkes invited the earl and Colonel Berkeley, his second, to dinner the evening before the duel. Was this Olympian bravado, a studied pose, an attempt to disconcert his antagonist, or a genuine display of that attitude of off-hand indifference to life and death which was deemed the appropriate stance? Wilkes left an account of the events in a letter to Lord Temple.[7] The pen is rarely mightier than the sword, but the writer has the power of the fashionable portraitist to arrange the scene and to place the subject in the most flattering pose. Wilkes records that on arrival, he found Lord Talbot highly agitated, subject to violent mood swings, at one point attacking Wilkes as a murderer whom he hoped to see hanged but then whining and pleading with him to accept that he was responsible for, and regretted, the outrageous accusations that were the cause of the present impasse. When Wilkes refused to comply, Talbot went into a temper and demanded that the duel take place immediately, that evening, not postponed until the following morning. Wilkes assented, asking only time to 'settle some important business relative to the education of my only daughter, whom I tenderly loved'. That done, Talbot proposed that the engagement take place inside the hotel room, but this idea was rejected and the party moved into the garden. They stood eight yards apart, and fired, but both missed. The evening's proceedings then took another twist, as Wilkes reported:[8]

> I walked up immediately to his Lordship, and told him, that now I avowed the paper. His Lordship paid me the highest encomiums on my courage, and said, he would declare everywhere that I am the noblest fellow God had ever made. He then desired that we might now be good friends, and retire to the inn to drink a bottle of claret together, which we did with great good humour and much laugh.[9]

Contemporary critics were withering in their jeers at both men, who had fallen short of the demands of honour. The more plausible conclusion is that neither wished to fight in the first place, and were relieved to get off so lightly.

Or perhaps not, for in November the following year, Wilkes found himself on the field of honour in Hyde Park, staring at a pistol in the hands of Samuel Martin, a Member of Parliament and a loyal subject of the king who was offended at the disrespect Wilkes had yet again shown His Majesty. There were also various insulting, unsigned references in the *North Briton* which Martin took, probably correctly, as referring to him. Contemporaries had no doubt over whom Wilkes had in mind with his reference to the 'secretary of a certain board, and a very apt tool of ministerial persecution, who, with a snout worthy of a Portuguese inquisitor, is hourly looking out for carrion in office, to feed the maw of the insatiable vulture... Neither the tenderness of age, nor the sacredness of sex, is spared by the cruel Scot.' Wilkes was not given to euphemism or understatement, and Martin showed equal spirit, if lesser inventiveness, in branding Wilkes a 'stabber in the dark, a cowardly and malignant scoundrel'. When they met, four shots were fired, with Wilkes being struck in the abdomen. Martin offered to help him but Wilkes, with the gallantry expected of a gentleman, shooed Martin away, warning him run off to avoid arrest. In the event, the engagement did neither man any public harm. The Speaker ordered the House of Commons' official surgeon to assist Wilkes' recovery, while Martin, after a period in exile in Paris, was promoted to higher ministerial office than he had previously occupied. The two men exchanged cordial messages. Gentlemanly bullets when not fatal were often a prelude to good fellowship.

At times the language of honour and the gentleman was employed in situations which now appear to be downright hooliganism. In 1765, the fifth Lord Byron, great uncle of the poet, known in his own time as the Wicked Lord and judged by Horace Walpole to be insane, had a disagreement in a tavern with William Chaworth, a neighbouring landowner, over the best way to manage game on an estate. Byron held that the question was best left to nature, but Chaworth thought it necessary to protect the land from poachers. The conversation moved on, but Byron was dissatisfied and sought the views of other diners who told him it was a silly business and to forget it. Believing that Chaworth had treated him 'in a slighting and contemptuous manner', Byron could not let the matter rest, took Chaworth aside and invited him into an adjoining room where he told him to draw his sword. In the ensuing melee Chaworth received a fatal wound, but his last recorded words were, 'My Lord, all I have to say is, that you have behaved like a gentleman.' And in the manner of the time, he had. There is no reason to believe that any animosity had previously existed between the two, but vanity, revenge or simple bloody-mindedness can be made to look like offended honour when the orthodoxy of the times requires it.

Byron was charged with murder, tried by the House of Lords, found not guilty of murder but guilty of manslaughter and discharged.[10] It could be added that the poet Byron later wrote that he would have been tempted to behave in similar manner in the same circumstances. In a letter written in Ravenna in 1820, he asserted that if he had been insulted by Henry (Orator) Holt in the way his friend Hobhouse had been, he 'would not have descended to call out a miscreant who won't fight - but would have passed my sword-stick through his body - like a dog's and then thrown myself on my Peers - who would I hope - have weighed the provocation.'[11]

Another writer who found himself, unwillingly, duelling in circumstances unforeseen by the *code duello* was the Irish playwright, Richard Brinsley Sheridan. The dispute concerned a young woman, Elizabeth Linley, who in her late teens had already established herself as a highly promising soprano and was one of the most admired and desired beauties of the age. Her father recognized his daughter's extraordinary talent and took on the role of her impresario, seeing her rare qualities as an economic resource to be exploited. At the same time, Elizabeth attracted amorous attention, welcome and unwelcome, from other men, including Sheridan's elder brother Charles, but the most unwelcome attention came from Thomas Matthews, who was already married. The young lady had no interest in his insistent advances, but her rejection of his suit led him to threaten blackmail. Worn out by her father's demands on the one hand and the threats from Matthews on the other, Elizabeth thought of joining a religious order but instead she turned to the females of the Sheridan family for help. For reasons which are not clear, they recruited Richard rather than Charles as her defender. He planned a scheme for a flight to France which has the adventurous, rumbustious complexity of the plot of one of his later comedies, but perhaps the flight was an agreed elopement. While attempting to find sanctuary, he asked her to marry him. They found an accommodating *abbé* to conduct a wedding ceremony, but this was invalid as both were under the legal age. In Lille, Elizabeth's father, who had some concerts lined up and had no wish to lose the income, caught up with them and took her back to England. The newlyweds had decided to keep their marriage secret so Sheridan made his way home separately and the couple remained apart in England.

Their return brought Matthews back into Sheridan's life. He had no honour to defend and had no legal or moral status but he posted a notice in the *Bath Chronicle* labelling Sheridan a liar, a scoundrel, a ne'er do well etc. Sheridan heard of the defamation and faced Matthews in London. All bluster and swagger evaporated as Matthews struggled to convince Sheridan that he had been misled. Back in Bath, Sheridan discovered that Matthews had been lying, so he returned and demanded a duel, to be held in Hyde Park at dusk on 4 May. The etiquette of honour did not automatically instil the *sang-froid* or the self-command needed to stand poised facing a gun, but the mechanism had its own momentum and Matthews now found himself entangled. Trapped and plainly terrified, he tried every possible stratagem to postpone or cancel the duel, but this was not easily accomplished. The established procedures and formalities saw him turn up at the agreed time and place, but he must have presented a forlorn, pitiable sight as he prevaricated, equivocated and temporized, objecting to every ground chosen by the seconds until the light failed. He was given no respite and was prevailed on, or bullied, to accept that the duel had to go ahead and could take place indoors in a nearby tavern. The two met face to face in an inner room where Sheridan quickly reduced the man to helplessly begging for his life. The seconds forced the door and made the two desist. Matthews made a written apology.

But even that was not the end of the matter. Matthews was persuaded that his good name had been sullied and that his honour required a fresh duel. Surprisingly and needlessly, Sheridan agreed. This time they met at dawn, near Bath, but this was a more serious matter. The field was muddy and both men fell to the ground with their swords broken, but continued struggling. Matthews kept his blade in his hand and stabbed Sheridan repeatedly, calling on him to surrender, which his opponent, although covered in blood, slashed on the face and body and pinned to the ground, refused to do. Matthews believed he had killed him and fled the field, but Sheridan survived and was carried away to receive treatment. Elizabeth had heard of the fracas and rushed to his side, declaring she was his wife. Sheridan made a good recovery, but the couple were again forcibly separated and he was packed off to undertake a course in Law. Almost a year later the families relented and the pair were officially wed.

Aware of the grotesquerie of the duel, Sheridan used the experience in *The Rivals*, more farce than comedy of manners. The basic plot concerns the travails of Lydia Languish who wishes to have the freedom to marry for love, but the ravelling and unravelling of multiple mistaken identities leads to the climax of a ludicrous duel fought for reasons no one fully understands. The adversaries are Bob Acres, who is in love with Lydia but finds himself, however reluctantly, pitted against a fiery Irishman, Sir Lucius O'Trigger. When he arrives at the ground, Acres admits he does not feel 'quite so bold as (he) did somehow', and tries to have the two take up positions as far apart as possible: 'forty yards is a good distance,' he pleads. Sir Lucius reproaches him and tells him to consider his honour, a request which causes some confusion in Acres: 'Ay true my honour. Do, Sir Lucius, edge in a word or two every now and then about my honour.' The matter is resolved when a group including Lydia rush to the ground to prevent the duel taking place. They are partly successful but only at the cost of creating more confusion and involving Sir Lucius in a separate duel. Acres invites the whole party to a feast, and all live happily ever after.

The duel in Hyde Park in 1779 between Charles James Fox and William Adam also ended with a feast. Fox was leader of a reforming political faction, gadfly to the Establishment, three times foreign secretary but never prime minister. A notorious womanizer, roisterer and gambler, he led a private life that stretches the meaning of the word 'colourful'. Being a heavy drinker and bon viveur, he was portly in body, something which would be significant in his duel. William Adam, an altogether more sober character, was related to Britain's most distinguished family of architects and had enjoyed a successful career in the law and politics in Scotland and England. He sat for a stately portrait by Sir Henry Raeburn, making him every inch a gentleman and landowner with his estate stretching out behind him. In politics, he was a royalist and member of Lord North's Cabinet, and objected when Fox, in a particularly snide comment, reminded King George of the misfortunes visited on Charles I and James II, monarchs who were respectively beheaded and exiled. He also took exception to complaints about the conduct of the American War, but the final straw was Fox's jeer that 'bad as the ministry were, it was not certain that the nation would be at all bettered by taking their opponents.' Adam requested Fox to clarify that the judgement did not reflect on him personally. Subsequent correspondence did not produce the desired clarification or retraction so a duel was deemed necessary.

Duellists at the time customarily stood not face-on to their opponent but turned to one side to reduce the target, so when Fox took up his position looking directly at Adam, he was advised to move. Unperturbed and showing the necessary degree of nonchalance, he replied, 'I am as thick one way as the other.' Gentlemanly etiquette was observed throughout, with Fox declining the opportunity of first shot. He was slightly wounded by Adam's shot, fired back but missed, as did Adam with his second shot. Fox then fired in the air saying that he had never meant any personal affront to Mr Adam or to any other member of the company. Duly mollified, Adam declared that Fox had 'behaved like a man of honour', and the two men formed a lasting friendship. A contemporary cartoon satirized the affair by portraying Adam in full Highland dress shooting at Fox, with foxy features and human dress. The spoof caption enjoyed a pun with a line from Genesis: 'And ADAM had Power over all the Beasts of the Earth.'

'And ADAM had Power over all the Beasts of the Earth.'

James Gillray's cartoon of the duel between Fox and Adam (Wikimedia Commons)

Fox, however radical he was, was no opponent of duelling and later served as second to the Earl of Lauderdale when he faced General Arnold. That matter was settled peacefully when the earl declined to take aim at the general, who missed with his only shot. The earl had just survived a similar encounter with the Duke of Richmond. The nobility of the British Isles would appear to have had little free time to attend to their legislative duties in the House of Lords.

Both Fox and Sheridan, who had given up theatre in favour of a political career, were fully involved in the impeachment process in 1786 against Warren Hastings, ex-Governor General of Bengal, who was charged with 'unwarrantable and criminal practices' against the East Indian Company and against some Indian Begums (Muslim women). Although not the reason for his indictment, Hastings himself had fought a duel in 1780 in Kolkata (then Calcutta) with Sir Philip Francis, a member of the governor general's Council. The duel was not known in India until the British imported it, and the street in Kolkata is still named Duel Avenue. Francis had been an implacable opponent of Hastings, causing the latter to circulate a minute in which he accused Francis of being 'void of honour' in both public and private conduct. To be accused of being 'void of honour' was already inflammatory, but the sting was the reference to the private sphere. Francis was known to be conducting an affair with a married woman, and had actually appeared in court in 1779 on a charge of adultery. He had been arrested under the window of his paramour with a foldable ladder.

The attack on Francis' honour could not pass unremarked, so he called Hastings out. The projected duel itself was not devoid of elements of comedy which might have appealed to Sheridan the playwright. Neither man had had any grasp of the regulations governing the duel, and had to rely on their seconds for hastily arranged tuition. It was agreed that they would use the previous year's Fox-Adam duel as a template to fix the distance between the men and the number of shots to be fired, but it then transpired that neither had much experience in the use of firearms. Francis claimed never to have handled a gun and Hastings that he had done so very rarely. As the guns were being loaded by the seconds it was found that Francis' powder was damp, so he had to request a supply, gallantly provided by the Hastings camp. They took up their positions and while Francis missed his target, Hastings shot Francis in the body. He fell to the ground screaming he was dead. Hastings ran towards him, exclaiming, 'Good God! I hope not.' Francis survived, and Hastings served out his term as governor general. Francis issued no further challenge, but his accounts of Hastings' rule provided much of the material for the impeachment process, although the accused was acquitted after a trial lasting seven years.

There were many routine duels in the remaining years of the century, but two in particular aroused more than usual disbelief and comment because of the status of the parties involved. The first in 1789 involved Frederick, Duke of York, best remembered outside military circles as inspiration of the song 'The Grand Old Duke of York', but at the time second in line to the throne and commander in chief of the Army. His adversary Colonel Lennox was no commoner, but holder of several aristocratic titles in England and Scotland, including that of Duke of Richmond. He later saw service at Waterloo, and his wife was the celebrated duchess who threw a ball the night before the battle. For the duel, his second was the Earl of Winchilsea, who later fought a duel with the Duke of Wellington, while later the same year Lennox himself met and wounded Theophilus Swift, an Irish poet, who had upset him by certain derogatory remarks in a pamphlet.[12]

The duel with the Duke of York was the product of little more than mess-room tittle tattle. The duke was overheard to say that 'Colonel Lennox had heard words spoken to him at Daubigny's, to which no gentleman ought to have submitted', the implication being that Lennox had been too craven to respond appropriately. The script thereafter could have written itself, except that Lennox made the odd mistake of approaching the duke to seek an explanation when he was on parade, and received the expected rebuke that this was not the appropriate time. Lennox enquired about the appropriate time and received the gnomic reply that the duke would not shelter behind privilege as a member of the royal family, and that 'when not on duty, he wore a brown coat, and was ready, as a private gentleman, to give the Colonel satisfaction.' He was, in plain language, one of the boys, or an officer and gentleman who would do what was required of him. The colonel wrote round to find if anyone had any recollection of injurious words being spoken in the club, and when the replies were in the negative he reported back to the duke, asking him to withdraw his statement or else don his brown coat or whatever garb he preferred and prepare to give Lennox satisfaction. The duke chose the latter option, so the two met on Wimbledon Common. Seemingly, the duke stood erect and did not fire at his opponent, while Lennox's shot cut out a curl - the reports are very specific that it was a curl - in the royal hair. Both men retired unhurt into a maelstrom of public bewilderment and derision, with more than the usual production of mocking cartoons. This may have been the bourgeois view, but the duke's colleagues in the military were mainly of the view that his actions were right and proper.

The year 1798 saw Pitt the Younger, then prime minister, engage with George Tierney, a fellow MP but a follower of Fox and sympathetic to the French side even during the war with France. James Gillray caricatured him standing alongside a guillotine in a public square in Paris, wearing the Phrygian cap which was the standard head-dress of a French revolutionary. Pitt introduced a bill to strengthen the Navy, a measure opposed by Fox's party. As a delaying strategy, Tierney requested more time for deliberation, but Pitt attacked Tierney's motion as showing a lack of patriotism. All this appears no more than normal party political manoeuvring, but Tierney chose to take Pitt's reaction as a personal affront and, as affronted gentlemen did, drew up a challenge. Pitt could have laughed the matter off or responded in a haughty tone that this request was absurd and beneath him at a time of national crisis, but he accepted. The two men met on Putney Heath at the unusual time of three o'clock in the afternoon, but no doubt they both had busy schedules and struggled to fit in a duel between division bells. It was agreed that no more than two shots would be fired on either side, but in the event both men missed (deliberately?) with their first shot, fired the second in the air, and there was an end of it.

King George rebuked Pitt severely. However, the royal criticism contained enigmatic words of semi-absolution, 'perhaps it could not have been avoided,' and there's the rub. Was duelling an obligation once a challenge had been issued, or even before that if honour had been offended? The matter was under debate in France at that time, but in the radically different context of the French Revolution. Duelling had been banned during three successive reigns, those of Louis XIV, XV and XVI. Louis XIV's edict in 1679 actually prescribed the death penalty for duelling but this was never imposed. In the same edict he established a Court of Honour to adjudicate in all gentlemanly conflicts, a measure which impressed Tobias Smollett, but the court was rarely convoked. The very idea of seigneurial honour was plainly incompatible with the outlook of new forces which came to the fore in 1789, particularly when the Third Estate declared itself the National Assembly and invited the clergy and nobility to join them. That was the year when feudal rights were abolished and the Declaration of the Rights of Man and the Citizen was promulgated. The first article read, 'Men are born and remain free and equal in rights. Social distinctions can be founded only on the common good,' and these were statements of historical significance and of immediate importance for society and government in France. In the name of equality and fraternity, and to demonstrate the rejection of the suppressed order, the fashions and codes of the old regime were to be suppressed in favour of plain dress. Citizens replaced gentlemen and serfs, and the concept of honour had no place, at least in principle.

'At the commencement of the Revolution duels were not deemed necessary,' writes J.G. Millingen,[13] but although they were viewed in revolutionary circles as a relic of the regime which had been overthrown, it was not so easy to extirpate the practice, especially when so many conflicts over the right to the position of citizenship and over the role of the monarchy were still unresolved. A duel in 1790 between Charles Malo François Lameth and Armand Charles de la Croix de Castries, partly provoked by political differences and partly by personal antipathy, aroused great interest, as demonstrated by the flurry of partisan pamphlets and prints it occasioned. One of the latter is reproduced on the cover of this book. Of the two combatants, the former had previously been a count and the latter a duke, but their titles were no longer recognized and both were members of the National Assembly, although their rank was re-established with the Restoration. The biographies of the two men are in miniature a history of the fluctuating fortunes of many in those days. Lameth had fought in the American War of Independence and was elected to the Assembly as representative of the nobility but could be viewed in modern terms as a constitutional monarchist who wanted the Assembly to have ultimate power. Castries had been an officer in the army and if he supported the abolition of privileges, he remained a royalist.

The pamphleteers, one of whom was named Toulouse de Lautrec and whom it is beguiling to view as an ancestor of the artist whose brush with duelling is recounted later, differ somewhat in their account of the quarrel and duel. Lameth had allied himself with the Jacobins and was one of the triumvirate whom Carlyle dignifies as 'great in speech, thought, action'. It appears that when Lameth turned up at the Assembly a M. de Chauvigny, or Sauvigny, a partisan of the other side, accosted him with insults and a challenge which Lameth ignored. However, Castries intervened to issue his own challenge which Lameth felt he could not refuse. The two chose to fight with swords, but let us entrust the description of the duel to Thomas Carlyle's incomparable prose: 'And so, as the shades of dusk thicken in that Bois-de-Boulogne, we behold two men with lion-look, with alert attitude, side foremost, right foot advanced; flourishing and thrusting, stoccado and passado, in tierce and quart; intent to skewer one another.'[14] In plainer language, Lameth made a lunge but missed his mark, leaving himself open to a parry from his opponent, who pierced him in the arm. It was feared that Castries' blade was poisoned or that the loss of blood would be fatal, but Lameth recovered. He had made himself a favourite of the masses, who in retribution for his wound sacked Castries' town house but did not harm his wife and children. They insisted that their pockets be searched as they made their exit to ensure that although much damage had been done, nothing had been stolen. Mirabeau pointed to this restraint as an example of the new system of values. 'Such is true honour, which the prejudices and atrocity of gladiators can never display.' The civic authority in Paris took advantage of the moment to petition the National Assembly to outlaw duelling entirely, which it did but with no greater success than that enjoyed by its royal predecessors.

1 T.H. White, *The Age of Scandal*, London: Penguin, 1966.
2 J.G. Millingen, *The History of Duelling*, London: Bentley, 1841, vol. 2, pp. 29-31.
3 Stephen Banks, *A Polite Exchange of Bullets*, Woodbridge: Boydell Press, 2010, pp. 17-19.
4 Victor Stater, *High Life Low Morals: The Duel That Shook Stuart Society*, London, John Murray, 1999.
5 Quoted by Millingen, *op. cit.*, vol. 2, p. 30.
6 Quoted in Markku Peltonen, *The Duel in Early Modern England: Civility, Politeness and Honour*, Cambridge: Cambridge University Press, 2003, p. 190.
7 The letter to Lord Temple is reproduced by Millingen, *op. cit.*, p. 69.
8 'Hyde Park', *Old and New London*, vol. 4, London: Cassell, Petter & Galpin, 1878, pp. 375-405. URL: http://www.british-history.ac.uk/report.aspx?compid=45205. Date accessed: 31 May 2020.
9 Millingen, *op. cit.*, vol. 2, pp. 67-76.
10 Elizabeth Longford, *Byron*, London: Hutchinson, 1976, p. 5; Edna O'Brien, *Byron in Love*, London: Weidenfeld & Nicolson, 2009, p. 7; Millingen, *op. cit.*, pp. 61-6.
11 Lord Byron, edited by Leslie A. Marchand, *Selected Letters & Journals*, London: Pimlico, 1993, p .229.
12 'Theophilus Swift', *Dictionary of National Biography 1885-1990*, vol. 55.
13 Millingen, op. cit., vol. 2, pp. 230-2.
14 Thomas Carlyle, *The French Revolution: A History*, London: Chapman & Hall, 1837, vol. 2, chapter 3:3.

8

'CREATIVE MAYHEM'
THE AMERICAN DUEL

Some of the first colonies in North America were founded by refugees looking to escape persecution or intolerance at home, others by men and women hoping more simply for greater prosperity, but the early generations aspired to live out their days, as exiles do, in conditions as similar as was feasible to those they had left behind. No new intellectual or moral structure can ever be constructed on a ground zero, so the ships carrying the colonists across the Atlantic were well stocked not only with specimens of flora, fauna and livestock but also with copies of the Bible and works of literature and philosophy. The plants took root and the cattle adapted to the New World, sometimes embellishing the unfamiliar environment, at others damaging it. The same could be said of the imported culture and the accompanying institutions of religion, law and politics. The early criminal law was in all material respects the common law of England, moral standards were those of Christian Europe and the culture of the elites kept pace with developments in the Old World, especially at the time of the Enlightenment. Inevitably these invisible imports included contemporary prejudices, *idées fixes* and superstitions, the norms of the code of honour and the duel among them. Some ministers of religion and progressive thinkers expressed their antagonism in the same terms as their counterparts in Europe, but duelling made a successful transition to America.

The inner core of those who settled at a spot they named New Plymouth consisted of a Puritan community who aimed to establish a godly society free of the constraints put on their beliefs and religious practice back home under James VI & I. All signatories of the Mayflower Compact were expected to observe the highest moral standards, so it is startling to discover that the first recorded duel fought in the New World occurred in that Massachusetts colony in 1621, just one year after the Pilgrim Fathers disembarked, and that it involved two men, Edward Doty and Edward Leister, who had actually sailed on the *Mayflower*. The duellists were servants in the employ of one Stephen Hopkins, who appears to have been an inn-keeper. The fact that people of that confession became involved in a duel is the first surprise, and the second is that the men were servants, that is, members of the lower orders. Traditionally, duelling was an activity reserved for gentlemen.

Not much is known of the character of the two men although they were both allegedly 'rowdy'. They fought not with pistols but with sword and dagger, one of the methods of single combat taught by Saviolo at his fencing school in London. Both received wounds, one to the arm and the other to the thigh. Fighting being regarded as immoral or criminal in the colony, the two men were brought before a tribunal which sentenced them to be chained together and left without food or drink for twenty-four hours. It was a harsh sentence, causing their employer to take pity on them and intercede on their behalf with the governor, who granted them a pardon.[1]

Although this event is amply documented, the normally authoritative Don C. Seitz post-dates the first American duel by more than a century to 1728, coincidentally on the same site, Boston Common. In 1719 Massachusetts had passed a law explicitly banning duels, under pain of loss of political rights, an act which may lead the sceptical observer to wonder how many duels had occurred to make legislation necessary, and in any case the law did not protect Benjamin Woodbridge, found dead early one October morning in 1728 with a stab to the chest which had gone right through his body. Seitz writes that 'Boston had never been so excited in its hundred years of existence', and a coroner's court was immediately convoked. The seconds were summoned and Henry Phillips, a merchant in the city who had been seen with a wound in one hand, was indicted, but he had already made his escape on a British warship.[2]

From Gentleman to Cowboys

Doty and Leister were the first in a long line. A complete chronicle of American duelling would date from New Plymouth in 1621 to take in the 'creative mayhem practised by American duellists',[3] including both traditional duels of honour and more unruly shoot-outs based on 'frontier attitudes and frontier weapons', such as the celebrated gunfight on 26 October 1881 which pitted the Earp Brothers against the Clanton-McLaury gang at the O.K. Corral in Tombstone, Arizona. The western duel appealed to the public imagination and became a Hollywood staple in films such as *Shane* or *High Noon* and countless other B movies. In recent years, these movies have been subjected

to earnest analysis by critics, not all of them French, so their omission here is due not to some high-minded scorn but rather to respect for a topic which would alone fill a volume.

Some commentators have suggested that the Second Amendment to the Constitution which established the right of every American citizen to bear arms made duelling easier and more frequent, but it is hard to sustain this view. Many American duels were fought not with readily available weapons but with elegant duelling pistols which had to be sought out, and a superficial knowledge of European duelling indicates that ease or difficulty of access to weaponry made no difference. The American version of the duel did acquire characteristics of its own, although it should be noted from the outset that there were internal divergences between the northern states and the South. There were several variations from European habits: duels in America were mainly fought by the pistol rather than the sword, but a range of weapons, including the Bowie knife or the rifle, could be employed; a wider range of insult was taken as justifying the duel; a more imaginative style of reply was devised; 'posting' was invented as an alternative response to an offence (see below); bruised honour was not the only justification for a challenge; and a specifically American *code duello* was eventually drawn up.

The central difference from Europe, however, was a process of democratization, in that duelling was practised by men of all walks of life, unlike in the old continent where the principle that duelling was reserved for gentlemen was unchallenged, largely because that class alone was considered to have honour to defend. In Europe, any gentleman who received a challenge from a man of a lower caste was entitled to dismiss it with disdain. Some European social critics observed with disapproval that men of the lower orders had taken to issuing challenges as a means of raising their status or giving themselves airs and graces above their station, and the drafters of duelling protocols advised intending duellists to be on their guard against this wholly reprehensible trend. These class-based standards did not apply in the New World, although Andrew Jackson did decline a challenge in Tennessee on the grounds that his putative opponent was no gentleman. Perhaps fewer gentlemen were among the huddled masses who made America their home, or perhaps, as noted later by de Tocqueville, hierarchical notions of society were progressively undermined by the nature of the new economy and the greater social mobility it entailed.

This did not, of course, signify that an artisan or farm worker could insult his betters with impunity. On some occasions the defamed individual commissioned thugs to execute condign punishment, but it was totally in order for him, as for his European counterpart, to exact retribution by himself by assaulting the vulgar miscreant in the open with no real fear of recrimination from magistrates or police agencies. The normal weapon was the horsewhip, itself an aristocratic implement used by European sporting classes, or perhaps a cane or a swagger stick. The beating imposed was not merely a symbolic act of humiliation, and there are instances of victims being left bloodied and traumatized, with bones broken. As an instance, in 1798 a committee was established to oppose the growing French influence on American political life, and in a report of a meeting in New York it was stated that James Jones, a Republican, was present when he was not. He demanded to be told the name of the reporter responsible for this error. It turned out to be Brockholst Livingston, a Federalist, son of the Governor of New Jersey. The offended Jones attacked him with a cane. The matter might have ended there, but Jones overstepped the mark by 'tweaking the nose', an unpardonable insult on both sides of the Atlantic. Livingston then 'called out' Jones, who was killed. Livingston got off scot-free and indeed went on to serve on the Supreme Court from 1807 to 1823.

A novelty introduced by Americans nursing a grievance was 'posting', a form of self-vindication especially popular in those cases where a person receiving a challenge declined to accept it. The offended person would write out his complaint or accusation and 'post' it in a public place, insert it in a newspaper or distribute it as a handbill, setting out the wrong suffered and branding his rival a coward, a liar or a rascal, terms which would require vindication in a duel, but that was the purpose of the exercise. Major Truman, an authority on American duelling, suggests that 'posting originated with General James Wilkinson, whose challenge to Congressman John Randolph in 1807 was disdainfully declined by the haughty Virginian.' Randolph, a descendent of one of the 'First Families' of the State of Virginia and thus as near to an aristocrat as the Republic could produce, refused to recognize the validity of Wilkinson's challenge, causing Wilkinson to publish around Washington a grandiloquent post: 'HECTOR UNMASKED: In justice to my character, I denounce to the world John Randolph, a member of Congress, as a prevaricating, base, calumniating scoundrel, poltroon and coward.' Randolph, or Hector, remained unbowed but the habit caught on.[4]

In Europe, with a high measure of hypocrisy, the United States acquired the status of nation most prone to duelling. The otherwise staid historian Andrew Steinmetz wrote excitedly that:

> America is the country where life is held cheaper than anywhere else. There duels, or 'difficulties', are off-hand diversions. But when men fight in the States, they fight in earnest. There is no objection to fowling pieces, to rifles, to bowie-knives... In the hotels at Washington and elsewhere, you may see the marks of bullets on the walls, shots that missed, or that went through a man leaving him dead on the floor.[5]

However over-fired was Steinmetz' style, the sober contemporary American historian Jack K. Williams confirms that already in the eighteenth century 'duels among gentlemen were recorded in New York, Illinois, Pennsylvania, Massachusetts and elsewhere.' He adds that one South Carolina editor covered a trio of duels in Camden in one week in 1817.[6] Happily, Steinmetz was able to offer the reassurance that 'a man, taking care to be reasonable, may pass through the States most comfortably', but the image of America as a violent land plainly appealed to British readers.

In its edition of 17 January 1808, the *Glasgow Herald* opined that 'the rage for duelling in America seems now beyond all precedent. Scarcely a day passes in New York without an event of this kind, and in other parts of the United States the infatuation is equally prevalent.' In fact, the 'infatuation' was equally prevalent in Britain at that date, but it is always preferable to flatter a nation's self-esteem by denigrating other peoples. Another Scottish journal, *The Sentinel*, reported that 'Dr Randall and Lieut Hull, both of the American army, lately fought a duel at Penascola. The latter was shot thorough the heart.' There were duels of equal brutality nearer home, but these stories confirmed the condescending view of the primitivism of American society which would later be confirmed by such celebrated Victorian visitors to the US as Charles Dickens and Fanny Trollope.

European Legacy

Despite the radical break in political structure that Independence achieved, the cultural parameters within which duelling was tolerated, or necessitated, had been fixed before Independence and would persist after the restoration of peace. In politics as in society, the newly independent Americans were keen to distinguish their robust Republican ways from the more decadent manners of royalist Europeans, and anything that reeked of those cultures was open to forthright condemnation. But no new intellectual structure can ever begin from a tabula rasa. The old structures may be crumbling, but some parts of the masonry will always be transported from the ruins, perhaps unintentionally, to bolster the new edifice. The writers of Republican Rome, principally Cicero and Plutarch, gave the Founding Fathers and the succeeding generations august models to aspire to in the political arena, but in the day-to-day competition for place and power, the new men found themselves in a sea of radical uncertainty. They could, in theory, have constructed their own cultural framework, created their own narratives, but instead, the new Republican American intellectual deferred to the sophistication of Paris and London in social and economic, if not political, mores. Willy-nilly, the ethical and civil standards, codes and manners of the Old World remained integrated into the habit of mind and hierarchy of values of the New World. Precisely because they were so deeply seated as to be regarded either as part of Christian heritage or as common sense, Renaissance and Enlightenment requirements of gentlemanly conduct were not subject to sceptical questioning.

This ingrained conservatism of mind and conscience was visible in no other realm so strongly and irrepressibly as in that relating to codes of honour, with its consequent necessity of recourse to duelling. Legislatures and courts of law had been set up in the colonies from the outset, but when honour was at stake they were as likely to be shunned as they had been in Europe, leaving the offended gentleman the only option of seeking redress via an established social code or the pseudo-courts of received opinion. On certain occasions, honour offended was, in the Americas as in Europe, the justifying pretext rather than the genuine motive for the duel, especially in the political arena.

Duels are recorded before the Declaration of Independence. The first recorded in North Carolina took place on 18 March 1765 and involved two British officers, Alexander Simpson and Thomas Whitehurst, who fought over a local woman.[7] Many other duels are chronicled in the history of that state, but a watershed was reached in 1802 with the Stanly-Spaight encounter, an event which involved a mixture of political rivalry and offended honour but which also exposed yet again the contradictions in public opinion on the duel in itself. Richard Dobbs Spaight was a distinguished figure in the political life of North Carolina. Having served with the American Army, he represented the state in the Continental Congress and Constitutional Convention, and became in turn governor and congressman. His record seemed secure enough to guarantee his re-election to Congress even after switching sides in the 1800 election from Hamilton's Federalist Party to the Democratic-Republican group. In the event he lost his seat to a noisy young upstart, John Stanly, who denounced him for pursuing 'the crooked policy of being occasionally on both sides'. Two years later, Spaight stood for the Senate, but Stanly re-appeared to launch a series of attacks which might have been wounding but unremarkable in a later age of democratic electioneering. Claiming his honour had been offended, Spaight issued a challenge, which was refused, but he followed up with another, and this time Stanly responded by 'posting', accusing his rival of demonstrating 'a spirit, malicious, low & unmanly'. In his turn Spaight produced a handbill which branded Stanly 'a liar & scoundrel', and announced that he was 'in readiness to give him satisfaction'.

The two met in September on the outskirts of New Bern in the presence of some three hundred spectators. Neither man was a particularly good shot, and the first three rounds left them both unharmed. The seconds requested them to stop, but they refused and on the fourth exchange Spaight was struck and died the following day. Some of the dead man's friends attempted to bring a charge of murder against Stanly, but he appealed directly to the governor who obviously regarded the duel as having been fought in compliance with the code of honour, and pardoned him. The state's General Assembly dissented from the governor's acquiescence and in November passed an Act outlawing duelling and establishing exclusion from public office as punishment for a challenge or for a duel which ended without loss of life, and the death penalty 'without benefit of clergy' when one party was killed.[8]

Legislation tended to be as ineffectual in America as in Europe, and on those rare occasions when duellists were brought to court, they were likely to find a sympathetic jury of their peers. Illinois would appear to be the only state which actually executed anyone for murder in a duel. The original offence was far removed from any consideration of honour, but illustrates the extent to which by 1818 the duel had become an automatic recourse in all strata of society. Alphonso Stuart, a lawyer, owned a stretch of property next to that held by William Bennett, whose horse had the irritating habit of straying onto Stuart's cornfield. Provoked beyond measure, Stuart ordered his farmhand to teach it a lesson, which he did by wounding the animal. An outraged Bennett was goaded to issue a challenge, which Stuart accepted, seemingly deluded into believing this to be a mock encounter. They chose rifles, took up a position twenty-five yards apart and Bennett shot Stuart dead. He was arrested, but Illinois had only attained statehood the previous year and had no relevant laws. The Legislature approved an emergency law, but in the meantime Bennett had bored a hole through the wooden wall of the prison in which he was confined and escaped. He remained at liberty for over two years, but revealed his whereabouts when he made contact with his wife and children. He was apprehended, tried and sentenced to death by hanging. His execution drew the largest crowd seen in the history of the state, mainly sympathetic to his plight. The ambiguity in public opinion is evident in the local newspaper's report: 'Poor Bennett! He lost his life for the love he had for his family. He stated on the scaffold that he was willing to risk his life for the pleasure of once more greeting his wife and children. He also denied that he had put the bullet in the gun that killed Stuart.'[9]

While no class or occupation had a monopoly, most duellists came from the ranks of journalists, politicians and lawyers. Joanne B. Freeman writes that there were as many as seventy violent clashes involving one, or more commonly two, congressmen. One of the most notorious, fought in 1838 between Congressmen Jonathan Cilley of Maine and William Jordan Graves of Kentucky, aroused a wave of public nausea. Cilley, a Democrat, launched an attack in the House of Representatives on Colonel James Watson Webb, editor of the Whig *Morning Courier and New York Enquirer*, alleging that the newspaper took a soft editorial line on corruption. The dishonoured Webb reacted in the expected way with a challenge, which Cilley refused to accept since a newspaper editor was beneath his notice. Webb then prevailed on Graves to act as his second and deliver the challenge on his behalf, but Cilley again declined. The affair took a new twist when Graves decided that he himself had been offended by Cilley's manner, and issued a challenge on his own behalf. Cilley, a stickler for etiquette, consulted the terms of the *code duello* and felt obliged to accept. The two congressmen courteously declared they had no quarrel with each other, but agreed to meet with duly appointed seconds who were also members of Congress. Rifles were the chosen weapons, eighty yards apart the initial distance, with the agreement that they could advance on each other, shooting at will. The first two shots missed their targets, but Graves' third

James Watson Webb (Library of Congress, Washington DC)

pierced one of Cilley's arteries, causing him to bleed to death. He was thirty-five and had a wife and three children. Graves' only penalty was a motion of censure in the House. A Bill to ban duelling in the District of Columbia was approved by the Senate but voted down in the House, although a subsequent Bill passed smoothly. It was Webb who became the main object of public anger, with two of Cilley's fellow Whigs threatening to cane him. He was depicted in contemporary cartoons armed for self-defence with cane, musket, knife and pistols.

California duelling reflects the adventurous history of the territory in its early days before and after it was incorporated into the United States after the Mexican wars. Life was made more turbulent at one level by the bullish optimists, assorted renegades and roughs of several nations who flooded there for the Gold Rush (1849-53), and at another by virulent political disputes over whether California should be a free or a slavery state. Tussles of whatever kind and with whatever outcome between gold-rushers went largely unrecorded, but there were other better chronicled duels fought by businessmen, newspapermen, lawyers and law-makers. In its edition of 15 June 1853, the *San Francisco Evening Journal*, reporting in a matter-of-fact way on three duels that had taken place in recent days, concluded that 'duelling seems to have become almost an epidemic among us'.[10] One duel in the report involved 'Hon. Messrs Gwim and McCorkle, members of Congress' who fired three shots 'ineffectually' before their seconds intervened. Truman adds the information that the two men 'were fighting under a misapprehension of the facts', and that once this was cleared up they made peace. Another report concerned the duel between John Nugent, a journalist of the *San Francisco Herald*, and Alderman Hayes, who wounded his opponent in the right arm. Dr A.B. Crane was less fortunate and died after a duel with Edward Toby. The newspaper gave no details of the cause of the quarrels, and if the reports were written in the straightforward style later used to report traffic deaths, the newspaper did express its disapproval some days later by proposing that 'if everyone that fought a duel were to stand in the pillory, it would quickly lessen the number of these imaginary men of honor, and put an end to so irrational a practice.' In October, it was able to inform its readers that the law could be of some value, since 'Mr J.M. Warner and Mr Chas. B. Grant were held to bail yesterday in the sum of $1,500, the former for giving and the latter for accepting a challenge to fight with deadly weapons.'

Yet two duels involving prominent citizens made it clear that the law was not able to eliminate duelling. George Pendleton Johnston had been both a US court commissioner and later member of the Californian Assembly, and as such had been a supporter of anti-duelling legislation, which adds a certain poignancy to his participation in a duel in 1858 with William I. Ferguson, himself a state senator. The two had met in a bar, where Ferguson made a joke about some ladies of Johnston's acquaintance. This may have been crude macho repartee but it was too strong meat for the delicate sensibilities of his drinking partner. An argument ensued, escalated out of control, a challenge was issued, and they agreed to meet on Angel Island, the beautiful and now peaceful island in the Bay which had become the favoured site for settling scores. They took up a position ten paces apart but this was reduced after the first and second shots so they must have been almost face to face for the third, but both still missed. That should have been that, but Ferguson rejected Johnston's repeated demand for an apology, and at the fourth round Ferguson was badly wounded in the leg. He refused an amputation which might have saved his life, and three weeks later he died. His body lay in state in the state capitol. Johnston was charged with murder, but was acquitted after successfully pleading that Ferguson was responsible for his own death by refusing medical advice. On his death in 1884, *The San Francisco Evening Post* was fulsome in its praise of his character, lauding him as 'the type of the Southern Gentleman ... honorable to a fault', and as displaying 'chivalrous conduct'.

Appeals to the spirit of chivalry recur in the nineteenth-century United States, perhaps due more to the popularity of Walter Scott than to a command of medieval history. No doubt some element of old-fashioned chivalry could be detected in a defence of a lady's honour, but none in the employment of such an idiom on other, more material affairs. The issue that tore California apart in the years preceding the Civil War was slavery, and this issue led to the infamous duel between David Colbreth Broderick, previously a member both of the Californian and the National Senate, and David Terry, chief justice of the California State Supreme Court.[11]

Broderick had moved from New York at the height of the Gold Rush and bought *The San Francisco Herald*, a purchase which caused trouble and led to a duel in 1852 which ended without casualties. He and Justice Terry had been good friends and members of the same party until they fell out over the admissibility of slavery in California, Broderick being opposed and Terry favourable. They made fiery speeches on opposing sides at a Democratic Party convention in 1859, after which Terry issued the challenge. The fact that he had been a judge and that duelling was illegal did not dissuade him, although to appease his conscience he resigned the night before the duel. Their first attempted meeting was broken up by the police, but they agreed to rendezvous again near Lake Merced. Broderick's gun misfired. He respected the codes which laid down that a misfire should count as a shot, so he stood upright, making him an easy target for Terry who shot him in the chest. He died immediately. His passing was widely mourned, although the official orator at his funeral declared that 'the code of honour is a delusion and a snare: it palters with the hoes of a true courage and binds it at the feet of crafty, cruel skill.' Terry was tried for murder but was acquitted. He was later killed by a bodyguard hired by a judge who was in fear of his life from Terry's threats.

The code of honour, like the language of chivalry, was still quoted but often respected only in the breach and adduced as dignified endorsement of conduct which had no savour of honour. In this context, it is worth considering the career of Andrew Jackson (1767-1845), military leader in the Creek War of 1813-14, hero of the Battle of New Orleans (1815) where he defeated a larger British army, and seventh President of the United States. He remains one of the most controversial figures in American history, with historians radically divided over both his political achievements and his personality. James Parton opens his biography of the man with a string of striking paradoxes: 'A democratic autocrat. An urbane savage. An atrocious saint'.[12] Alexis de Toqueville, too, was plainly disturbed by his lack of principle and unscrupulousness, and even Don C. Seitz, tolerant of all duelling, was moved to refer to 'the savage Jackson' when instancing the mercilessness he once displayed.[13] Discussion here will be limited to his record as a duellist, which was well out of the ordinary.

According to some, admittedly unprovable, calculations he was involved in perhaps as many as one hundred duels in various capacities, as attendant, as second and as principal. In his character and outlook he personifies the wholly unsavoury aspects, by no means limited to the United States, not of the high-minded code but of the actual practice of duelling. There are, notably in military history, many other such individuals, often revered as national heroes, whose acts, on sober assessment, arouse considerable unease in the observer and who display a high degree of malevolent sociopathic traits: narcissism, deviousness, emotional detachment or Machiavellianism, however grandly disguised. More than any other individual, Jackson can be taken as representative of a caste of man whose willingness to fight is dictated not by codes of honour but by idiosyncrasies and deviances of character. His was not a unique case, but Jackson thrived in an age and society which viewed the violence which is duelling as part of a normal pattern of behaviour, and he himself gloried in duelling to an unusual degree.

As a legacy of an early duel, Jackson had lodged in his body a musket ball which could not be removed, and that malign presence can be taken as a symbol of the centrality of duelling in his life. It has to be added that Jackson, for all the ferocity of his language and the multiplicity of his duels, killed only one man, Charles Dickinson, in a dispute in 1806 which began as an argument over horses. Each man owned a horse of which he was particularly proud, and they agreed to put their qualities to the test in a race with $2,000 at stake, and a forfeit of $800 in the event of either man pulling out. Dickinson did decide not to proceed and agreement was initially reached over payment until one Thomas Swann appeared on the scene. Swann may simply be one of those who enjoy loitering at the foot of the gallows or guillotine, but he first goaded Dickinson to renege on his deal and then became so deeply embroiled in the dispute with Jackson that he issued a challenge in his own right. Jackson was not devoid of grand standards, and being unconvinced of Swann's status as a gentleman, he declined the challenge, limiting himself to administering a caning.

Undaunted, Swann continued to goad Dickinson to take action against Jackson, so accusations of cowardice, mendacity and conduct unbecoming a gentleman were made. There were also insinuations concerning Jackson's wife, who had been divorced under the law of Tennessee to allow her to marry Jackson. Her married status was legal but she suffered

THE DUEL.

Andrew Jackson kills Charles Dickinson, woodprint, 1834 (Library of
Congress, Washington DC)

the same social ostracism as did Anna Karenina in a similar
situation. Slurs concerning the couple circulated. A substantial
correspondence, which is highly enlightening on the mentality
of duellists, ensued but a piece of collateral damage caused by
this group letter writing was that some members of the retinue
of the two asides fell out and challenged each other. Eventually,
agreement was reached between the two protagonists on a duel
to the death. Dickinson was a renowned sharp shooter, and bets
were laid on his eventual victory. On the day, Dickinson fired first
and did strike Jackson, but he remained standing. Dickinson, as
required, held his ground, making himself an easy target but
Jackson's gun misfired. Under the code of duelling that should
have been his shot and the seconds should have stepped forward
to prevent him firing again, but Jackson readjusted his gun and
shot Dickinson, who died shortly afterwards.

Jackson found time in 1813, while an officer engaged in war,
for a private shoot-out in Nashville, Tennessee with two brothers,
Jesse and Thomas Benton. Jesse Benton had previously fought a
duel with William Carroll, whose promotion in military ranks by

Jackson was widely resented by Benton, and had led to related
challenges and canings. Jackson acted as second for Carroll in
a duel with Thomas Benton, but his own deep enmity with the
Benton brothers culminated in a fracas in Nashville, where shots
were fired, a horsewhip brandished and sword sticks wielded.
Jackson received a bullet wound in the shoulder which was so
severe that surgeons recommended amputation. 'I'll keep my
arm,' Jackson retorted, presumably in tones fitting a seasoned
warrior, and he did. He also kept the bullet in his body for the
rest of his life.

The dubious privilege of being regarded as 'the most
distinguished meeting that took place in the United States'
has been disputed by two encounters. Recently that garland
has been granted to the Burr-Hamilton encounter, discussed
in the following chapter, but previously it was bestowed on the
duel in 1826 between Henry Clay and John Randolph, whom
we have already met.[14] Randolph's bearing throughout was as
majestic as that of a French nobleman facing the guillotine. The
resplendent personalities of both men, whose portraits now
hang unremarked on the walls of provincial galleries, make
them seem scarcely flesh of our flesh. They were by any standard
citizens of high distinction, and were both experienced duellists,
Randolph having fought his first duel while still a student, and
Clay having several duels to his (dis)credit. Clay had been a
member of both the House of Representatives and Senate and
was on three occasions a candidate for the presidency. He lost
to John Quincy Adams in 1824 but was promoted by him to
the position of secretary of state, an office he held at the time
of the duel. Randolph was senator for Virginia, and Clay's crime
in his eyes was accepting, or perhaps soliciting, an invitation to
attend the 1825 Congress in Panama called by Simón Bolívar
to establish some harmony among the newly independent
republics of Latin America. Randolph and other senators
believed that the Senate had been demeaned by the failure to
seek its authorization before accepting the invitation, and in
a fiery speech he denounced the 'combination of the Puritan
(Adams) and the blackleg (Clay)' responsible for this move.

Clay set in motion the normal gentlemanly manoeuvres and appointed General Thomas S. Jessup to seek out an explanation and an apology. Randolph was entitled to plead that comments made in the Senate were guarded by special privilege, but the stout-hearted senator agreed to waive such rights. Jessup noted that throughout Randolph's 'bearing was ... that of a high-toned, chivalrous gentleman of the Old South'. Each step between gentlemen even, or indeed especially, when leading to a duel had to be legitimized by the code of honour, strengthened by the lexicon of chivalry, and as such Randolph accepted Clay's challenge. Delicate points of rights and entitlements were debated among the seconds over the following weeks, but the decision was that the challenge was permissible and the agreement was reached that the meeting would take place in Virginia, although duelling there was illegal. Randolph preferred to have his blood shed there, but he also decided that he himself would fire in the air.

The night before the duel, Benton, Randolph's second, called on Clay and provides a moving portrait of family life, with Clay's wife and three children innocently unaware of what lay ahead. Meanwhile, another insider, Colonel James Hamilton, paid Randolph a visit and discovered him engrossed in reading Milton's *Paradise Lost*. How else should a Christian gentleman pass what may be his last evening on earth? He was still intent on going to the field at the due time but not firing. In view of this resolution, Hamilton recruited the assistance of Clay's second to beg Randolph to draw back from what could only be an act of suicide, but before he would engage them in discussion on the next day's business, Randolph treated them to a learned discourse on the beauties of John Milton's poetry. He would not be shaken on his purpose of turning up but firing in the air, conceding that he might change his mind if he saw some devilish expression in Clay's eyes.

The duellists met as agreed. The first mishap was that Randolph's pistol, held downwards, went off prematurely and this would have given Clay entitlement to a free shot but, ever the knight and gentleman, he waved aside this right. He took his own gun from his assistant on the field, who happened to be the Senator for Louisiana, Josiah Johnson. The first shots went wide, but the two men insisted that honour was not satisfied and chose to exchange another round. Clay's shot went close enough to tear Randolph's coat but missed, while Randolph shot in the air. At this point, the two men shook hands, and even exchanged a joke with Randolph telling Clay that he owed him a new coat. 'I am glad the debt is no greater,' replied the senator from Kentucky.

Anti-Duelling Moves

Anti-duelling sentiments among philosophers and ecclesiastical bodies had as long a history as duelling itself, but in nineteenth-century America this opposition hardened. Committees were formed, sermons preached, pamphlets written and speeches delivered inside and outside legislatures but the underlying problem persisted. Public opinion remained at best ambivalent and so reluctant to regard duellists as criminals. Courts often turned a blind eye, the blinding caused by the lingering gleam of the codes of the gentleman.

Some clergymen are recorded as attending duels, but ecclesiastical opinion was hostile. The General Assembly of the Presbyterian Church in 1805 gave 'consideration to the unhappy prevalence of duelling in the United States', and did what its members could to 'discountenance and abolish this practice'. They resolved unanimously that 'the duellist is a murderer', and authorized the publication of all forty-eight pages of a sermon, *The Remedy for Duelling*, delivered by the Rev Lyman Beecher, father of Harriet Beecher Stowe.[15] As an addendum, the leaflet carried a stultifying, rhetorical address made by the same clergyman to the Anti-Duelling Association of New York, calling on the citizens of the city no longer to 'permit a crime, the reproach of our land, the scourge of our peace, to stalk the streets openly and impudently through our streets.'

Other notable appeals from pulpits included *A Sermon on Duelling*, preached in Baltimore by the Rev Frederick Beasley in 1811. The plain title belies the flights of eloquence which may have tested the endurance of the congregation. In its published version the oration runs to some fifty-eight pages. The reverend took as text the lines from Exodus 'Thou shalt not kill', and lest anyone entertained any doubts he announced in his opening line his intention to 'inveigh against the barbarous custom of DUELLING. This custom has become so prevalent in this country that it has ceased to excite in us that horror which a Christian people should feel for a vice which is so flagrant and presumptuous an outrage against the laws both of God and man.' A more widely heard voice was that of Mason Locke Weems, familiarly known as Pastor Weems. A prolific writer, he secured his place in literary history with his hagiographical lives of early American statesmen, notably George Washington, in which he preserved for posterity the uplifting tale of the young Washington and the cherry tree he could not lie about felling. Weems' contribution to the anti-duelling campaign came in 1821 with the publication of *God's Revenge against Duelling*, or, *The Duellist's Looking Glass: Exhibiting that Gentlemanly Mode of Turning the Corner, in Features altogether Novel, and admirably Calculated to entertain and instruct the American Youth*. The pastor had a formidable familiarity with God's schemes and had detected *God's Revenge* against other acts, firstly *Against Murder* (1808) and later *Against Adultery* (1815). The threat of God's revenge did not exercise the hoped-for deterrent effect, as all three crimes or sins continued to be perpetrated in America as elsewhere, but the aim of these tracts was to strip duelling of the allure in which in bedecked itself as an assertion of honour, and of the implicit claim of the *code duello* to superiority over the Bible.

There were anti-duelling moves in New Orleans where, perhaps under inherited French influence, an almost medieval proposal was made to establish a 'court of honour' to redress any slights or slurs. A visitor in 1834 reported, however, that the city witnessed 'more duels than there are days in the year'.[16]

That same year also saw the British proto-sociologist Harriet Martineau stop off in the city as part of her two-year sojourn in the US. She reported favourably on gatherings of anti-slavery groups but was more sceptical of nascent anti-duelling movements. If her book published in 1837 is a reliable guide, these initiatives faced formidable odds, since she writes that members of one such committee in New Orleans quarrelled with such ferocity during a meeting she attended that they struggled to keep their pistols in their holsters.[17]

A Mississippi law of 1835 required the victorious side in a duel to pay the medical or funeral expenses of the victim. The legislators in Virginia decreed that principals or seconds would be ipso facto deemed insane, and their property assigned to a trustee for administration. The District of Columbia outlawed duels in 1839, a necessary measure granted the number of duels and fights involving elected representatives. Under Kentucky's constitution of 1850, anyone taking up political office was and is required to take an oath which runs: 'I being a citizen of this State, have not fought a duel with deadly weapons within this State nor out of it, nor have I sent or accepted a challenge to fight a duel with deadly weapons, nor have I acted as second in carrying a challenge, nor aided or assisted any person thus offending, so help me God.' Tennessee introduced an anti-duelling law in 1874 in response to public outrage over an altercation between Moses J. Wicks, Mayor of Knoxville, and Captain William Rule, editor of the local *Journal*. The mayor took offence at an article and issued the challenge which the editor initially ignored, duelling being contrary to his principles. Undaunted, the mayor returned with cries of greater and greater stridency, causing such public disquiet that a Grand Jury was summoned. It commended Rule's restraint and ordered Wicks to desist. A law was passed outlawing duelling and containing a clause similar to that in Kentucky requiring intending attorneys to take a special oath to forswear duelling. It had been shown that some 90 per cent of duellists in Tennessee were members of the legal profession.[18]

The American Way

Such moves met fierce resistance from pro-duelling activists, however, who continued to disguise their aims in stately language. A distinctly American code was deemed necessary, particularly by John Lyde Wilson, who set out to find an American solution to an American dilemma. A disconcerting figure who embodies many of the most troubling characteristics of the age, Wilson was a stalwart supporter of slavery and a prominent figure in a Lynching Club, membership of which was restricted to those who had been present at a lynching. He practised law in South Carolina and served in the state's legislature before becoming governor in 1822, but on demitting office and resuming his seat in the Senate, he was threatened by Thomas S. Grimké with impeachment for alleged improper use of public money. Wilson responded with the standard challenge to duel, but in the event the matter was settled without guns being fired. While researching the duel, he discovered in the Irish barrister Jonah Barrington's autobiographical *Sketches* the Clonmel Code of 1777, with the regulations listed in an appendix.[19] He was impressed but decided that the US required a code of its own, and in 1838 published *The Code of Honor, or Rules for the Government of Principals and Seconds in Duelling*. His precepts parallel the Clonmel Code, but his own views were given in the four lengthy paragraphs of introduction which constitute an unembarrassed and unashamed defence of duelling, although he covers his back by proclaiming from the outset his purity of purpose:

> To publish a Code of Honor, to govern in cases of individual combat, might seem to imply that the publisher was an advocate of duelling, and wished to introduce it as the proper mode of deciding all personal difficulties and misunderstandings. Such implication would do me great injustice. But if the question be put directly to me, whether there are not cases where duels are right and proper, I would unhesitatingly answer there are.

He adds that 'nine duels out of ten originate in the want of experience in the seconds', and this ignorance he is out to remedy, but his overall defence of the principle of duelling is uncompromising. It was already commonplace to compare the right of an offended individual to take up arms to the entitlement of a nation to defend its interests by waging war against an oppressor, but Wilson goes beyond that cliché to base the justification for the duel on an instinct for self-defence detectable in nature. Even plants will put up a struggle to survive when threatened by the encroachment of a parasite, and on that observation Wilson advances the theory that

> ... the principle of self-preservation is co-extensive with creation; and when by education we make character and moral worth a part of ourselves, we guard these possessions with more watchful zeal than life itself, and would go further for their protection.

He moves on to confront Christian moral objections that had special force in the Bible-based Protestantism of the southern states.

> If a man be smote on one cheek in public, and he turns the other, which is also smitten, and he offers no resistance, but blesses him that so despitefully used him, I am aware that he is in the exercise of Christian forbearance, highly recommended and enjoined by many very good men but utterly repugnant to those feelings which nature and education have implanted in the human character. If it was possible to enact laws so severe and impossible to be evaded, as to enforce such rule of behavior, all that is honorable in the community would quit the country and inhabit the wilderness with the Indians... Those, therefore, who condemn all who do not denounce duelling in every case, should establish schools where passive submission to force would be

the exercise of a commendable virtue... But I very much
doubt, if a seminary of learning was established, where
this Christian forbearance was inculcated and enforced,
whether there would be many scholars.

With no evasion or double-speak, Wilson is at his most
Machiavellian in giving equal status to two moral codes,
Christian belief and the code of honour. He does not reject
the former in the abstract, but for life in society he prefers
the latter. The Biblical injunction to turn the other cheek,
and the ethics of the gospel will, he writes, make communal
life impossible. He was unlikely to know that Machiavelli had
reached the same conclusion, but he goes on to advance the
idea that the imposition of temperate Christian ethics would
compel men to take refuge 'in the wilderness with the Indians'.
Indians are plainly taken as primitive savages, perhaps even
part of the primitive state of nature to which human beings
would be reduced if they were denied the opportunity to strike
back. Wilson's basic tenet is that since 'character and moral
worth (are) a part of ourselves', we are entitled to defend them
at any cost, even by taking life. However cunningly disguised,
this is a restatement of the law of the stronger party. For all his
protestations of distaste for duelling, he provided the duellist
and his attendants with not only a user's manual but also an
ethic to placate their consciences.

Having attended to the moral doubts, Wilson moves onto
procedure, providing eight chapters, each tidily subdivided
into numbered sections, which provide a practical guide for the
perplexed duellist. He gives instructions to the party receiving
a preliminary warning of a pending challenge, outlines the duty
of the challenger and 'challengee' and their respective seconds
for every stage of the preparatory phase, advises on behaviour
at the field, lays out rules on who should be in attendance and
explains how arms should be selected, loaded and presented.
The American duellist now had his own home-made handbook,
but having given this information, Wilson suddenly remembered
that he should be discouraging the duel and so in his final

chapter, jarringly out of place, he reverts to his initial stance to discuss 'degrees of insult and how compromised'.

Fashion in morals and culture were in any case changing. John K. Williams records that two young lawyers met in 1877 in Savannah, but they were reluctant duellists who put off meeting until nightfall, but by then the encroaching darkness became a problem for one party who suffered from myopia, as the other gallantly accepted, so they decided to call the whole thing off. Seitz records a later and, he believes, final American duel which occurred in 1883. Richard F. Beirne, editor of the Richmond *State*, faced William C. Elam, editor of the rival *Whig*. Elam was bending over at the wrong time and received a bullet in the buttock. The comment Williams made on the Savannah duel could be applied to both: 'the code of honor died a less than honourable death.' If not dead, it was dying.

1 Alexander Young, *Chronicles of the Pilgrim Fathers*, New York, Cosimo Classics, 2005, p. 201. See also the various numbers of *The Mayflower Quarterly*, published by the General Society of *Mayflower* Descendants).
2 Don C. Seitz, *Famous American Duels*, New York: Thomas Y Crowell Company, 1929, pp. 48-51. This work is one of the classic histories of the American duel, together with Major Ben C. Truman's *The Field of Honour* (1884); the sections relating to America were edited by Steven Randolph Wood as *Duelling in America*, reprinted San Diego CA: Joseph Tabler Books, 1992. See also Barbara Holland, *Gentlemen's Blood: A History of Dueling from Swords at Dawn to Pistols at Dark*, New York: Bloomsbury, 2003; Joanne B. Freeman, *Affairs of Honour*, New Haven CT, Yale University Press, 2002.
3 Truman, *op. cit.*, p. 18.
4 *Ibid*, pp. 26-7.
5 Andrew Steinmetz, *The Romance of Duelling in All Times and Countries*, London: Chapman & Hall, 1868, vol. II, p. 298.

6 Jack K. Williams, *Dueling in the Old South: Vignettes of Social History*, College Station TX: Texas A&M University Press, 1980. See also William Oliver Stevens, *Pistols at Ten Paces*, Boston MA, Houghton Mifflin Co, 1940; Bertram Wyatt-Brown, *The Shaping of the Old South*, Chapel Hill NC, University of North Carolina Press, 2001.

7 Richard Rankin, 'Dueling', in William S. Powell, ed., *Encyclopedia of North Carolina*, Chapel Hill NC: University of North Carolina Press, 2006.

8 Diane Bell-Kite, *The Stanly-Spaight Duel*, https://www.ncpedia.org/history/stanly-spaight-duel, 2010.

9 www.museum.state.il.us/RiverWeb/landings/Ambot/Archives/transactions/1901/Stuart-Bennett_20Duel.html

10 Truman, *op. cit.*, p. 102; see also https://www.sfgate.com/bayarea/article/Historic-duels-in-San-Francisco-9208235.php .

11 https://www.cschs.org/wp—Newsletter-Spring-Justice-Terry

12 James Parton, *Life of Andrew Jackson*, New York: Mason Brothers, 1860.

13 Seitz, *op. cit.*, p. 123.

14 The case is examined by Don C. Seitz, *op. cit.*, pp. 227-50; and by Truman, *op. cit.*, pp. 88-93; see also the anonymous *The Great Duellist: a Sketch of the Duelling Practices of the Hon Henry Clay*, Boston: J. Leavitt & Alden, 1841.

15 https://archive.org/details/remedyforduellin00beecrich/page/n7/mode/2up

16 Williams, *op. cit.*

17 Harriet Martineau, *Society in America*, 3 vols., London: Saunders & Otley, 1837; reprinted by Cambridge University Press, 2009.

18 Seitz, *op. cit.*, pp. 29-30.

19 Sir Jonah Barrington, *Recollections and Sketches*, London: Henry Colburn, 1827.

9

'THIS LAMENTABLE AFFAIR'
THE HAMILTON-BURR DUEL

The main complaint of the internal narrator in Gore Vidal's *Burr*, a novel later incorporated into a series given the portfolio title *Narratives of Empire*, is that he 'doesn't seem able to catch the right tone' for the fictionalized biography of Burr he is to write. He settles for a detached, sardonic approach appropriate for an observer who aspires to remain non-partisan, but his voice occasionally falters as the events demand. After a few lines on Aaron Burr's second marriage in 1833, he proceeds in a flat journalistic prose which belies the extraordinary events he lists:

> In 1804, Colonel Burr - then Vice-President of the United States - shot and killed General Alexander Hamilton in a duel. Three years after this lamentable affair, Colonel Burr was arrested by order of President Thomas Jefferson and charged with treason for having wanted to break up the United States. A court presided over by Chief Justice John Marshall found Colonel Burr innocent of treason but guilty of the misdemeanour of proposing an invasion of Spanish territories in order to make himself emperor of Mexico.[1]

It is surprising to hear Barbara Holland in her history of American duelling casually refer to the 'once famous' Burr-Hamilton duel, an event that 'nowadays few American remember anything about', especially since the duel had been given prominence by Joseph J. Ellis' much praised book *Founding Brothers*, published before her work. The biography *Alexander Hamilton* by Ron Chernow followed shortly afterwards, and was the inspiration for the 2015 musical *Hamilton* by Lin-Manuel Miranda, a maxi-success first on Broadway and then around the world.[2]

This show brought the duel between the two men roaring back to public attention first in newspapers, then in theatre journals and finally in more rarefied academic periodicals where supposed inaccuracies, dubious timelines, questionable depictions of character or misleading interpretations were severely brought to task. No matter. For most people, knowledge of history, whether of the Trojan War or the Tudor court, is more likely to be gleaned from Hollywood movies, TV serials or popular fiction than from serious tomes authored by conscientious historians.

Historians of the early days of the American Republic, conscientious or otherwise, are themselves at odds over virtually everything regarding Alexander Hamilton and Aaron Burr - their characters, their vision, their political intentions, their actual achievements, their beliefs and even more the motivations which finally drove them to fight. That duel was not caused purely by some single rash act or isolated offence viewed as unpardonable under the prevailing moral and social code, since the two had vied with one another all throughout their lives. The deep divide in personality, background and perspective on life combined with their aspirations to fame and power goes a long way, Joanne Freeman writes, to help 'understand the fire and fury of the Burr-Hamilton rivalry and the reason they cut such wide paths through the imagination of their peers'.[3] The two were life-long opponents who embody the clashing myths, values and delusions of a new Republic which wished to differentiate itself from European aristocratic models, but who are now doomed to be paired forever, like Iago and Othello. But which is Othello and which Iago?

Hamilton embodies the combination of *fortuna* and *virtu* which Machiavelli judged indispensable for success in politics, where the first represents the hand an individual is dealt and the second his skill in playing that hand; the former is a gift arbitrarily bestowed by a power beyond human reckoning, and the latter the personal exploitation of intellect, imagination and foresight or power and ruthlessness. After an unpromising start, Hamilton benefited from the intervention of fortune at various, crucial points in his life. Not American by birth, he was born in 1755 or 1757 - there is no consensus over the actual date - on the Caribbean island of Nevis of a displaced Scottish father, James Hamilton, and a local woman of French Huguenot descent, Rachel Fawcett. In his autobiography, John Adams, no friend of Hamilton, put the matter accurately, if brutally, when he described him as the 'bastard brat of a Scotch pedlar'. In the opening lines of the musical, Miranda explains Hamilton's origins in similar terms: 'a bastard, orphan, son of a whore and a/Scotsman, dropped in the middle of a forgotten/Spot in the Caribbean.'

James Hamilton deserted his family and Rachel endured much in her life, including being briefly compelled by poverty into prostitution, and a period in prison after being accused of adultery. She died in 1768, leaving Alexander Hamilton an orphan, but he received the decisive lucky break of his life when he was given employment by American merchants who later, plainly impressed by the young man's native abilities, had the philanthropic urge to send him to New York, where the company had its main base. They ensured that he was given an education at the institution which became Columbia University, where he enrolled for the study of law in 1773. This happened to be the year of the Boston Tea Party and, still in his teens and newly arrived in America, Hamilton authored pamphlets in support of the colonists' claims and joined the American militia on the outbreak of war.

Aaron Burr was born in 1756 in New Jersey to a family who were relatively prosperous and prominent in church and academic circles, but he was orphaned at a young age and seemingly suffered maltreatment at the hands of the relatives who took him in. If the origins of the two men were widely different, their first independent steps were eerily similar. Burr studied theology at Princeton in the broadly Calvinist tradition, but switched later to law. When he heard of the first clashes between British and American troops at Lexington, he dropped everything to enlist and took part in an expedition to Quebec, which was British territory. Having made his mark, he was promoted to captain and appointed to George Washington's staff, but he found the atmosphere stuffy and only lasted a couple of weeks before returning to the front line. Hamilton too moved between a posting as aide-de-camp to George Washington and as an officer in the field. The two men's paths may have crossed in August 1776 when, shortly after the Declaration of

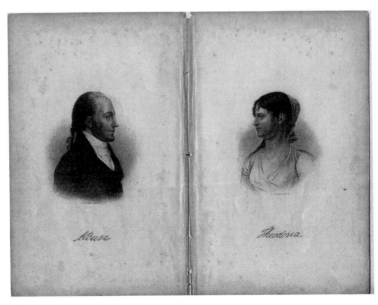

Aaron Burr and his daughter Theodosia, date unknown (Museum of American Science/Wikimedia Commons).

Independence, Hamilton's unit was trapped in Manhattan by British warships until he was rescued by a detachment led by Aaron Burr.[4] Both men had distinguished military careers and both served both as combatants and as assistants on Washington's personal staff. At the end of the hostilities both moved to New York, both decided to practise law, and both became involved in politics but on different sides.

Hamilton married Elizabeth Schuyler in 1780. It was a successful marriage, even if Elizabeth had to endure her husband's infidelities. The couple had eight children. Burr had been conducting an affair with Theodosia Bartow Prevost before he married her in 1782 on the death of her husband. She died in 1794. Only one daughter, Theodosia, survived into adulthood, and Burr's close relationship with her was a subject of gossip and even of insinuations of incest, and these may have been a factor in the lead-up to the duel with Hamilton.

Hamilton carved out a prominent position for himself at city and national level.[5] He served in the New York State Legislature, represented the city on the Congress of the Federation and wrote fifty-one of the essays which made up The Federalist Papers, a work which remains a fundamental document for the Constitution of the United States. He founded the Bank of New York and in 1789 was invited by Washington to join his government as Secretary to the Treasury. He was dogged by allegations of corrupt practices during his time in office. His initiatives and policies, such as the assumption by the national government of state bonds issued during the war, were of necessity divisive, and would return to haunt him later.[6] Two main factions or proto-parties were emerging: the Federalists, of which Hamilton was undisputed leader, and the Democratic-Republicans, which included Thomas Jefferson and Burr among its number. The Federalists found themselves under attack as being variously too European or too aristocratic in outlook, too pro-British and even as harbouring pro-monarchist sentiments. Hamilton resigned from the Cabinet in 1794, partly for private reasons to do with his wife's health, but also because he found public office insufficiently remunerative compared with his legal practice, to which he returned. Far from retiring totally into private life, he remained a significant figure in politics.

After his military service Aaron Burr too set up his own legal practice in New York, and also took a full part in public life. He sat in the New York State Assembly, became state attorney general in 1789 and was later elected senator for New York, ousting Philip Schuyler, Hamilton's father-in-law, an outcome which riled Hamilton. Burr stood for president in 1796, but came a distant fourth. In September 1799 he founded the Manhattan Company, the second commercial bank formed in New York, a move which deepened the antagonism between him and Hamilton. In the 1800 presidential campaign he was again a candidate, going head to head with Thomas Jefferson, but the vagaries and complexities of the electoral system in force at the time meant that the two men tied for votes in the Electoral College, with the result that the decision was left to the House of Representatives. After no fewer than thirty-six rounds of voting, Jefferson was elected president, but under the then Constitution Burr automatically became vice-president, basically a powerless sinecure. As the next elections drew near it was clear that Jefferson would never countenance Burr as vice-president, so he put himself forward for the position of Governor of New York State, but was again unsuccessful. Burr believed that Hamilton had actively campaigned against him, an allegation Hamilton never denied. These are the standard outlines of politics in a democracy where the advocacy of ideals and hopes for reform are matched by the darker facts of the disappointment of failure and having to endure the braggadocio of victorious opponents.

The lives of the two men moved on parallel, sometimes overlapping, paths. However, as Joanne B. Freeman makes clear in her authoritative study of this period, the politics of the new Republic had elements which were wholly sui generis and which produced a toxicity of their own. It is not completely out of place to note that the musical Hamilton finds place in its plot for three duels, all historically attested. The first involved

Charles Lee and John Laurens in 1778 when both were in the service of Washington during the war, but Burr and Hamilton were in the wings. Lee was outraged when he was dismissed by Washington, and pilloried Washington behind his back. He was recipient of two challenges from Washington supporters, and in fact would have had a third from Hamilton had not Washington intervened to veto it. The duel with Laurens went ahead, and ended with Lee receiving an injury but surviving. In the musical both Hamilton and Burr are portrayed as being seconds, but that is poetic licence. In history Hamilton alone took on that role.[7]

That event occurred in the conditions of war, but the cultural parameters within which duelling was tolerated or necessitated had been fixed before Independence and would persist after the restoration of peace. Americans had inherited the code of honour from their European forebears, but the circumstances which could lead to the duel in eighteenth-century America were if anything more plentiful. Freeman argues that reputation, the limping sister of honour, was of greater import in the new Republic than elsewhere, and that it was more likely to be damaged by the insidious circulation of gossip.[8] 'Gossip was everywhere... The power of gossip was its ability to savage one's reputation now and forever, a double threat for the posterity-minded founding generation.'[9] This situation was aggravated by the fact that the ruling elite of pioneering Constitution builders were a highly literate group, skilled in rhetoric, adept in the polemical tirade and always willing to take to print. They were prolific in their output of public letters, articles in the burgeoning press outlets as well as in handbills and little pamphlets attacking and mocking their rivals. The image built up over the generations by American biographers and historians, or indeed by judges in the Supreme Court, of the Founding Fathers as selfless Sages requires some revision, although by and large they remain worthy of their allotted place in the empyrean of higher thinkers reserved for selfless philosopher-kings. A mindset formed by the reading of Cicero, the philosophy of John Locke and the deliberations of the French and Scottish Enlightenment

thinkers was one part of their intellectual armoury, but they were
also highly disputatious and given to individual striving. They
were learned and cultured, but as prone as lesser men to forming
and re-forming cliques, to nurturing enmities, to believing the
worst of that day's antagonists and to seeking confirmation in
whispers and gossip for that negative opinion. During the War
of Independence, Edmund Burke coined for the rebellious
colonists the adjective 'umbrageous', that is, easily moved to
taking umbrage when provoked by real or imagined slights. This
characteristic remained observable among politicians near to,
or maliciously excluded from, the centres of power of the new
Republic.

Hamilton himself was highly umbrageous, both as giver
and receiver of umbrage. He was surrounded by men such as
John Adams and Aaron Burr, who were perfect foils and with
whom he engaged in life-long vendettas. The level of vitriol
in his pamphlets and letters is astonishing, especially towards
Adams who was an enemy both in political and personal
terms. In 1800, Hamilton published a venomous, signed piece
on *The Public Conduct and Character of John Adams, Esq* when
the presidential campaign was in full swing and when Adams
was leader of the party to which Hamilton officially proclaimed
allegiance. Adams had defeated Jefferson in 1796, but he lost
in 1800. Quincy Adams may have exaggerated the role of
Hamilton and Burr jointly in bringing about his father's defeat,
but however strange bedfellows they might have made, he was
right in identifying the shifting relationship of interest which
allowed political figures to come close at times only to veer
away when the dice spun in another direction. By 1804, when
Burr stood for the governorship of New York, the Federalist
Party, headed by Hamilton, published a one-page leaflet headed
Aaron Burr!, where the exclamation mark can be considered the
most raucous, sarcastic piece of punctuation in history. The text
itself was coruscating from the opening line where he compared
his adversary to Catiline, the arch-conspirator of Roman history,
denounced for his treachery by Cicero. Hamilton made a similar
charge, in rhetorical terms Cicero would have relished, against

Burr, who 'stands confessed in all his villainy. His INVETERATE HATRED of the Constitution of the United States has long been displayed in one steady, undeviating course of HOSTILITY to every measure which the solid interests of the Union demands.' Burr's political perfidy was accompanied by allegations of debauchery at the expense of 'numerous unhappy wretches who have fallen victim to this accomplished but too successful debauchee'. Burr declined to reply, although this pamphlet was symptomatic of the toxic air circulating in the years before the final duel.

Both Burr and Hamilton had acquired their own experience of 'affairs of honour'. Hamilton came close to fighting a duel in 1790 with South Carolina Representative Aedanus Burke, who insulted him by the use of the ritualistic formula, 'giving the lie to Colonel Hamilton', words which all the experts on duelling agreed must inevitably lead to a challenge, although on this occasion the matter was patched up. Not long after, he had a virulent quarrel with James Nicholson, who committed the supreme outrage of calling Hamilton a coward, another offence which normally could only be pardoned after bloodshed. Once again the duel was avoided, but the taunt was repeated in 1795, when Nicholson had become a leading light in the Republican faction. The two men took opposing views of the Jay Treaty, which was meant to restore harmony with Great Britain which was then at war with revolutionary France. Hamilton supported the measure while Nicholson and his Republicans viewed it as an act of degrading appeasement. When Nicholson organized a demonstration in New York to protest against it, Hamilton went to meet the demonstrators in an attempt to placate them. Nicholson scoffed at Hamilton and told his fellow demonstrators to disregard him since he had previously shown his lack of manliness by declining a duel with him. Never notable for his self-control, Hamilton challenged Nicholson to a duel there and then. When Nicholson's supporters backed him, Hamilton challenged them one and all, and even extended the challenge to the 'whole detestable faction'. One Republican, Maturin Livingston, stepped forward to pick up the gauntlet. Hamilton rebuffed him saying that he had business with Nicholson but once that was settled, he would be happy to accommodate his new adversary. If the Hamilton-Burr duel was deemed worthy of being staged as a musical, this incident would find its most suitable dramatic form in a movie starring John Wayne.

The dispute was not settled on the public highway. Correspondence was exchanged over the following days, with Hamilton adducing Nicholson's 'unprovoked rudeness' and insulting words as leaving him 'no option but that of a meeting with you, the object of which you will readily understand'. Of course he would. Hamilton begged for a week's postponement because of previous commitments, but this request was awkward for Nicholson who had sobered up after the mobbing and sent an exquisitely worded reply. 'The publicity of the affair & the unusual visit of your friend (Hamilton's second) have however unfortunately occasioned an alarm in my family & may produce an inquiry.' He requested Hamilton's assistance to enable him to deal expeditiously with the family alarm, and went on, 'you will therefore perceive that my situation will be rendered extremely disagreeable unless your interview takes place before that time.' He could have been requesting an alteration in the date for a coffee and a chat, but his tone shows that, having recovered his poise, he was acting in accordance with protocols which required a display of gentlemanly courtesy and insouciance towards an opponent whom he might kill or by whom he might be killed. The brutal word 'duel' could not be employed in these urbane exchanges, where a more genteel euphemism, like 'interview', was de rigueur. In the event, the seconds did their job and the interview was avoided. Nicholson asked Hamilton to accept that his intemperate language 'proceeded from a misapprehension of the nature of his (Hamilton's) interposition in the altercation', and claimed he had no recollection of having cast any aspersions on Hamilton for having 'declined a former interview'. In consequence he 'regrets the pain which it (his imputation) must have occasioned to Mr Hamilton'. Peace and harmony were restored, no shots were fired and the two men lived to fight another day - literally.

According to the most reliable accounts, Hamilton was involved in eight affairs of honour, most of which ended in ritual apologies, while Burr totted up a mere four. The name John Barker Church, Hamilton's brother-in-law, continually crops up in exchanges between the two, and not only because he was the owner of a fine set of duelling pistols which he generously made available for use by friends. He used them himself in 1799 in a duel with Burr. They would come out of their case on two occasions when the Hamilton family required them, and who knows on how many other occasions? However, in 1797 Church was, together with none other than Aaron Burr, instrumental in preventing a dispute between Hamilton and James Monroe from spinning totally out of control and onto the field of honour. The origins of this dispute went back to 1792 when Monroe was a member of a committee charged with investigating allegations against Hamilton for embezzlement of public funds while he was Secretary of the Treasury. Hamilton protested his innocence, but was compelled to confess that he had been involved in some underhand dealings as a consequence of his affair with a married woman, Maria Reynolds. Her husband had connived at his wife's relationship with Hamilton but had then made use of his knowledge to blackmail Hamilton and request his help in certain suspicious deals. At the time, the committee of enquiry accepted Hamilton's version but decided to keep a record of the proceedings which would not, however, be made public.

Five years later, an account of the case backed by the original documents appeared in the press. Hamilton believed that the journalist had been briefed by Monroe and confronted him in person. Unconvinced by Monroe's denial, he accused him of lying. Monroe countered by calling Hamilton a scoundrel. Such terminology had an acknowledged place in the gentlemanly vocabulary of honour and dishonour, and was thus a conscious challenge. The later choreography which entailed the appointment of seconds, negotiations, the choice of weapons and agreement on time and venue was not fully recognized at that date either in Europe or the US, so in the heated atmosphere in the room where they met both men agreed to proceed to a duel as soon as weapons could be produced. Church, who had accompanied Hamilton, was a stickler for the emerging code, and intervened to argue for delay. The time thus gained permitted further discussions, and Church's pistols remained in their cushioned case, for the moment.

Tellingly, Monroe never withdrew the accusation of the misappropriation of public funds, so the case simmered over the summer. In August, Hamilton published an astonishing pamphlet with the anodyne title *Observations on Certain Documents* in which he set out to rebut charges of financial wrong-doing, but in which he laid out in explicit detail the course of his adulterous affair with Mrs Reynolds. A decade or so later, when Victorian morality was dominant, such a scandal would have put an end to his career, but he was writing in the late Enlightenment, when such misdemeanours were of lesser moment. In the pamphlet he admitted that he had submitted to blackmail to keep her husband quiet. To complicate matters further, he publicized his differences with Monroe, who had once again to react. His first letter to Hamilton was confused and obscure, leaving Hamilton unsure whether or not it amounted to a challenge, but he made it clear that if that were the case, he was ready to take it up. Monroe then turned to Aaron Burr, expressing the hope that he could 'settle this disagreeable affair finally', and adding that he had 'entire confidence in (his) judgment, honour and friendship'. Burr was plainly equal to the request, and the dispute was resolved.[10]

Hubris and Tragedy

In the following years relations between Hamilton and Burr and their families and factions deteriorated even further, with tragic outcomes. It is tempting to exit from the frame of American politics at the turn of the eighteenth and nineteenth centuries, with its political struggles between families and factions, and to place the enmity between Hamilton and Burr in a more ancient context. Perhaps only Aeschylus, the poet who chronicled the fate of the House of Atreus, could have had the insight to penetrate the mentality of these two men and to shed light on the tragic forces which drove them ineluctably to confront a destiny neither would have chosen. Both seem entangled in their version of the perpetual 'struggle of man with more than man', in the words of Sophocles. Like Orestes or Oedipus, they were subject to the inner flaws and outer forces which together constitute fate and which compelled them to pursue their own variation of the classical Greek force of destiny. The term hubris (overweening pride) from the Aristotelian dissection of tragedy is relevant to the final acts of this American drama. Hamilton, who was capable of subtler self-analysis than his opponent, came to recognize that Burr too had his rights. On his death bed, he wrote the enigmatic words, 'I have found for some time that my life must be exposed to that man.'[11] There is no analysing the imperative 'must' in purely rationalist terms.

The sins of the father were first visited on the son, Philip Hamilton, born in 1789, the eldest of eight siblings. Like his father he studied law and began in his teens to dabble in politics. Family biographers agree he was a lively lad, a 'brisk blade about town', as Don Seitz puts it.[12] He may have been drinking when in November 1801 he went with a friend, Richard Price, to the theatre where by chance, pure chance, he ended up in a box alongside one occupied by George Eacker, a young lawyer and a supporter of the Burr faction of Republicans. That was the year that saw Jefferson become president with Burr as his vice-president after a bitterly contested campaign. Some months previously, Eacker had made a widely reported speech in which he had attacked Hamilton for having misused public office and for plotting to overthrow the Jefferson government by force. Hamilton and Price invited themselves at the interval into Eacker's box, making a nuisance of themselves and causing Eacker to shout out: 'It is too abominable to be publicly insulted by a pair of damned rascals.' The choice of vocabulary may have been careless or may have been deliberate. 'Rascal' was a forbidden, duel-provoking word between gentlemen.

Both groups repaired to a tavern, as suggested by other friends, although such a venue seems guaranteed to pour oil on fire. There was no reconciliation or apology, so Price issued his challenge, followed by Hamilton with his. Eacker accepted both. In another age, what would have been an episode of rowdy behaviour dismissed as adolescent hooliganism was now, in accordance with the prevailing culture, destined to turn tragic. Since New York had banned duelling the venue was fixed as Weehawken in New Jersey, a neighbouring township on the River Hudson with a rocky ledge overhanging the water. The ledge has long since collapsed, but there is a plaque nearby which records that some eighteen duels took place in that place.

Eacker faced Price first, but evidently neither was a good shot, as they each fired three times and missed. The seconds intervened to say that honour had been surely satisfied, but both dissented so a fourth shot was allowed, but this too was harmless. They then deserted the field, but Eacker still had a challenge outstanding with Hamilton. The seconds attempted unsuccessfully to invite the two to reconsider what all parties agreed was no more than a minor incident of youthful, male bravado. Hamilton knew he was the offender but could not bring himself to apologize, although it was afterwards said that he planned to shoot in the air. They met the following day and Hamilton was seriously wounded with the first shot. He was rowed back to the city and his parents summoned. A witness reported that on arrival he saw 'poor Phil, pale and languid, his rolling, distracted eyeballs darting forth flashes of delirium. On one side of him on the same bed lay his agonised father; on the other, his distracted mother.' Philip Hamilton died on 25 November 1801. Seitz wrote that so great was his father's grief that he had to be supported at the graveside, but adds the haunting remark that for Hamilton senior his 'son's death was as a shadow cast before.'[13]

There were two other duels fought in that lengthening shadow. John Swartwout was a Burr supporter, while DeWitt Clinton was a Hamilton man. In 1802, aged thirty-three, the latter's CV already included membership of the state legislature and candidacy for the Senate. He protested when Swartwout alleged that Clinton's opposition to Burr was grounded on 'personal and selfish motives', and called out his rival as 'a liar, a scoundrel and a villain'. Any one of that triad would have been sufficient to set the duo on the dismal road to the field of honour. As Marx famously said, history repeats itself, first as tragedy and then as farce. The Philip Hamilton tragedy having been acted out, the new duel is more fortunately characterized by its elements of farce or harlequinade. The *Sacramento Daily Union* gave a full account of the episode some seventy years later in a retrospective look at Clinton's career, when it branded their duel 'the most remarkable affair of the kind that ever occurred - out of Ireland.' Ireland had, fairly or unfairly, acquired a reputation as the land of foolish duellists.

On the day, the first three shots were fired with no injury inflicted. The seconds, perhaps moved by tedium as much as by duty, suggested after each round that enough was enough, but neither man would have it, so the guns rang out a fourth time, this time leaving Swartwout with a wound to his left leg. Clinton helpfully stated he had no animosity against his rival but, being a man of honour, Swartwout declared he preferred to continue unless he received a written apology, which Clinton declined to give. They resumed their positions and Clinton struck Swartwout on the same leg. Swartwout wished to soldier on, but the seconds were more resolute and Clinton threw down his gun. Referring to Clinton, the Sacramento journal concluded that 'he was brave to rashness, and ambitious beyond measure; but he lived up to the standard of his day, and acquitted himself of every Trust with honour and distinction.' DeWitt Clinton served as Mayor of New York several times between 1803 and 1815, and in 1812 he was a candidate for the presidency, losing to the incumbent, James Madison. Fighting a duel was no bar to high office.

The shadow covered yet another duel when in early 1804 William Coleman shot and killed Captain Jeremiah Thompson. Coleman too had studied law and had once been a member of the same legal firm as Aaron Burr, but by 1804 he was an ally of Alexander Hamilton and was invited by him to edit the *New York Evening Post*, which Hamilton had founded in 1801.

Coleman's opponent was a Burr supporter but politics were not the immediate cause of the challenge. James Cheetham was editor of the rival *American Citizen* and used its columns to allege that Coleman had had an illegitimate child with a black woman. The seriousness was plainly not in the extra-conjugal relationship itself but in the inter-racial nature of the union. The inevitable challenge was issued but, duelling being illegal in New York, an interview was banned by court order. There the matter might have rested had not a Captain Thompson stepped forward to allege that Coleman himself had manoeuvred this ban, thereby showing himself a coward. The word 'coward' was taboo, necessitating a new challenge. The encounter took place in what is now downtown Manhattan. Thompson was shot, Coleman fled, and the dying Thompson refused to reveal the identity of his opponent since he had been, he said, fairly treated. He abided by the gentleman's code to the end. Coleman returned and remained a Hamilton loyalist, later serving as an intermediary with Burr.

This was a curtain raiser to the main event of that year, the Hamilton-Burr duel itself. Burr was in office as vice-president, but his relations with President Jefferson had never been cordial and he knew he would not be on the same ticket as the incumbent at the next election. He convinced himself, perhaps accurately, that his hopes of progress were being thwarted by gossip and slander put about by a faction headed by Hamilton. He stood for Governor of New York State but lost. He asked to be dispatched as Ambassador to France, but Jefferson refused to appoint him. Already in a state of some sensitivity to insinuations allegedly emanating from the Hamilton camp, he was made aware of a published letter written by Charles D. Cooper to Philip Schuyler, Hamilton's father-in-law. Cooper took issue with Schuyler's rebuttal of a previous article in which he (Cooper) had claimed that Hamilton had defamed Burr as 'a dangerous man and one who ought not be trusted with the reins of government.' That charge might have been dismissed as the normal currency of party political slanging, but it was followed by a second allegation made all the more sinister by its imprecision. Cooper claimed to be aware of a 'still more despicable opinion which General Hamilton has expressed of Mr Burr'. Historians have advanced the most varied theories on this enigmatic phrase, the most common being that it was a reference to Burr's supposed incestuous relationship with his daughter. The fact of incest was never proved, nor was the exact nature of the damaging accusation itself ever revealed, but the publication of these opinions, true or slanderous, was more than a man of honour could bear. Burr's dilemma was that whatever the veiled charge was, it was evidently gross and would undoubtedly diminish him in his own day and in days to come. In any reasonable regime of truth and falsehood, not just in the narrowly defined terms of eighteenth-century courtesy and discourtesy, Burr had a point and was entitled to expect clarity.

In the face of Burr's demands, Hamilton prevaricated. He conflated the two accusations and waffled about degrees of meaning for the word 'despicable'. He accepted that the first accusation could be read as implying that as a man aspiring to public office Burr was 'despicable', but over the mysterious second accusation he indulged in vague semantics to the effect that the phrase '"still more despicable" admits of infinite shades, from the very light to the very dark'. In his view, 'between gentlemen, despicable and more despicable are not worth the pains of distinction.' He further wondered why Burr expressed no objection to the merely 'despicable' opinion, leaving him (Hamilton) without an objective standard by which to judge the unstated but apparently 'more despicable' assertion. In his words, 'I deem it inadmissible on principle to consent to be interrogated as to the justness of the inferences which may be drawn by others from whatever I may have said of a political opponent in the course of fifteen years competition.' Hamilton himself was hardly displaying gentlemanly candour.

Burr was unimpressed, and moved the discussion away from quibbles over degrees of meaning onto the treacherous central terrain of 'the laws of honour and the rules of decorum'. Friends and emissaries, Nathaniel Pendleton for Hamilton and William Van Ness for Burr, were called into action as counsellors as well as bearers of missives. They also held their own private discussions, as pre-duelling formalities required. Hamilton judged Burr's reply rude and in a brief response on 22 June requested it be withdrawn since its terms did not permit him to give the 'direct avowal or disavowal' requested. The scurrying from house to house with verbal or written communications continued, interrupted by the demands of day-to-day living as one or other of the principals had to attend to business outside New York. The two men were obliged to keep confidential their increasingly acrimonious discussions and the likelihood of the impending 'interview', not least because they were afraid of stirring up legal and political opposition which would have surely put paid to their plans. The negotiations lasted over a full month, during which the two men carried on routine business and family life, and even met at a dinner given by the Society of Cincinnati, a club of veterans of the War of Independence. John Trumbull, an artist who had painted several portraits of Hamilton, was present and left in his Memoirs an account of the contrasting behaviour of the two men that evening.

> The singularity of their manner was observed by all, but few had any suspicion of the cause. Burr, contrary to his wont, was silent, gloomy, sour; while Hamilton entered with glee into all the gaiety of a convivial party, and even sang an old military song.

Subsequently there was some acrimonious dispute over which song Hamilton actually sang. Some of those in attendance distinctly remembered him giving voice to 'The Drum', while others were equally clear in their recollection of his powerful rendering of 'How Stands the Glass Around?' The question has remained unresolved, but no challenges were issued over the question.

Away from the festivities, Hamilton claimed to be racking his brains to recall the conversation Cooper was referring to and the exact terms in which his witticisms or sallies were couched. He told Burr's emissary that 'the conversation to which Dr Cooper alluded turned wholly on political subjects and did not attribute to Col. Burr any instance of dishonourable conduct nor relate to his private character.' This was a private denial but not a public apology, and as such was not felt to be adequate. The tone of the letters continued to be invariably polite and diplomatic, opening with expressions of humble gratitude for the honour done by the other in writing, but the underlying hint of menace was never far from the surface. By 27 June, Van Ness sent on Burr's behalf a letter which went over the ground already covered, repeating the basic point that since Burr had 'reason to believe that General Hamilton had used expressions derogatory to his honour, he would (sic) have had the magnanimity to retract them.' No offer of retraction was made, so while 'Colonel Burr disavows all motives of predetermined hostility', he nonetheless feels 'as a gentleman should feel when his honour is impeached or assailed'. Hamilton, who had always declared his aversion to duelling, did make one more effort and drew up a final missive which he gave to Pendleton to hand to Van Ness, but he declined to accept it. The letter is extant and in it Hamilton states:

> General Hamilton has been ready to enter into a frank and free explanation on any and every object of a specific nature; but not to answer a general and abstract inquiry, embracing a period too long for an accurate recollection, and exposing him to unpleasant criticism from, or unpleasant discussions with, any and every person who may have understood him in an unfavourable sense... To this therefore he can never submit.

There was now no alternative to the duel, or at least none that was feasible to men of that culture in that age. Hamilton now devoted himself to putting his affairs in order and left ten assorted documents and memoranda in the care of Nathaniel Pendleton.[14] The first was a tender letter to his wife in which he told her of his intention not to fire. 'The scruples of a Christian have determined me to expose my own life to any extent rather than subject myself to the guilt of taking the life of another. This must increase my hazards and redoubles my pangs for you. But you had rather I should die innocent than live guilty.' Being a scrupulous man, in addition to his will he outlined the properties he owned, made such provision as he could for his creditors and even gave a list of debts owed for services not tendered. The most eccentric letter was addressed to one George Mitchell, enclosing a lottery ticket. History does not record if Mr Mitchell's ticket was the prize winner, and history can only wonder at the mind which in those circumstances could attend to lottery tickets.

The document of greatest value, one which ranks alongside Casanova's pamphlet for its insights into the mind of a man who feels himself honour-bound to fight a duel, is given the prosaic heading *Statement on Impending Duel with Aaron Burr*. Internal evidence suggests that it was drawn up on 9 or 10 July 1804, in the final hours before the duel itself. Nothing in the whole literature of duelling is more confounding or stupefying than this document. Unlike Casanova's memoir, the Statement is a preliminary to action and shows the moral anguish of a man torn by conflicting imperatives. As with classical tragedy, these are all imperatives, not optional courses of action. What was its intended readership? His contemporaries? History? Hamilton was a tenacious opponent of duelling, as he repeats throughout, and in his Statement he listed his obligations as a man, and reformulated the ethical codes to which he owed allegiance, all of which forbade duelling: his religious belief, family obligations and civil duty to creditors all argued against risking his life. To these he added a fourth consideration, that he was 'conscious of *no ill-will* (his emphasis) to Col. Burr, distinct from political opposition'. The conclusion was that he would 'hazard much, and (could) possibly gain nothing by the outcome of the interview.' However, in the last analysis these could not be determining factors, since 'it was, as I conceive, impossible to avoid it. There were intrinsic difficulties in the thing, and *artificial* (emphasis in the original) embarrassments, from the manner of proceeding of Col Burr.' Since he had already ruled out any other options, such as offering an apology, it was impossible to do other than face Burr. He was as ensnared by his own code as any tragic hero. The decisive intrinsic problems related to his own conduct towards Burr, which led him to believe he had a *duty* to Burr (my emphasis) to fight, since his 'animadversions on the political principles, character and views of Colonel Burr have been extremely severe.' He circles round the dilemma of offering an apology, but his conclusion is that 'enforcing all the considerations which constitute what men of the world denominate honour imposed on me (as I thought) a peculiar necessity not to decline the call.' The implications of the cryptic phrase 'what men of the world denominate honour' are profound: the consequences of pursuing the logic of 'honour' are thus attributed elsewhere, not to himself. He was the prisoner of a code from which he could not, and thus would not, free himself. He arrived at the desperate compromise that he would turn up at Weehawken at the appointed hour and fire in the air, but the decision not to aim at his opponent was not communicated to Burr.

The events of the day were reported in meticulous detail in the press, and the articles were collected in a volume edited by William Coleman whose exhaustive title was *A Collection of the Facts and Documents, Relative to the Death of Major-General Alexander Hamilton: with Comments: Together with the Various Orations, Sermons, and Eulogies, that Have Been Published or Written on His Life and Character*. Hamilton arrived first, the two men greeted each other formally, the distance of ten paces was measured out, pistols were loaded in full view of the principals and seconds, final instructions given and the shots exchanged. Burr's first shot struck Hamilton, who fell to the ground. Burr made to go up to him but was hurried from the field by his attendants. There was some confusion over whether Hamilton had in fact fired his shot, the physician present saying that Hamilton's gun went off into the air as he fell to the ground. Hamilton was still alive and was rowed back to his home, where further surgeons were summoned, but all agreed he was beyond recovery. He repeatedly said to his wife, 'Remember, my Eliza, you are a Christian.'

The Burr-Hamilton duel at Weehawken (Library of Congress, Washington DC)

The funeral was a grand affair, with all the notables of the day present and grand words spoken as the due ceremonial was played out. Eliza Hamilton was left to bring up the seven surviving children and to take responsibility for her husband's debts. She had to sell the family home, The Grange, which had been completed only in 1802, but was later able to re-purchase it. She lived to the age of ninety-seven. Burr was charged with murder in New Jersey, but the case was not brought to trial on account of the legal awkwardness that although Hamilton was shot in New Jersey, he died in New York. Burr never reproached himself for his part in the proceedings but his career in politics was over. He was stripped of his right to practise law in New York, but was able to complete his term as vice-president. Much later he was brought to court on other charges, including treason, but was never convicted. He kept on the move, first in America and then in Europe, and died on Staten Island in 1836.

The only man to take any comfort from the outcome of the duel was John Quincy Adams who became president in 1825 but who had always put his father's defeat in 1800 down to the joint efforts of Hamilton and Burr. When news reached him of Hamilton's death and of Burr's ignominy, he rejoiced in his diary, noting that it was appropriate that 'divine retributive justice' had intervened to bring about 'the murder of one of them by the other in a duel, and the irretrievable ruin of the murderer'.[15]

There may be doubts over the 'divine retributive justice,' but shorn of its malice it was a fair summary.

Honour and the Sword

1 Gore Vidal, *Burr*, 1973, London: Abacus, 2003.
2 Barbara Holland, *Gentlemen's Blood: A History of Dueling from Swords at Dawn to Pistols at Dark*, New York, Bloomsbury, 2003, p. 105; Joseph J. Ellis, *Founding Brothers: The Revolutionary Generation*, New York: Random House, 2000; Ron Chernow, *Alexander Hamilton*, New York: Penguin Press, 2004.
3 Joanne B. Freeman, *Affairs of Honor: National Politics in the New Republic*, New Haven CT: Yale University Press, 2002, p. 161.
4 Richard Sylla, *Hamilton: The Illustrated Biography*, New York: Sterling, 2016, pp. 31-2.
5 Broadus Mitchell, *Alexander Hamilton*, New York: Macmillan, 1962; Freeman, *op. cit.*
6 It is worth noting that Hamilton's initiative was cited as a precedent by the European Union in 2020 when in the aftermath of the Covid-19 outbreak the proposal was discussed, but rejected, of having the European Central Bank take over pandemic-related debts of individual national governments.
7 Hamilton Papers, consulted at https://founders.archives.gov/documents/Hamilton/01-01-02-0687.
8 Freeman, *op. cit.*, chapter 2 passim.
9 *Ibid*, pp. 66-8.
10 Papers of James Monroe. Consulted at https://academics.umw.edu/jamesmonroepapers/2015/09/03/the-near-duel-between-james-monroe-and-alexander-hamilton.
11 Quoted in Freeman, *op. cit.*, p. 168.
12 Don C. Seitz, *Famous American Duels*, New York: Thomas Y Cromwell, 1929, p. 70.
13 *Ibid*, p. 75.
14 These papers are now in the possession of Columbia University, and were consulted online at https://founders.archives.gov/documents/Hamilton/01-26-02-0001-0276. The *Statement* and the earlier correspondence are quoted in Seitz, *op. cit.*, pp. 80-101.
15 John Quincy Adams, *Diaries 1799-1821*, edited by David Waldstreicher, New York: Library of America, 2019.

10

THE VICTORIAN AGE

VULGAR INCIDENTS AND HONOURABLE ENCOUNTERS

'And yet duels are so common now that they are really vulgar incidents. We hear of men being shot in duels about nothing every day,' lamented Lady Delacour in *Belinda*.[1] The tones of mockery were still infrequent in 1810 when Maria Edgeworth's novel was first published, but ironic disbelief or rancorous repudiation of the duel became the more accepted attitude as the century wore on.

The position of gentleman in Georgian and Victorian society was highly prized, highly demanding and highly precarious. It granted admission to an inner elite, but also helped shield inept rogues, of whom the Earl of Cardigan was one egregious example; it gave a limited number of males licence to strut self-importantly across a national or local stage, but imposed certain behavioural obligations; it was jealously guarded, but could be easily forfeited, perhaps by some solecism, indiscreet remark, tasteless joke especially about a lady, or by inadequate response to a slight which may or may not have been intentional. Since his rank could be put in jeopardy by the malice of others, the gentleman had to guard his standing against members of the same caste. Friends could be transformed into enemies after false words were spoken, perhaps incautiously or injudiciously, and not regretted with sufficient candour. Those who failed to comply with unwritten standards could see themselves relegated to an area outside the confines of respectable society at a time when respectability had none of the dismissive connotations it later acquired. The fate of the Hon Bertie Cecil in Ouida's novel *Under Two Flags*, compelled to join the French Foreign Legion in the face of a false accusation which he could not refute for fear of injuring a lady's honour, stood as a warning, however exaggerated for the purposes of fiction, to any blackguard.

In the decades before and immediately after the accession of Queen Victoria the nature of honour was if anything more abstruse but its demands more urgent than before. The honour code, in all its contradictions, was strengthened by the nineteenth-century revival of religious practice and belief, especially in their quintessentially Victorian form of 'muscular Christianity'. Organized religion, aided by the stately example of the queen herself, was enabled to regain that social power it had largely lost with the Enlightenment. In reprimanding her wayward son, Edward Prince of Wales, Queen Victoria called on him to respect the three-fold standards of the Gentleman, the Christian and the Soldier, thus giving unchallengeable expression of an ideal. The duties imposed by the appeal to honour among the upper classes were not weakened by the philosophical or moral arguments of such men as the Rev William Paley or Jeremy Bentham. Some now forgotten divines and reformers thundered against the duel, but by the early nineteenth century it was becoming clear that the duel was an ingrained custom but also that offended honour was frequently no more than a respectable pretext for a course of action aroused by resentment, pique or irritation. Foibles, trivial provocations which in other times would occasion an argument, a cross word, a shouting match, a verbal clash or even the temporary or permanent rupturing of once amicable relations now required gentlemen to appoint seconds to arrange what was euphemistically called a 'meeting' with pistols, the sword having passed out of fashion.

It is a cliché nowadays to make the terms Victorian and hypocrite virtually interchangeable, but the Victorian ideal of life, whatever the gulf between pious aspirations and daily practice, was neither more nor less genuine than any other. There were, of course, warts in the nineteenth-century self-portrait. Acceptance abroad of slavery and of the Imperial oppression of those perceived as lesser breeds without the law, as well as the domestic exploitation of working people and disregard of degrading living conditions were condoned at the time and can now be taken as aspects of Victorian double think, but so was the ready recourse to institutionalized violence by gentlemen. The incompatibility between the call to turn the other cheek and the chivalric code which sanctioned 'calling out' had been noted by moralists in previous centuries but complacently ignored by those who felt drawn to the field of honour. The hierarchy of values which supported duelling remained intact until a change of attitude, culture or fashion occurred in Britain and elsewhere in Europe around mid-century.

Fighting Talk

In the first half of the nineteenth century the duel was viewed as part of the lifestyle of a gentleman and an officer, pardonable for a Christian. There were many such cases. In 1803, Captain MacNamara of the Royal Navy met Lieutenant-Colonel Montgomery in a duel occasioned by a fight between their dogs in Hyde Park while the officers themselves were out riding. The Newfoundland dogs may have infected the men with mad bites, for soon they were exchanging angry and thus dishonouring words followed by the established pre-duel rigmarole. In the ensuing encounter at Chalk Farm, MacNamara, who had previously fought duels in his native Cork, killed Montgomery. He was put on trial for murder, but having served with distinction in the Navy, he was able to call on several sea lords including Horatio Nelson himself to attest to his excellence of character. Killing a man in a duel did not represent a stain on that character. In his own address to the jury, MacNamara explained that as an officer

... to maintain any character in that station I must be respected. When called upon to lead others into honourable dangers I must not be supposed to be a man who had sought safety by submitting to what custom has taught others to consider as a disgrace. I am not presuming to urge anything against the laws of God, or of this land. I know that, in the eye of religion and reason, obedience to the law, though against the general feelings of the world, is the first duty, and ought to be the rule of action; but in putting a construction upon my motives, so as to ascertain the quality of my actions, you will make allowance for my situation.

He was probably the first to make a legal plea explicitly based on twin codes of law, not criminal and civil, but divine law and the code of honour. The two enjoyed equality of status, so that observance of the one could not imply infringement of the other. He further appealed to the jury to accept that as an officer he required to be seen as being of unimpeachable character, so begged to be excused of the crime of murder. The judge was not wholly convinced and said that manslaughter was the only possible verdict, but the jury disagreed and acquitted him. He resumed his rank and naval duties in the Napoleonic War.

Major Campbell was less fortunate in the trial of 1808 after his duel with Captain Boyd in Armagh, where the two were posted. Once again, the *casus belli* was an unremarkable dispute, on this occasion in barracks about the correct manner of issuing a command. Nothing more. In later reports it was said by Campbell that Boyd had spoken in a peremptory, thus dishonourable, way but the substance of the exchange has been recorded: 'Captain Boyd, do you say that I am wrong?' Captain Boyd replied, 'I do. I know I am right by the King's orders.' The allegation was strong, too strong, so the two repaired to an adjoining room where shots were fired and Boyd was found slumped in a chair. Campbell made every effort to elicit a statement from the dying man that everything had been fair, but this Boyd initially refused to give, repeating that Campbell was 'a bad man', before relenting and saying that he forgave him and even 'felt for him'.

Campbell fled from Ireland and hid out in London, but a year later he surrendered to the authorities, bolstered by a belief that he would be found guilty of nothing more than manslaughter. His defence too was based entirely on good character, but this plea, surprisingly, cut no ice with judge or jury and he was condemned to death, although with a recommendation of clemency. His wife travelled from Ireland to London to plead his cause with the king, and managed to gain admittance to Windsor Castle, only to discover that the king had gone to bed. The queen agreed to receive her and showed every sympathy with her plight, but a hurriedly convened council decreed that the law should take its course. Campbell reportedly faced his fate with Christian fortitude, and after his request to face a firing squad was rejected, he was hanged in Armagh where the offence was committed. His body was taken back to his native Ayr, where it arrived on the very day his wife made her return from London. He was one of the very few sent to the gallows after a duel, whatever the penalty laid down by the law.

This duel and its outcome were widely reported, but this was not standard practice for every loss of life. More common were the few, sad lines in a newspaper, such as: 'the duel between Mr Romney and Mr Leckie, students attending medical class at Edinburgh University, resulted in Mr Leckie receiving a wound from which he died.' It was, it would appear, a humdrum affair, of no great importance, nothing to disturb the peace of the citizenry.[2]

Journalists and writers viewed their own activities, including their own duels, with greater gravitas and ensured that they were duly reported. A number of nineteenth-century duels had their origins in slanging matches between rival journals, of which there were many. The most celebrated periodical of the day was the *Edinburgh Review*, whose editor, Francis Jeffrey, was drawn into a farcical duel in 1806 with the Irish poet, Tom Moore. Jeffrey ran an unfavourable review of Moore's *Odes and Epistles* and on a visit to London he made some scornful remark over dinner on Moore's likely opinion of him, but the remark came to Moore's ears, causing him to demand satisfaction. Neither man made a likely duellist, and they seem to have been incredulous at finding themselves in that position, but remedy there was none. On the day they had difficulties procuring pistols but discovered that they were over-provided with bullets. They sauntered about bantering amicably as the seconds struggled to load the guns and actually failed in Jeffrey's case. It was all wasted effort, since before shots were exchanged the duellists were arrested and trotted off to Bow Street, where they patched up their disagreement. Byron included some scoffing lines in *English Bards and Scotch Reviewers*, even adding in a footnote that 'on examination, the balls of the pistols were found to have evaporated. This incident gave occasion to much waggery in the daily prints,' he wrote.[3] On reading these lines, Moore then proceeded to challenge Byron to a duel, but Byron laughed the matter off and the two men became good friends and spent time together in Italy.

There was no waggery over the duel in 1809 between Lords Castlereagh and Canning, when both were cabinet ministers and the Napoleonic War was underway. This was not a case of a single offence to gentlemanly honour, for the two men had been over the years prickly colleagues at best, divided by personal rivalry and ambition. In a later age they would have vented their spleen in private gatherings or by briefing against each other to tame journalists, but in their day the duel was part of the natural order. Castlereagh has been dealt with by history more severely than Canning. It is difficult for any man to divest himself of the image imposed by Shelley in *The Masque of Anarchy* with the famous lines: 'I met murder on the way / he had a mask like Castlereagh.' The appropriateness of that mask has been questioned, most recently and cogently by Giles Hunt in his study of the duel, but the shadow remains.[4] Both men's origins were in the Anglo-Irish Ascendancy class, both made an unsteady ascent through British political ranks so that at the time of the duel Castlereagh was secretary for war and Canning foreign secretary in the same Cabinet. While Canning was viewed as a Liberal and Castlereagh as a Tory, on many matters they saw eye to eye, and perhaps had there been a prime minister of even average competence they would have continued that way, but the Duke of Portland was universally considered to be out of his depth and incapable of maintaining harmony among his ministers.

Canning became disillusioned with government policy and several times offered his resignation, but King George III refused to accept it. Finally, as an alternative, without informing the man himself, he proposed that Castlereagh be removed from office. When he learned of these developments, Castlereagh was outraged but did not react immediately, instead delaying to gather information and presumably to take advice before issuing his challenge. The information he was given aggravated the situation, for it transpired that most of Castlereagh's colleagues were in agreement with Canning that it was better for him to go. His challenge was contained in a lengthy letter in which the word 'honour' appeared several times, although on a more sober assessment the issue was *hubris* or wounded pride. Wilberforce, an independent witness, judged the letter 'a cold-blooded measure of deliberate revenge'.[5] Castlereagh objected not to the dismissal request as such, but to the fact that he had been kept in ignorance of it. Had he known how he was regarded, he 'could not have submitted to remain one moment in Office without the entire abandonment of my private Honour and public duty'. He went on to upbraid Canning: 'You knew I *was* deceived, and you *continued* to deceive me.' The gentleman's code was as constricting as a ball and chain. Canning spent the evening before the encounter in the conventional way clearing his desk, and writing a loving letter to his wife. His adversary, showing the greater aplomb expected of the aristocrat, is said to have chatted about opera in his carriage on his way to the appointed place.

Castlereagh had the reputation of being an excellent marksman but Canning had never fired a shot in his life. The men made the usual statement of having no personal grievance, fired and missed, but on the second exchange Canning received an injury to the leg. Castlereagh helped him off the field. Shortly afterwards, when Portland was forced out of office, both Castlereagh and Canning resigned, although later they resumed their careers.

During his career in Irish politics before his move to Westminster, Castlereagh was one of the proponents of the Act of Union between the British and Irish parliaments, a move opposed by Daniel O'Connell, who made his debut in the political arena with a speech to the Catholic Association opposing the merger. O'Connell was subsequently garlanded with the title of the Liberator, and no revisionist history has questioned his right to such a status, but there has been some reconsideration of his views on the use of violence. It was believed that his first-hand observations of the French Revolution had led him to espouse an almost Gandhian belief in non-violence, but a biography by Patrick M. Geoghegan has cast doubt on this stance, at least in his early life.[6] In the period following his return from France in 1790 and after the execution of the king in 1793, he made the gnomic entry in his diary that duelling had 'a certain charm'. He was plainly caught in two minds, as were many at the time, between the romance and the reality, so while the duel still seemed to him on balance unacceptable, he noted that it gave a man 'independence', and in consequence was attractive 'even to many thinking minds'.[7] Perhaps the attractiveness and the appeal of independent action were enhanced by the experience of life under a system of government and law which were deliberately weighted against interests of the majority.

However, in his subsequent political campaigning he became more resistant to the charm and more hostile to political and personal violence, at least until he tangled with John D'Esterre in 1815. D'Esterre was a member of Dublin Corporation, a body dominated by the Protestant Ascendancy class, while O'Connell had become recognized as leader of the nationalist movement, and as such he was feared and detested in the ruling circles. Their antipathy towards him was heightened when he attacked the Corporation for its treatment of Catholics and branded it a 'beggarly' body. Perhaps D'Esterre took this description personally, or perhaps as an ex-marine lieutenant and an expert marksman he was pressured by his fellows to provoke O'Connell in the hope that a duel would ensue and that D'Esterre could see him off once and for all. D'Esterre did not move immediately, and even when the speech was reported, he allowed some eleven days to elapse before he wrote to O'Connell to ask if the news was accurate. O'Connell initially declined to enter into correspondence and refused to confirm or deny the accuracy of the report. He may have been attempting to manoeuvre his way out of the situation, but his personal position was made more complex by certain factors, including the contemporary need, to which he was not immune, to preserve honour. He had in the recent past avoided a fight, leaving him open to accusations of cowardice, and had no wish to see that reputation reinforced. D'Esterre pursued the matter relentlessly. Having failed to make progress with the challenge, he decided that a horsewhipping would be adequate punishment and one evening went looking for O'Connell in central Dublin, but when a hostile crowd gathered, he judged it judicious to seek refuge in a safe place. The quarrel festered and eventually O'Connell's resolution snapped and he sent a missive deliberately formulated, or so it must be presumed, in offensive terms, thus making a duel inevitable.

The agreed time was the unusual hour of three-thirty in the afternoon, the place near Naas in County Kildare, the antagonists to hold fire until the signal was given after which they could walk forward and shoot at will. D'Esterre shot first and missed. O'Connell too was skilled in gunfire, and with his first shot struck D'Esterre in the lower part of his body, in an area which the delicacy of the times would not allow to be too precisely identified. It was a serious wound causing the victim to bleed profusely, and he died two days later. As a gentleman, he exonerated O'Connell from any blame and protested that he nurtured no animosity towards Catholics. Unbelievably O'Connell faced no legal proceedings at all over this act, while his standing among his followers was enhanced. He attempted to make reparation to the widow who was left with three children, but she declined his offer although she did accept an allowance to help with her daughter's education. O'Connell never fought another duel, although he was challenged. He also put on a glove or wrapped the hand that fired the fatal shot whenever he went to mass.

A poster of O'Connell, 'Champion of Liberty', Pennsylvania, 1847 (Wikimedia Commons)

The following year, an anti-duelling booklet entitled *Friend of Peace*, displaying a style of tortured thought which was common in thoughtful pro- and anti-duellists alike, was published in Edinburgh.[8] The author was obviously a clergyman, and what gives the work its individuality in that age is his embrace of a form of hesitant pacifism. The work was formally occasioned by the Hamilton-Burr duel, and takes the form of an imaginary dialogue between the President of the United States and one Omar, described as 'an officer dismissed for duelling'. Omar is an odd name to have chosen, and the paradox of his personal situation as a cashiered officer is not explored, nor are the reasons for his duel explained, but the central concern in the debate is the contradiction between the president's support for war between nations but opposition to the duel. While he will dismiss officers like Omar for duelling, he holds that war is necessary and justified since 'the *honour* of a nation will not allow a government to submit to insult or aggression'. Omar counters by saying that 'in duelling one life will *probably* be lost and that two might *possibly* be lost, while in war 60,000 lives or more may be ended.' Where is the honour or the logic, he asks?

The president bases his opposition to duelling on a belief that 'the offences in general, or the ground on which duels are fought, are hardly worth the notice of a man of noble and magnanimous mind.' He continues, '...by a conformity to this custom men do not even rise above the petulant and ferocious nature of the brute creation.' Omar objects that 'an appeal to arms in vindication of honour is no more necessary on the part of a nation than on the part of a military or any other gentleman. Dishonourable and ruinous sacrifices are made in the name of that PHANTOM called HONOUR.' The president argues that he has shown his unhappiness over duelling by the ban imposed on the military, but he is unwilling to go further and take action over duelling in civil society. Being a politician, he declares that he is bound by public opinion: 'popularity is the only element in which such a murderous custom can thrive or even live among men of reflection ... only let the custom become disreputable and it will wither away like a weed pulled up by the root and exposed to the heat of the sun.'

Public opinion was the new battlefield for the duel, as it was over the abolition of slavery. Parliament, especially the House of Lords, still had a majority who would not countenance the outlawing of either, but the tract is symptomatic of a tentative shift, even if there was no consensus that duelling was disreputable, or that honour was a phantom. The duel was illegal in most countries but was still recognized as an obligation even by men like Sir Walter Scott, who had earlier advised on circumstances in which an affair of honour was unavoidable. Sir Walter was an involved observer of a duel in 1821 instigated unwillingly by his son-in-law, J.G. Lockhart, but fought by John Scott (no relation) and Jonathan Christie. This was one of a series of political-literary duels fought at a time when a remarkable plethora of disputatious periodicals flourished. After the *Edinburgh Review*, two of the most

prominent were the Whiggish *London Magazine*, edited by
John Scott, and the longer established, Edinburgh-based,
Tory-supporting *Blackwood's*, which counted Lockhart among
its contributors, although he had no editorial control. These
publications carried work by the most distinguished writers of
the age, but the polemics between them were often virulent.
John Scott took to berating *Blackwood's* and Lockhart in
particular, causing the latter to reply in kind, if with greater
wit. It was a complicating factor in all these pseudo-literary
disputes that articles were by convention unsigned, meaning
that identifying authors of offensive contributions was left to
detective work or guesswork on style and beliefs. John Scott
and Lockhart became embroiled in attacks and counter-
attacks, until Scott unequivocally identified Lockhart as author
of pieces to which he objected, meaning that he was, as Harriet
Harvey Wood puts it, 'according to the customs of the day, not
only entitled but obliged to demand satisfaction'.[9]

If the participants were well versed in the requirements
placed on them as gentlemen, they were innocents in the
actual mechanics of duelling, an anomalous but not uncommon
situation and proof of the hold of the convention in the abstract.
Lockhart appointed Christie as his second, and travelled from
Edinburgh to London to make himself available for a duel. Scott,
however, temporized to an extent which comes as no surprise
to later generations but did startle his contemporaries. He was
caught in a real dilemma. It is easy but anachronistic to excuse
his hesitation as natural fear, but he was also, as O'Connell
had been, anxious to live up to contemporary expectations
and be free of all damaging taint of unmanly or ungentlemanly
cowardice. The prospects facing him were equally pernicious,
death or shame. In exasperation, Lockhart left London to return
home, where his wife was due to give birth to their first-born.
In his absence, Christie took up his cause with undue zeal and
over-committed himself in his diatribes. He in his turn was
invited to apologize, refused and on this occasion Scott felt his
reputation would be ruined if he shirked a second time. Christie
accepted the challenge.

The sheer ignorance shown by principals and seconds of the routine protocols contributed to the unfolding tragedy. The meeting took place at Chalk Farm in February in the evening when it was already dark. With exquisite courtesy, Christie noted that Scott had positioned himself prominently in the moonlight making him an easy target, but he refused to take any unfair advantage and called to Scott to move, which he did. Christie then deliberately aimed away from Scott, who may or may not have fired deliberately at him. The point was disputed later, but in terms of the Clonmel Code what had occurred should, or at least could, have ended the matter, but the seconds were not *au fait* with the regulations. Seemingly a proposal was made by one of the seconds for the two men to shake hands, but it may have been unheard. Scott may also have been unaware that Christie had deloped with his first shot, but Christie's second believed that Scott had fired in his direction, and ordered Christie to aim at Scott, which he did, wounding him so seriously that he died some days later. Before being removed from the field, Scott stated, 'Whatever may be the issue of this business, I beg you will bear in remembrance, that everything has been fair and honourable.' Few duels present such a muddle of initial pig-headedness, sleep-walking, submission to unquestioned but conventional standards of gentlemanly values, innocence and ignorance and then final brutality. Both men give the impression of automata wound up and released, but left devoid of freedom of will.

Christie and his second fled, but returned when the case was called at the Old Bailey to face a charge of wilful murder, for which the sentence was death by hanging. In the event, the law applied by Lord Chief Justice would appear to have been the code of the gentleman rather than the common law of England. Both Christie and his second pleaded not guilty, and their barristers led only evidence relating to character and public conduct, not to the duel itself. The presiding judge, incredibly, left open the possibility that the perpetrators were persons unknown who had then fled, but the central point in his summing up was that the verdict in cases of duels could be either manslaughter or murder, depending on whether the accused fought in 'the heat of blood', which would constitute manslaughter, or in cold blood, that is, on 'a false notion of honour' and thus murder. He drew the attention of the jury to the last words spoken by the dead man that everything had been 'fair and honourable', but having planted that idea in their minds, he stated that the implicit idea of honour in those words had no legal weight. He underlined that Christie himself wondered why he had been allowed a second shot, and suggested that 'having forborne to take aim' the first time, he might have fired his second shot under an impulse of immediate anger, meaning that it was legally manslaughter. If they were in doubt, the judge recommended the jury 'to take the side of mercy' and to take into account 'the excellent characters which the prisoners had received'. The charge to the jury is confused and confusing, wayward in its logic but, like the duel itself, is a perfect insight into an uncertain code. The jury brought in a verdict of not guilty. In the circumstances to have done otherwise might well have left them liable to a charge of contempt of court.[10]

A similar cast of writers and men of letters, including Lockhart and Walter Scott, were in the wings in 1822 for Scotland's most famous duel which pitted Sir Alexander Boswell, son of James Boswell, against James Stuart of Dunearn. The dispute was triggered by journals but had its deep origins in the unsettled, acrid politics of Scotland in the post-Napoleonic War period. Boswell was a heart-and-soul Tory, briefly MP for a 'rotten borough' in Devon and awarded his baronetcy by Lord Liverpool when he resigned his seat. He was author of some volumes of verses and songs, some of which are still part of a traditional repertoire, but had also a talent for satirical and scurrilous squids which he practised on political adversaries.[11] For reasons which are not altogether clear, the main target of his scorn was James Stuart of Dunearn, a moderately prominent Whig.

Stuart was derided and vilified anonymously in *The Beacon*, an Edinburgh Tory journal, and demanded that the editor, Duncan Stevenson, identify the author and apologize. When he

refused Stuart administered a horse-whipping on the editor in
the light of day on the High Street in Edinburgh. No criminal
action of any kind followed but Stevenson challenged Stuart
to a duel. Since it was established that a gentleman could not
accept a challenge from a social inferior, Stuart disdained even
to reply. *The Beacon* went out of business, but was succeeded
by a Glasgow journal, *The Sentinel*, and Stuart found himself
once again the object of sneering comments, some in the form
of mild jibes but others more insidious. All boundaries were
breached when it published verses entitled 'The Two Jamies',
the first a Jamie Macdonald 'who keeps a gin shop', but the
second scarcely veiled:

> Who's this too but Stuart well known for the Cow-art,
> Of oxen the feeder, of Frank the delight?
> In specification he's up to the true-art
> A bully by day and a justice by night!

In an attempt to unmask the writer, Stuart actually burgled
the offices of *The Sentinel* and was dismayed to discover that
the author of the verses was none other than Boswell, whom
he considered a friend. A duel was inevitable but could not be
held in Edinburgh since the sheriff got wind of the quarrel and
issued a ban. The two parties crossed the Forth to Kirkcaldy
and met at dawn outside the town. Although Stuart, another
innocent in a strange land, had never handled a pistol, his first
shot struck Boswell in the collar bone. He lingered on in what
must have been excruciating agony for two days before dying.
He was laid to rest in the family mausoleum in Auchinleck. The
Ayr Courier reported that more than 11,000 people, including
members of the aristocracy, attended his funeral.

Stuart fled to France, but returned for the trial for which he
had engaged two of the finest minds of the Scottish Faculty of
Advocates in its most glittering period, Francis Jeffrey, editor of
the *Edinburgh Review* and with experience of a farcical duel, and
Henry Cockburn, author of the *Memorials of His Time* and other
works, one of which was a pioneering pamphlet on the threats

to the environment of Edinburgh. Cockburn wrote that Stuart's trial aroused more interest than any other 'Scotch trial of my time'. A fellow Whig and an orator of some repute, Cockburn underlined to the jury that Stuart was 'a gentleman connected with the foremost families in the land', before declaring that 'the law of Scotland, which was founded on humanity and common sense, never condemned except where the mind was guilty' and that was not the case with Stuart who had acted 'under a moral necessity', meaning that a 'verdict of not guilty would be most grateful to humanity'. The judge emphasized 'the ample and fair testimonies which had been tendered in favour of Stuart' and 'the distressing feelings of mind he had experienced since that fatal moment'. It was practically an instruction to the jury to acquit, which it did without even withdrawing to consider the verdict. Sir Walter used the case as model for the duel scene in *St Ronan's Well*.[12]

In November 1829, the editors of two rival Edinburgh newspapers, Dr James Browne of the *Caledonian Mercury* and Charles Maclaren of *The Scotsman*, fought a duel in the streets of the city. The *Caledonian Mercury*, published three times a week, had since 1720 enjoyed a monopoly in Scotland's capital until the upstart *Scotsman* was founded in 1817, initially appearing only on a Saturday. Maclaren was appalled at the 'unblushing subserviency' of the existing press and in the restless days following the Napoleonic War declared his paper's support for the extension of the suffrage and Catholic emancipation, as well as his determination to expose corruption, reaction, nepotism and privilege. He had not a thick enough skin to disregard the attacks from his rival, and the two met at dawn and exchanged shots, which both went wide, but in defiance of gentlemanly manners they refused to shake hands before returning crestfallen to their offices to continue sniping in print.[13]

The aristocracy was not to be left behind. The Dukes of Bedford and Buckingham, the Marquis of Londonderry twice, the Duke of Wellington while he was prime minister, Lord Castlereagh again, and the Earl of Cardigan some fourteen years before leading the infamous Charge of the Light Brigade at the

Battle of Balaclava all took to the field of honour in the 1820s and 1830s. The Dukes of Bedford and Buckingham were first in 1822. Bedford fired into the air allowing Buckingham to walk towards him to assure him that there was no man he was less inclined to fight with, had he not been compelled to challenge him since 'a public man's life is not worth preserving unless with honour'. The offence related to a speech given by Bedford where he had implied corrupt behaviour by the other who was out to curry favour with the government. This particular duel, like others at that time, caused controversy, expressed in a pamphlet with the weighty but unambiguous title, *The folly and wickedness of duelling exposed: to which is prefixed a letter to the Duke of Bedford on the duel between his Grace and the Duke of Buckingham.*

These censorious words had no impact on Lord Londonderry, who in 1824 condescended to meet the lowly Ensign Battier. Londonderry was colonel of 10th Royal Hussars and forbade Battier to dine with other officers in the regimental mess. Battier made his distress public, but Londonderry haughtily ignored Battier's protests, including his public allegation that his commanding officer 'sheltered himself under his rank'. He refused even to say whether or not he had intended any slight on Battier's honour, until the sheer barrage of protests became too much for him. Disregarding the mismatch of rank, he met Battier in Hyde Park. Londonderry fired one shot, Battier's gun misfired and the seconds called a halt, but there were further ramifications. The king received a report and expressed 'his concern and displeasure' not at duelling as such but at an officer of Londonderry's rank committing himself to a duel with an inferior.[14] The Duke of Wellington reported that the Duke of York, who had plainly forgotten his own duelling days, wanted to have Londonderry put on trial, but Wellington himself considered this a futile gesture. He was blasé about the incident since 'the probability of the Hussars having to fight a duel or two (was) of no consequence'.[15] The unfortunate Battier's name was removed from the army's pension list. He approached Sir Henry Hardinge, who had been Londonderry's second, in the street, waved a whip at him and told him to consider himself horsewhipped. This pitiable gesture from a humiliated man of the lower class ended the matter.

Ridicule and contempt

Ridicule and cartoon depictions of duels, satirical and contemptuous in equal measure, now appeared frequently. Derision was heaped on the Duke of Wellington when it was announced in March 1829 that he had engaged in a duel with the Earl of Winchilsea. The hero of Waterloo was then prime minister and his government had finally implemented Catholic Emancipation, but this measure was repellent to the earl who in a letter to the press denounced the law as one of a parcel of 'insidious designs for the infringement of our liberties, and the introduction of Popery into every department of the state'. Wellington could not stand idly by and called on Sir Henry Hardinge, a duelling enthusiast who had been second to the Duke of Londonderry, to act as intermediary, with Lord Falmouth performing the same task for Winchilsea. Each side employed the standard courteous expressions about having the honour

The Duke of Wellington, dressed as a monk, meets the Earl of Winchilsea, by William Heath (The British Museum)

to address the other with letters and memoranda, but no words were withdrawn and no apology was forthcoming, so honour was still offended, satisfaction still required, and the outcome was foretold. The two men met on Battersea Fields. Wellington took aim perhaps intending to miss, while Winchilsea ostentatiously fired in the air. A final communiqué was drawn up by the two seconds, or perhaps had been prepared in advance, and sent to the press. In it Hardinge offered on Winchilsea's behalf the apology he had been invited to give at the outset, although the earl amended one or two fiddling points which rang out like the final notes, diminuendo, in an operatic libretto. It is worth noting that there was plainly an inner pool of experts whose names recur in various capacities in duel after duel.

The Marquis of Londonderry was out again on the field of honour, or at least on Wimbledon Common, in 1839 to face Henry Grattan, son of the celebrated Irish nationalist leader of the same name. Grattan himself was no tyro, having been second in one duel and principal in another, the latter with Lord Clare after he objected to a remark Grattan had supposedly made about his (Clare's) father. Clare missed with his one shot while Grattan deloped, and then admitted he had been in the wrong all along. The cause of the Grattan-Londonderry encounter was political, if bizarre. Londonderry had been offended by an article in which Grattan alleged that the queen's life would not be safe if the Tories got into power. The Tory Londonderry replied that Grattan had shown himself to be 'base and infamous', to which Grattan countered that although he was merely reporting a judgment of Daniel O'Connell's, he would assume responsibility. On the field, Grattan fired and missed while Londonderry fired in the air. This duel caused a group of clergymen led by the Dean of Ripon Cathedral to issue a precisely targeted but somewhat incoherent tract, *A Chapter on Duelling by One of the People Called Christians*.[16] The prime focus was Londonderry himself whom they accused of hypocrisy in claiming allegiance to the Church of England while being prepared to take up the gun. The author widened the field to express his opposition to duelling in general, and scoured

history to identify the first duellist whose passion prompted
him to engage in a question of honour. He concluded it was
'unquestionably Cain'. His gloss on that episode makes little
sense, and could have been employed by supporters of the duel:

> ... What is also very remarkable, the Greek of the
> Seventy (sic), in recording the challenge contains almost
> the words of modern duellists from the Marquess of
> Londonderry downward ... the language of the father of
> duelling is 'Let us go to the field.'

He was on stronger ground when he asserted that there was no
evidence of duels in classical times until late in the Roman Age
with Aeneas and Diomedes. There is, he writes, a distinction to
be drawn between ancient duels, which were 'national conflicts',
and 'the modern duel (which) is the fruit of personal and private
offence'. His heart produced stronger arguments than his head,
so after listing attempts to ban duelling in Christian history, he
concluded:

> Ridicule and contempt are the next means of putting
> down a ridiculous and contemptible custom. Oh for a
> Cervantes in the nineteenth century to arm and equip
> some barber (sic) duellist! We cannot understand by
> what process it is that a duel determines a lady's chastity
> a gentleman's veracity or a soldier's honour. Has the first
> for proofs of its existence the most skilful shots? The
> second the best swordsmen? And the third the most
> successful homicides?

The duke replied indignantly, stating in unequivocal terms the
now familiar argument of the twin moralities: the clergy should
attend to preaching the gospel while 'soldiers must fight to uphold
the altar and the throne' and gentlemen to defend their honour. In
the ethics of muscular Christianity the code of the gentleman had
equal status to the Ten Commandments. That was one of the last
confident statements of a code whose appeal was weakening.

In the imaginary dialogue, *Friend of Peace*, mentioned above, the fictional president had expressed similar hopes, believing that the custom of duelling would 'wither away' once it lost the popularity it currently enjoyed 'among men of reflection'. No single individual did more to further the process of withering than James Thomas Brudenell, seventh Earl of Cardigan, an aristocrat of unusual arrogance of bearing and a military man of extraordinary incompetence. He made two significant entries into British history, firstly his duel in 1840 and his subsequent appearance before a jury of his peers in the House of Lords, and secondly his command of the Light Brigade whose charge into the Valley of Death at the Battle of Balaclava in 1854 he led. It is piquant to observe that had the duel, or the subsequent trial for an offence which carried the penalty of transportation, gone differently, English literature would have suffered the not insupportable loss of Tennyson's heroic poem, 'The Charge of the Light Brigade', and history would have been freed of that act of murderous futility.

As an officer he was a pitiless martinet, lacking all humanity, brutal with rank-and-file soldiers and condescending with fellow officers. Shielded by title, class and wealth, he could dismiss most hostile criticism in the press but was riled by an article in the *Morning Herald* in 1838, and called out the editor. The challenge went unheeded.[17] A further, highly critical letter appeared in the *Morning Chronicle*, signed 'An Old Soldier' and in fact written by Captain Harvey Garnett Phipps Tuckett, an ex-officer in Cardigan's regiment. The full name was to be of decisive importance in the subsequent trial. Apologies were demanded, refused, challenges issued and a duel held in September 1840 on Wimbledon Common. The first exchange was harmless but Tuckett was injured in the second, bringing the duel to a close. It was a sign of the changed climate that both parties were arrested. When he was brought before magistrates, Cardigan stated, 'I have fought a duel; I have hit my man I believe, but not seriously.' Cardigan demanded his right to be tried by a jury of his peers in the House of Lords. The first Gilbert & Sullivan operetta, by chance entitled *Trial by Jury*, was not staged until 1871, but this solemn trial can be regarded as a forerunner.

Since no death had occurred, Cardigan was charged only with a felony: 'firing a loaded pistol with either intent to murder, or to maim and disable, or to do grievous bodily harm'.[18] The prosecution was led by the attorney-general who was able to reassure the assembled lords that 'on the present occasion the charge against the noble prisoner at the bar does not imply any degree of moral turpitude, and that, if he should be found guilty, his conviction will reflect no discredit on the illustrious order to which he belongs.' He tried the patience of his listeners by expatiating on the legal niceties of duelling, clarifying that if 'any person or persons shall wilfully and maliciously shoot at any person in any dwelling-house or other place, he shall be adjudged guilty of felony, without benefit of clergy.' The operative word, he explained, was 'maliciously' and thus 'no act of shooting, will amount, under this statute, to a capital offence, unless it be accompanied with such circumstances.' Cardigan was, it appears, charged with firing a gun at another man, but not maliciously. The attorney-general went on to acquit the accused earl 'of anything unfair in the conduct of this duel'.

> Something has been said respecting the noble earl's pistols having rifle barrels, whilst those of Captain Tuckett had no such barrels. However that may have been, I have the most perfect conviction that nothing but what was fair and honourable was intended. Nor do I suppose that there was any grudge, any personal animosity, any rancour or malignity on the part of the noble earl towards his antagonist. Whether the noble earl gave or received the invitation to go out, I believe his only object was to preserve his reputation, and maintain his station in society as an officer and a gentleman.

The facts of the case were not in dispute but witnesses were called and cross-examined, with one odd omission. The attorney-general omitted to summon Tuckett himself to give evidence or to be identified, and here either the law showed itself to be in Dickens' term, 'an ass', or else the attorney-general showed himself to be to be deviously indifferent to justice. The indictment identified Cardigan's opponent as Harvey Garnett Phipps Tuckett, but the challenge had been issued to a Captain Harvey Tuckett. Could the lords assembled as jury be certain that the two were one and the same? They did have the card left at the scene of the crime, but since that was in the name of Captain Harvey Tuckett, it was inadequate. The card might refer to someone other than the person named by the indictment. On these grounds, the Earl of Cardigan was acquitted unanimously on a public vote of the House of Lords.

The verdict caused public outrage. 'Let his head be cropped and let him be put on an oatmeal diet,' thundered *The Times*.[19] The very idea of the duel now came under public scrutiny in a changed climate. A new culture was beginning to take root. Societies were established to campaign against Gambling and Strong Drink among the working classes, and against Duelling among their betters. The notion of the gentleman underwent a transformation, the cult of honour fell into disrepute and fashions in the resolution of disputes underwent a sea-change. It has been plausibly proposed by Stephen Banks that in Britain this change is due to 'the increasing influence of the middle classes, as signified perhaps by the Reform Act 1832'.[20]

More duels were fought, the last recorded duel on mainland Britain taking place in 1852, but it involved two French citizens, so did not count. The romance of duelling, the ethics and etiquette of the gentleman, the call to defend honour by the sword or the pistol were judged incongruous and incomprehensible by a new society dominated by blunt, bluff businessmen for whom the accumulation of wealth and not the inheritance of a title were the badges of honour. In March 1844, we find none other than Sir Henry Hardinge, now Secretary of State for War, announcing to the House of Commons that the queen viewed duelling with abhorrence. Perhaps Sir Henry was no more than a political weather-vane: he certainly knew that of which he spoke, and sensed which way the wind was blowing.

1 Maria Edgeworth, *Belinda*, London: J. Johnson, 1810, chapter. 4.
2 *The Glasgow Herald*, 26 July 1805.
3 Andrew Steinmetz, *The Romance of Duelling in All Times and Countries*, London: Chapman & Hall, 1868, vol. II, pp. 196-202.
4 Giles Hunt, *The Duel: Castlereagh, Canning and Deadly Cabinet Rivalry*, London: I.B. Tauris, 2008.
5 *Ibid*, p. 132.
6 Patrick M. Geoghegan, *King Dan: The Rise of Daniel O'Connell 1775-1847*, Dublin: Gill and Macmillan, 2008.
7 *Ibid*, p. 54.
8 D. McAllam, *Friend of Peace*, Edinburgh, 1816.
9 Harriet Harvey Wood, *Lockhart of the Quarterly: Prince of Biographers*, Edinburgh: Sciennes Press, 2018, pp. 97-117.
10 J.G. Millingen, *The History of Duelling*, London: Bentley, 1841, vol. 2 pp. 245-252.
11 *The Poetical Works of Sir Alexander Boswell*, Glasgow: Maurice Ogle & Company, 1871.
12 John Chalmers, *Duel Personalities: James Stuart versus Sir Alexander Boswell*, Edinburgh, Newbattle Publishing, 2014; Michael Moss, *The Duel between Sir Alexander Boswell and James Stuart*, Newcastle upon Tyne: Cambridge Scholars, 2019.
13 Albert Morris, 'The Editor Who Fought a Duel', *The Scotsman*, 30 June 2005, p. 14.
14 Millingen, *op. cit.*, p. 283.
15 *Encyclopaedia Britannica*, 1911 edition, p. 642.
16 *A Chapter on Duelling by One of those People Called Christians*, 2nd edition, London: James Fraser, 1840, pp. 14-24.
17 Stephen Banks, *A Polite Exchange of Bullets*, Woodbridge: The Boydell Press, 2010, p. 218.
18 *The Trial of James Thomas Earl of Cardigan for Felony*, Published by Order of the House of Peers, London: William Brodie Gurney, 1841.
19 *The Times*, 29 September 1840.
20 Banks, *op. cit.*, p. 219.

11

QUIRKS, FOLLY AND BOGUS DUELS

The Irish gentlemen who drew up the 1777 Clonmel Code believed they had introduced civilizing measures into the practice of duelling and had established rules of decorum which raised fighting with swords or pistols above a plebeian brawl. They were convinced they had resolved all disputed questions, whether relating to the nature of offence, delivery of challenge, appointment and duties of seconds, rules of civility on the day, suitability of venue and choice of weapon. Their protocols were, with minor variations, respected in all western countries whenever men met to protect or assert their supposed honour, or simply to seek satisfaction for some wrong done, but the human imagination is as unbounded as the human capacity to nurse grievance. Almost every aspect of the process - provocation, venue, weapon or implement, distance apart - would be in certain cases twisted and distorted.

Bizarre, innovative means for settling scores were devised, defying all logic, expressing some kink of character, or showing some satanic whimsicality. The occasions for duelling expanded, and there are records of duels provoked by supposedly hostile glances, by unguarded words, by 'nose-tweaking' (a gross affront), by fights between owners' dogs, by exchanges between lawyers in courts of law, by opinions expressed in newsprint, by misguided compliments to ladies, by rumoured criticism, by singing the wrong song, by accusations of cheating at cards, by misdemeanours in horse-racing, by the disputed pronunciation of a Greek word,[1] by wholly random challenges to complete strangers by men spoiling for a fight or by the discontent of

221

seconds over the misconduct by their principals.[2] The duel also took a range of forms: guns fired in darkened rooms, stabbings inside horse-drawn coaches, billiard balls hurled as weapons, men tied by the hand to each other in graves, opponents separated by the length of a handkerchief held by one hand but wielding a dagger in the other. Such encounters strain credulity, but the records are for the most part reliable.

One of the duties of seconds was to fix time and place, but many cities had established venues for duelling: the Bois de Boulogne in Paris, Hyde Park in London, Phoenix Park in Dublin, Weehawken near New York, Angel Island in the bay off San Francisco, Bladensburg near Washington for congressmen, Kirkcaldy across the Forth from Edinburgh, but there were cases where some inventiveness was required to avoid the attention of the authorities, if the authorities were indeed interested. A small island like Malta when under the rule of the Knights of St John presented a tricky problem. Strict anti-duelling laws

Duelling ground in New Orleans, c1900 (Library of Congress, Washington DC)

had been introduced in the sixteenth century by Grand Master de L'Isle Adam, but a visitor walking along Strait Street, that is Narrow Street, in Valletta can still make out bullet holes in the walls of the buildings on either side. That was the venue of choice since it was easy for seconds to close off the street at either end, allowing determined duellists to battle away until blood was drawn.[3]

There were always some imaginative or disdainful spirits who created inventively or punitive schemes to show their distaste for the duel. An early case was the Duke of Melfi, nominated Viceroy of Piedmont in 1545 by the French King Francis I. To crack down on duelling, he gave an order that duels could be fought only on the bridge over the River Po, and specifically on the parapet, with the further provision that any knight who plunged into the water was not to be rescued. Jumping forward in the centuries, we find Jean de la Fontaine (1621-95), the celebrated writer of the *Fables*, devising a witty means of maintaining a friendship while outwardly conforming to the requirements of honour. His wife was a woman of great beauty as well as of unusual learning, and the recipient of compliments on both counts. There is a tale recounted by the unimpeachable scholar, George Saintsbury, that much scurrilous gossip was occasioned by the frequent visits she received by one Poignan, a close friend of La Fontaine. Alerted of the gossip, La Fontaine summoned and challenged the bewildered Poignan to a duel. Being a skilled swordsman, Poignan quickly disarmed his opponent and only then demanded an explanation for his strange conduct. La Fontaine referred him to the code of honour and said that he had been left with no option in response to public chatter about Poignan's supposed affair with his wife, but that now that they had met on the field of honour, their friendship could continue as before.

One anecdote associated with Abraham Lincoln has a basis, albeit a shaky one, in truth. In 1842 he criticized James Shields, then an Illinois state auditor, causing the latter to challenge him. Lincoln was one of the most improbable of all duellists, but agreed to meet his rival in Missouri, where duelling was not illegal. Lincoln was unskilled in weaponry, but exercised his right of choice to opt for the sabre. There are two accounts of the outcome, one poetic and one prosaic. The poetic version is that while they were limbering up, Lincoln stretched out to hack down a branch in an overhanging tree to show his reach and to allow the shorter Shields to rethink. Cowed by this sight, Shields withdrew. The prosaic version is that the seconds got together and negotiated an agreement which rendered the duel unnecessary. Matthew Arnold wrote that the superiority of poetry over prose lies in its access to 'higher truth and higher seriousness', but in this case the lower truth of prose has the seriousness of truth.

Irregular Duels

Jeffery Hudson (1619-82) was a dwarf who earned his living in the only way open to him, by becoming a celebrity freak, originally in the service of the Duke of Buckingham but later in the employ of Queen Henrietta Maria, wife of Charles I. She gave him the fond nickname of Lord Minimus, but he does not seem to have settled comfortably into the role of court jester and was irked at being the butt of jokes or the subject of mocking verses. He was certainly, as he would demonstrate, a skilled horseman and marksman, and during England's Civil War was made an officer in the army, a rank which pleased him, even if it is not clear what duties, if any, he performed. While in exile in France with the queen, Charles Crofts, a fellow officer, went too far in jeering at him, causing Hudson to challenge him to a mounted duel but with pistols not lances. Crofts turned up with a water pistol, Hudson with a regular gun with which he shot his opponent dead. He was initially condemned to death but the queen intervened and he was pardoned.[4]

Giuseppe Balsamo was better known as Count Cagliostro, a title to which he had no legitimate claim, and when he arrived in St Petersburg in 1780 he had already acquired a European reputation as alchemist, adventurer, magus, fraudster and practitioner of dubious medical practices. Sicilian by birth, he had travelled widely and had mixed in the highest circles in several European courts. Later that decade his notoriety was extended by his involvement at Versailles in the mysterious Affair of the Diamond Necklace which undermined the already faltering trust in the French monarchy. His sensational life, which would end with him going insane in a papal prison, later made him the subject of a novel by Dumas *père* as well as a debunking essay by Thomas Carlyle who damned him as the 'Quack of Quacks'.

Shortly before his arrival in Russia, he had founded a masonic lodge in London, and although the Tsarina Catherine herself was distrustful of freemasonry, his membership facilitated his integration into aristocratic circles in Russia. He offered his medical services to some noble families, and after curing the ailing son of Prince Galitzin he enhanced his status still further by declining the substantial sums of gold offered him in recompense. This was a shrewd move, but his success and growing popularity alienated Catherine's personal physician, a Scotsman, John Rogerson. Cagliostro's status did not impinge directly on Rogerson's position with the tsarina who according to rumour so trusted him that she employed him to vet prospective lovers for venereal disease. He may have viewed Cagliostro as an unqualified upstart, or the doctor may have been moved by nothing more dignified than jealousy. Cagliostro counter-claimed that Rogerson was worried about the exposure of his ignorance, but now that allegations had been aired there was only one way for offended gentlemen to settle the matter. The account we have of successive proceedings is provided by Cagliostro, who replied to Rogerson's challenge in flamboyant terms:

> If you come to challenge me as Cagliostro, I will call my servants and they will come and throw you out of the window; if you challenge me as a doctor, I will give you satisfaction as a doctor.

Rogerson's discomposure is easy to imagine, but he managed to reply that he was challenging the medical man. Cagliostro had his answer prepared:

> Well, we will not fight with the sword. Let us take up
> the weapons of doctors. You will swallow two capsules
> of arsenic which I will give you, and I shall swallow the
> poison you will give me. Whichever one of us dies will
> be judged by men to be the loser.

A sober product of the Scottish Enlightenment, Rogerson was
no match for a fluent scoundrel, so he backed off.[5]

The Earl of Barrymore made use of his knowledge of
questions of hygiene to discomfit an antagonist. The Brighton
races were once an important event in the calendar of London
Society, and for those not wholly engrossed in the actual races,
drinking dens offered an acceptable substitute. In one such
venue in 1806 the earl and an MP, Humphrey Howarth, shared
a glass or two, but as drink was taken the conversation became
less convivial and offence of an unrecorded nature was given
and resented. We owe our knowledge of the subsequent acts to
the diarist Thomas Creevey, a member of Charles James Fox's
party and thus presumably fully conversant with the demands
of honour and duelling. He writes that the two men agreed to
meet the following morning. Barrymore was an experienced
army surgeon and so was aware of the dangers not only from
bullets, which never improve health, but of infection resulting
from soiled fabric entering the flesh under the impact of a
shot. He chose the radically unfashionable sartorial style of
presenting himself stark naked for the encounter. This form of
attire had not been foreseen by the legislators in Clonmel and
horrified his genteel opponent, who was prepared to shoot dead
a decently clothed man but could not bring himself to dispatch
an undressed man. The MP's resolve faltered, and both men
fired in the air. Decency may have been outraged, but honour
was satisfied.[6]

Innovative technology was quickly pressed into service
to settle traditional disputes, such as those over women. The
possibility of flight in a 'heavier than air' vehicle intrigued
scientists and public in the late eighteenth century, and ascents
by balloon-and-basket by such adventurers as James Tytler

and Vincenzo Lunardi became sensational events which drew massive crowds. No one could reasonably have foreseen that ballooning would provide a means of exchanging gentlemanly gunfire, but such was the case in Paris in 1808. Monsieur de Grandpré and Monsieur Le Pique found themselves rivals for the hand of Mlle Tirevit, a dancer at the Paris Opéra. Her affections went firstly to Grandpré but she had a weakness too for Le Pique, and neither man was prepared to share her attentions. Her own inclinations were, as was normal, of little concern, and the two males decided, obviously, that a duel was the only way to resolve this dilemma, but incredibly they opted for a duel in the sky. Their reasons remain unclear. It would be good to know who bore the expense, but the fact is they acquired balloons, appointed seconds with experience as aeronauts, took off from the Tuileries gardens, sailed over Paris until they brought their balloons into sight of each other, at which point they both fired. Le Pique missed but Grandpré's shot punctured his opponent's balloon which crashed to the ground killing both occupants. Little is known about Mlle Tirevit's subsequent love life.[7]

If these two gentlemen took to the air to settle their differences, another pair of combatants took a more sedentary approach. Following the Restoration of the French monarchy in the aftermath of the defeat of Napoleon, there were many duels between supporters of the two sides, so the provocation which led to a duel between Benjamin Constant, the novelist and political thinker, and Charles-Joseph-Louis-Henri Forbin des Issarts, a member of the bodyguard of Louis XVIII, was conventional enough. In June 1822, Forbin des Issarts published a letter in a journal to which Constant took offence, so a challenge ensued but there was a problem. Constant suffered from rheumatism which made it difficult for him to stand. His gallant opponent agreed that he could remain seated for the duel, which would be fought with pistols, and so as not to take any unfair advantage decided that he too would sit. The two men took up a position in armchairs ten paces apart and fired at the same time but both missed. The seconds called a halt.[8]

Chairs were not the only break with tradition. The causes of
the duel in 1830 which brought together the renowned literary
critic Charles Augustin Sainte-Beuve and the editor of *Le Globe*,
Paul-François Dubois, remain unclear, since the two men were
acquaintances and Sainte-Beuve had actually contributed to
Dubois' journal. 'Rain stopped play' is the routine experience
of sportsmen, but these two heroes were made of sterner stuff
and were determined not to allow a downpour to disrupt their
plans. Sainte-Beuve held an umbrella in one hand throughout.
'I do not mind being killed,' he is reported to have said, 'but I
have no wish to get soaked.' He was neither killed nor soaked,
and indeed no blood was shed. The two men became firm
friends.

That incident was farce enough, but sometimes history is
played out not by tragedy followed by farce, as Marx suggested,
but as a small farce followed by greater farce, as occurred the
following century with one unlikely harlequin, Count Otto von
Bismarck, facing in Berlin an equally unlikely Pulcinella, Rudolf
Virchow, leader of the opposition Progressive Party. Bismarck
was Minister President of Prussia, but in 1865 he was struggling

Sainte-Beuve and his umbrella, illustration by Henri Dupray, *Harper's New
Monthly Magazine*, 1887 (Wikimedia Commons)

win support in the Landtag, the parliament, for an increase in expenditure on warships. His most vocal opponent was Virchow, scientist as well as politician, who advocated greater investment in public health. He drew attention to the fact that many deaths were caused by the consumption of sausages, then as now a popular food, when produced in unhygienic conditions. Virology was Virchow's field of expertise and he had previously identified Trichinella parasite, commonly known as worms, as an obnoxious presence in sausages and a likely cause of the spread of a very unpleasant disease. Bismarck was no match for his opponent on scientific matters and made no effort to refute him, but continued to press his case for public expenditure on armaments. In a debate, the exchanges grew heated and Bismarck declared himself offended but aroused laughter when he seemed to issue a challenge. There was no doubting the seriousness of his intention since his next move was to deliver a private letter containing a renewed call for satisfaction. His letters to Virchow are extant, so these facts of the challenge are beyond dispute, as is Virchow's refusal of a conventional duel.

That should have been the end of the matter, but thereafter things are murkier. The story goes that Virchow as the recipient of the challenge had the right to choose the weapons and he proposed a novel use of sausages. His proposal was that the two duellists sit down before a plate containing two sausages, one of which was harmless, but the other impregnated by the nasty, possibly fatal, virus Virchow had identified. Bismarck stared at the plate for a time, but then got up and stomped off at this ungentlemanly conduct. It is a dramatic, even illuminating, scene suggesting an unexpected sense of irony among the Prussian elite, but while the story has been recounted many times, the problem is that no one can trace any reference to it before 1893, almost thirty years after the challenge. There is a letter from Virchow declining to meet Bismarck, but no reference to the sausage duel.[9]

In 1890, Toulouse Lautrec was in Brussels for an exhibition of Les XX (a group of Belgian artists), but at the official dinner he overheard another artist, Henry de Groux, dismiss Van Gogh as a charlatan and announce that he would not permit his own canvases to be displayed in the same hall as those of Van Gogh. Whether this would have been the loss to art that de Groux imagined is a moot point, but Toulouse Lautrec took the matter to heart and challenged de Groux to a duel. Toulouse Lautrec often bemoaned his reduced stature, but this lack of height would have made him an awkward target from twenty metres and might have been an advantage. De Groux may have been an arrogant boor, but he revealed his heart of gold by backing down. The duel never took place.[10]

Provocations

If the manner in which duels were conducted showed imagination, the original provocation too could assume the most unexpected form. The dispute in New York in 1798 between James Jones, a Federalist, and Brockholst Livingston, a Republican, has already been recounted, but it is worth underlining that what drove them to their duel was the capital provocation known as 'tweaking the nose', Livingston's in this case. There was much public debate about how much of Livingston's nose had actually been touched and how firmly, but even if the extent and firmness were never established, a challenge was issued, and Jones died in the duel.[11] It was a heavy price to pay.

The turn of the eighteenth and nineteenth centuries was a turbulent time in the Caribbean, with the slave revolt in Haiti, disputes over imperial rule in the islands and naval battles between France and Britain. As happens in such circumstances, the human flotsam and jetsam of several countries came to the surface, and one such was Henri D'Egville, a man of mixed race who found refuge in Jamaica after fleeing from the nearby island of Hispaniola. At dinner one evening in 1817, he invited a fellow diner, Captain Stewart, to sing a Gaelic song. Stewart protested that although Scots by birth he had no knowledge of the language, but he was plainly a man of some cultural attainment and not wishing to disappoint his importunate host, broke out into a musical version of an ancient Greek poem by Anacreon. Who would know the difference? Someone in the company did, and reported back to D'Egville, who declared himself offended at this deceit. Stewart had previously killed a man in a dispute over a woman and had sworn never again to allow himself to be ensnared into a duel, but his resolve weakened when he was horsewhipped in public by D'Egville. He agreed to meet the other man but only in a specially dug grave where the two would face each other with a pistol in one hand, and one end of a handkerchief in the other to keep them close together. D'Egville's courage failed him and he fainted before the signal to fire was given.[12]

As already mentioned, in the decades of the post-Napoleonic Restoration the antagonism between former members of the Grande Armée and royalists reached a peak of ferocity. The cause of a strange duel between a Napoleonic officer, Colonel Barbier-Dufai, and a young member of the Royal Guard, Raoul de Vere, is said to have been the cockade the young man was wearing and which he refused to remove in spite of Barbier-Dufai's mockery. There are various accounts of the next move, some saying that Barbier-Dufai issued a challenge which was accepted, others that he initially declined a challenge when he realized the youthfulness of the royalist officer and only accepted when de Vere continued chivvying him. They drew swords in the street and his greater experience allowed Barbier-Dufai to disarm his adversary more than once, but without pushing home his advantage. Although he refused the opportunity of finishing off his rival in open combat, it appears it was Barbier-Dufai who proposed a new approach - that the two should flag down a carriage, climb in tied together by one arm but leaving the other hand free to wield a dagger. The coach was driven twice round the Place du Carrousel, and when the door was opened, de Vere was found dead and Barbier-Dufai still alive although severely injured by stab wounds in the chest. The state of the coach does not bear thinking about.

Black Humour

The outlook and mentality displayed by the Irish lawyer and memoirist, Sir Jonah Barrington (1760-1834) in his sprightly *Recollections* are worth recording since they are representative of a schizophrenic approach to the discussion and presentation of the duel which was widespread, and not just in Ireland.[13] Barrington's book is autobiography but widens out to provide a vivid portrait of Irish society in his own time. He was gifted with an ironic sense of humour which allowed him to look awry at the ways of the world in the manner of Somerville and Ross, or even of Flann O'Brien, and those ways included the duel. With one significant exception, he viewed the duel as mystifying but humdrum, one of the many aspects of the human comedy.

Some humourists conceal elements of cruelty beneath the guise of comedy, so it is worth emphasizing that Barrington in reporting on duelling was neither a pathological deviant

'Preparing for a Duel' by William Cruikshank, 1824, a comic view of the ritual
(The British Museum)

nor an evident sadist, but a well-integrated member of the Protestant Ascendancy class, a highly respected lawyer, a man accepted in the clubs and salons of Dublin society and one who crowned a successful career with the grant of a knighthood. His *Recollections* contain much valuable factual element, such as the 'distinguished list, which is only an abridgement' of duels fought by judges and senior lawyers. In a footnote he adds the important information that 'two hundred and twenty-seven noble and official duels have actually been fought in my climacteric', an assessment accepted by James Kelly, author of the definitive work on duelling in Ireland. His 'climacteric' is approximately the last decades of the eighteenth and the first of the nineteenth century, and his assessment refers only to 'noble and official' duels. There were many others which were of no interest to him, nor to us.

Some anecdotes in the *Recollections* are whimsically reported, and while this adds to the charm of the book, it is disconcerting to see that capriciousness of mind extended to the ritualized violence of the duel. However, he writes in different tones of a duel which had a tragic outcome affecting him personally, devoting a moving chapter to the encounter in which his brother William died. In 1788, at dinner in the home of General Hugh Gillespie (1766-1814), William became embroiled in a quarrel with another guest, an infantry lieutenant named Mackenzie, which got out of hand and led to a challenge being issued. Barrington's account differs from the official version in military histories which is based on the subsequent trial. Barrington holds Gillespie responsible for allowing the quarrel at his table to fester, for then acting as Mackenzie's second, and finally for insisting that the duel go ahead even when the two adversaries were prepared to be reconciled on the field. Shots were exchanged but missed their targets, and the men shook hands in the best gentlemanly tradition, but the truce did not hold. Barrington writes that Gillespie then fired at William Barrington, while the official version has it that the latter used 'insulting language and Gillespie then challenged him to fight across a handkerchief'. Whoever was responsible for the provocation, William was killed, Gillespie survived and fled to Scotland but returned for the subsequent trial. He was acquitted on the grounds of justifiable homicide, and went on to have a glittering career in the army. After his death in Nepal, a monument to him was raised in County Down and a statue erected in Westminster Abbey. With evident bitterness, Barrington writes, 'I will never set my foot in Westminster Abbey.'[14]

The tone of this report is totally at odds with his discussion of subsequent duels, including some in which he was involved. The impression is that having once experienced the reality of the duel, he thereafter preferred, like one of Chekhov's characters, to shield himself from unpleasant sights. He had a light talent for the detached, comic style which pre-empted the need to probe too deeply, and perhaps that allowed him to don a nonchalant mask. The mask slipped when his brother's life was sacrificed, but for the rest duelling was a fact of life, part of a gentleman's duty, regrettable like illness, but to be faced with *sang-froid* and recorded in whatever terms may be appropriate to the individual case. There is not in Barrington any indictment of the cult of duelling, nor could there be since he had been 'out' himself, but the extent to which he turns a blind eye or gives the complicit onlooker's smirk at the grotesqueness of the spectacle is unnerving.

More than any other man, Barrington spread the idea, myth or history, of the fighting Irishman, of Ireland as the land of duels. It is he who circulated the report that in Ireland 'the first questions asked as to a young man's respectability and qualifications, particularly when he proposed for a lady-wife were: "what family is he of?" and "did he ever blaze?"' He tells us every family had its own cupboard of private arms, that one of his own family heirlooms was a rapier handed down by grand-uncle Captain Wheeler Barrington 'who had used it frequently', and of the captain's friendship with one Jemmy Keogh who had 'unfortunately killed a cripple in the Phoenix Park, which accident did him great mischief'. He opens a section dedicated mainly to duelling with a pseudo-embarrassed admission that

'it may be objected that anecdotes of duelling have more than
their due proportion of space in these sketches', and that less
attention should be accorded to such subjects but then proceeds
to a eulogy of the 'fire-eaters', as the most enthusiastic of Irish
duellists and upholders of the *code duello* were named, revelling
in their deeds with gusto.

His own first duel was a comedy of errors. He reminisces
about 'a young gentleman of Galway, Mr Richard Daly, then a
Templar, (who) had the greatest predilection for single combat
of any person, not a society fire-eater, I ever recollect: he had
fought sixteen duels in the space of two years, three with swords
and thirteen with pistols.' To Barrington's surprise, although
they had never exchanged two words, he received a challenge
from Daly, which he felt obliged to respect without further
enquiry. His chosen second was a man who was Ireland's first
aeronaut known as Balloon Crosby. (Crosby later met his end
in distressing circumstances. A crowd gathered to see him do
an ascent from Merrion Square in Dublin, but the balloon
was caught in the wind, floated off over the Irish Sea and was
never sighted again.) The first problem with the projected duel
was that neither Crosby nor Barrington possessed a pistol but
Crosby did own some 'old locks, barrels and stocks'. The two
men sat up all night to mould them into some form of firearm
before they betook themselves to Donnybrook for the encounter.
When they met, they discovered that Daly had a squint which
made it hard to know what he was focusing on.

The situation was rendered more complex when Daly
realized that someone, namely himself, had blundered and he
had never actually had any dealings with Barrington. He wished
to withdraw, but at this point, to general dismay, Crosby stepped
forward with a copy of the Clonmel Code and referred them to
Rule 7 which stated that 'no apology can be accepted *after* the
parties meet, without a fire'. He then gave Barrington the urgent
if enigmatic advice, '*Medio tutissimus ibis*: never look at the head
or heels; *hip* the maccaroni! the hip forever, my boy! hip, hip!'
The impact of these words on Barrington can only be imagined,
if not comprehended. Since there was no appeal against the

decision of a second backed up by the universally recognized code, Crosby insisted they take their stance and fire, which Barrington did, striking his adversary who fell back. Crosby congratulated his shocked principal, but when they examined the fallen adversary they found that a brooch had prevented the bullet from piercing his skin. All was nearly resolved but when Barrington asked for an explanation of the challenge, Daly's second referred to Clonmel Rule 8, which stipulated that 'if a party challenged accepts without asking the reason of it, the challenger is never bound to divulge it afterwards.' The mystery would never now be solved.

This may all be a joke at his own expense, and the same talent is evident in the report of the duel involving one Frank Skelton and an unnamed exciseman. The backstory is once against worthy of Flann O'Brien. Mr Skelton belonged to that category which Barrington defined as 'half-mounted gentlemen', that is small, almost impoverished, landowners, and his complaint against an exciseman was that the latter had forced 'the butt end of a horse whip down his throat whilst he lay drunk and sleeping'. The exciseman explained himself by retorting that 'snoring at a dinner table was an offence to every member of the company', and therefore no apology was required of him. Skelton was seemingly a peaceable type perfectly happy to let sleeping dogs lie, but he was egged on by his companions to demand satisfaction. The two met and Skelton fired both his pistols, bringing down but not seriously injuring or immobilizing his opponent, who had not yet fired. Before the exciseman rose to his feet, Skelton took to his heels, pursued by his own second, who denounced him as a rascal and quoted as he ran the section of the Clonmel Code which required him to stand his ground after firing his own shots. Skelton was brought back, but his adversary could not support himself on his own two feet and asked to be allowed to lean against a tree, but this request was denied as having no precedent. The duel was abandoned. There was talk of a return match, but this evaporated when Skelton demanded the right of choice of weapons and chose fists. The other demurred, and the matter ended.

1 James Kelly, '*That Damn'd Thing Called Honour*': Duelling in Ireland, 1570-1860, Cork: Cork University Press, 1995, p. 176.
2 *Ibid*, p. 177.
3 Joseph Attard, *The Knights of Malta*, Malta: PEG, 1993, p. 102.
4 William Archbold, 'Hudson, Jeffery', *Dictionary of National Biography, 1885-1910*, vol. 28.
5 F. Ribadeau Dumas, *Cagliostro*, London: George Allen and Unwin, 1967, p. 72; Iain McCallan, *The Seven Ordeals of Count Cagliostro*, London: Century, 2003, pp. 88-98.
6 Thomas Creevey to James Currie, July 1806, in *The Creevey Papers: A Selection from the Correspondence & Diaries of the late Thomas Creevey, M.P.*, London: John Murray, 1903.
7 Barbara Holland, *Gentlemen's Blood: A History of Dueling from Swords at Dawn to Pistols at Dark*, New York, Bloomsbury, 2003, p. 83; ultimate source, Robert Chambers, *The Book of Days*, 1804, republished by Chambers Harrap, 2004, vol. 1, p. 809.
8 John Norris, *Pistols at Dawn: A History of Duelling*, Cheltenham, The History Press, 2009, p. 62.
9 *The Correspondence of William I & Bismarck: With Other Letters from and to Prince Bismarck*, vol. 2, London: F.A. Stokes & Co, 1903.
10 Marco Cavina, *Il sangue dell'onore: Storia del duello*, Rome: Editori Laterza, 2014, p. 242.
11 Joanne B. Freeman, *Affairs of Honor: National Politics in the New Republic*, New Haven CT: Yale University Press, 2002, p. 172; *The Pennsylvania Magazine of History and Biography*, vol. 7, 2006.
12 J.G. Millingen, *The History of Duelling*, London: Bentley, 1841, vol.1, pp. 389-90; Andrew Steinmetz, *The Romance of Duelling in All Times and Countries*, London: Chapman & Hall, 1868, vol. II, pp. 321-4.
13 Sir Jonah Barrington, *Recollections of Jonah Barrington*, Dublin: Talbot Press, 1918. Now available at https://archive.org/details/recollectionsofj00barriala/page/284/mode/2up
14 *Ibid*, chap. 13; Royal United Service Institute Journal, vol. 59, no. 438, 1914. Now available at https://www.tandfonline.com/doi/abs/10.1080/03071841409420130?journalCode=rusi19

12

'PISTOLS AND PETTICOATS'
DUELLING WOMEN

A visitor to the Prado in Madrid will undoubtedly spend time gazing in awe and dismay at the gallery's marvellous Goya collection, probably focusing on the artist's late works, such as *Los Caprichos* and the Disasters of War, with their gruesome depiction of human savagery and brutality. One such painting portrays two gigantic figures seemingly up to their knees in mud, swinging clubs at each other. These monsters rank with other unsettling subjects from the same period such as Chronos devouring his own offspring, with the difference that the combatants in this dark sketch bestride myth and history. The work has no title, but can reasonably be taken as a depiction of, or even a satire on, duelling, shorn of all romance, stripped of any echo of chivalry, bereft of all trace of honour or exaltation of virile pride.

In another room further along the corridor, the same visitor might be intrigued by a painting by Jusepe de Ribera, dated 1636 and entitled *Dos Mujeres* (Two Women), although the gallery's catalogue gives the slightly longer title, *Combate de Dos Mujeres*, (Combat of Two Women, but now routinely rendered in English as Women Gladiators). The subjects are dressed in brightly coloured, female attire which may be Roman. They are holding shields and wielding swords, but have no other armour and are inside an arena surrounded by spectators, all male and some armed, outside a wooden barrier. The presence of these onlooking men is a conspicuous instance of that 'male glance' which feminist critics have identified as a dominant if previously unremarked aspect in artworks featuring women, and which will be a factor in accounts of female duels. In Ribera's painting, one woman is prostrate on the ground, her sword having dropped from her grasp, blood flowing from a neck wound, her shield raised as her last protection, her expression conveying a plea for mercy which her antagonist, whose sword is about to come down on her fallen adversary, appears unlikely to grant.

There has been, as the alternative translations indicate, some dispute over the subject and the interpretation of the work. The fenced-off arena suggests that the combat was being fought in accordance with the rules of the joust by combat, except that the combatants are female. Some critics propose that the painting may be a depiction of a Roman gladiatorial contest, and this interpretation is given additional credibility by the fact that it was originally displayed as part of a series of scenes from ancient Rome. Gladiatorial contests were common in the Roman Empire, but the duel as such was unknown in classical times. There is ample evidence, for instance in writings of the historians Cassius Dio and Suetonius, of gladiatorial combats between women. The satirist Juvenal, who was both virulently misogynistic and opposed to the gladiatorial spectacle in every form, was scathing about the 'gladiatress', to use the form employed by the historian Michael Grant. Juvenal was particularly outraged by the participation of women from patrician families, and gave his contempt free rein in Satire VI. Grant's translation reads:

> What a great honour it is for a husband to see, at an auction
> Where his wife's effects are up for sale, belts, shin-guards,
> Arm-protectors and plumes! ...
> Ah, degenerate girls from the line of our praetors and consuls
> Tell us, whom have you seen got up in such fashion,
> Panting and sweating like this? No gladiator's wench,
> No tough strip-tease broad would ever so much as attempt it.[1]

There was a succession of edicts against the participation of women in gladiatorial shows, but these were ignored, as were later laws in the Christian epoch on duelling, until Septimius Severus put an end to all female contests in AD 200.

Ribera's painting has also been interpreted more tentatively as an allegory of Virtue slaying Vice, and certainly the female body, usually naked, has been employed in supposedly allegorical style to illustrate all manner of ethical dispute. Titian's *Sacred and Profane Love* from a century earlier and now in the Borghese Gallery in Rome is one such example. It is also possible, indeed probable, that Ribera used an actual event and enriched it with symbolic, didactic overlay. The Prado's own documents state that it is a depiction of a historically attested event, a female duel which took place in Naples, then under Spanish rule, between Isabella de Carazzi and Diambra de Pettinella over Fabio de Zeresola, with whom they were both in love. He may be the man leaning against the fence but crucially inside the arena, looking on, somewhat anxiously but impassively, and certainly making no move to intervene. He is indifferent to the outcome and is, one can assume, as willing to accept either woman as lover in the spirit of the aria, *Questa o quella a me pari sono,* sung by the libertine Duke of Mantua in Verdi's *Rigoletto*.

Female knights such as Bradamante, Angelica and Marfisa excited the imagination of the late Renaissance epic poets Boiardo, Ariosto and Tasso, as discussed in an earlier chapter, and artists were keen to illustrate the adventures and misadventures of these heroic female warriors. Angelica, the beautiful daughter of the King of Cathay, was a special favourite, and several artists, doubtless motived by purely aesthetic impulses, seized the opportunity to bring to colourful life scenes of her single combats, or of the love-in-war story between her and Medoro, or of her misfortune in being left tied naked to a rock. These soldierly women fought duels only in fiction, and no doubt there was a certain erotic piquancy in this fantasy for readers or listeners in Renaissance courts. Such audiences could also scoff at the shame of regular knights who found they had been bested by a rival who had seemed their equal but had turned out to be a mere woman.

The intrusion of erotic fantasy by male artists, poets or chroniclers into the depiction or reporting of female duels makes the reconstruction of history singularly difficult. It may have been responsible for some imaginative or titillating embellishment of actual events or poetic scenes, but it might also have caused the canon of such events to swell beyond the limits of reliable records. One writer on female duels in recent centuries has shown himself to be extremely sceptical and even contemptuous of extant accounts, doubting if there were ever any female duels.[2] That judgment is extreme, but there is no question that the number of female duellists is extremely low when set against the totally verifiable total of their male counterparts.

A Question of Honour

The whole subject of women and duelling and their role in regard to the code of honour is complicated by beliefs, which long outlived Juvenal, that women were in every sense the weaker sex, demeaned by, or even incapable of, any direct connection with violence. Treatises on honour invariably made women passive, and thus the ipso facto wronged partner in any wayward behaviour, sexual or other. Female honour, as had been uncontested since the earliest Italian treatises on the subject, lay in a lady's chastity, her virginity before marriage and her unswerving fidelity in marriage. In chivalric and gentlemanly culture, the courtly lady was viewed much more as the Madonna than as the whore. G.K. Chesterton put this viewpoint succinctly, if whimsically:

Feast on wine or fast on water,
And your honour will stand sure,
God Almighty's son and daughter,
He the valiant, she the pure.[3]

241

Any deviation from the path of purity into what would be termed whoredom would be ruinous not only for the reputation of an individual woman, but also for that of her husband, or family in the case of an unmarried woman. Female honour, if impugned, demanded to be defended, but not by her. A woman could, in other words, provoke a duel, but any slight on her honour had to be, and could only be, avenged by the dominant male among her relatives, or by a volunteer champion.

Especially in Southern Europe, a man's honour was dependent on his wife's or sister's conduct. His honour was entrusted to her and to her steadfast adherence to abstinence before marriage and to socially sanctioned sexual behaviour in marriage. (It was plainly unthinkable in Italy or Spain that the honour of a genuine *mamma* could be in any way compromised since it was unthinkable that she could be prey to sexual desire.) In defending his wife's reputation, in avenging an allegedly dishonourable act by a sister or daughter, the male was in reality defending his own honour. A woman who had sex with a man not her husband could be regarded as a quasi-whore, or as a weak woman seduced and misled by a predatory male. It goes without saying that there could be some truth in the second allegation, when a woman had been lied to and mistreated by a mendacious Don Juan on the prowl for sex without fuss or commitment, but in other cases the woman could have been a willing partner. Seduction was assumed to have occurred irrespective of the attitude of the woman, and there are many instances of honour duels fought by husband, father, brother on behalf of a woman who might end up grieving for some lost love slain by an intrusive, self-righteous relative.

There is an irony in the fact that two men could fight either over a woman whom both wished to love and cherish, or alternatively over a woman in the family who had dishonoured them by her private sexual conduct. J.G. Millingen, in a chapter specifically devoted to 'Duels between French Women', explains the predicament of female dependence and male obligation with Victorian forthrightness: 'that women, who can mostly get silly people to fight for them, should not fight themselves is natural', but then adds the rider that 'there are instances on record in which ladies have shown their determination to avenge their own wrongs.'[4] It is worthy of note that, whatever 'the determination to avenge their own wrongs', there is no record of a challenge issued by a woman to defend her modesty and honour against malicious rumour. In some occasions, women did fight over a man loved by both contestants, but more frequently the *casus belli* was a personal insult or offence.

Female duellists are by definition exceptional characters, usually with an extravagant life-story, an additional factor which makes it difficult, particularly with those from an earlier age, to disentangle fact from overlays of excited fiction. Several historians have encountered this difficulty with Marie-Catherine de Villedieu (c1640-83), a prolific writer whose works included *Memoirs of the Life of Henriette-Sylvie de Molière*, a semi-autobiographical novel which includes a duel between the heroine and a rival. The name of the protagonist has caused some writers to believe that Henriette-Sylvie was a character in a play by Molière or even a lover of the playwright. When the duel was fought both women were dressed in male attire, a common ploy. Perhaps there was such a duel, but the event is recorded in a work of fiction.[5]

It is similarly unlikely that the first so-called 'petticoat duel' in London, allegedly fought in 1792, actually took place, although as much energy has been spent in searching for proof as was expended in the quest for the Holy Grail. The story satisfies neatly - too neatly - patronizing male sniggering over female behaviour. In the accepted version, Mrs Elphinstone was a guest of Lady Almeria Braddock and paid her hostess the gauche compliment that it was clear that she *'had been a beautiful lady'*. Lady Braddock rose in indignation at the scarcely veiled insinuation contained in the pluperfect, and demanded an apology which was not forthcoming. The two women followed male etiquette, appointed seconds and met in Hyde Park. With the first shot, Lady Braddock's hat was ripped by a bullet, while her own opening sally missed entirely.

The two then cast aside their pistols and drew their swords, thrusting and parrying until Mrs Elphinstone received a wound in her arm which was considered sufficient satisfaction for the malign words spoken, and proceedings ended there. It may be curmudgeonly to let the facts interfere with a good story, but regrettably no researcher has located a Lady Braddock in the eighteenth century.

Legend and history are frequently difficult to disentangle, and in no case is this truer than with Julie d'Aubigny (c1673-1707), who certainly did exist and is better known by her stage name, La Maupin. Unsurprisingly, she has been the inspiration for several novels, the most famous of which is by Théophile Gautier, as well as films and even one modern musical. The multi-coloured events of her complex biography cannot be contained in the space available here, but the material facts are that she was bi-sexual, a cross dresser, a trained fencer, an opera singer, and had a string of male and female lovers. She was condemned to death on two occasions but received royal pardons. She is reputed to have killed or wounded ten men in duels, and once to have killed three men in succession. On that occasion she was attending a ball dressed as a man when she was attracted by a lady and kissed her, to the annoyance of three robustly male suitors. Annoyed at their response, she

Mademoiselle Maupin de l'Opera

Anonymous print, c1700 (Wikimedia Commons)

challenged and slew all three of them in turn, or perhaps simultaneously. She was pardoned by Louis XIV but left for Brussels where she resumed her career in opera, and later became lover of the Elector of Bavaria. She may or may not have become a nun, but certainly died in a convent in Provence while still in her early thirties.[6]

Another all-female duel was occasioned by an instance of poor diary management which would have strained credibility in a boulevard farce, but was perpetrated by the secretary of Louis François Armand Vignerot du Plessis, third Duc de Richelieu (1696-1788). Coincidentally he had inherited his title, originally conferred on the famous cardinal-statesman, as a result of another duel fought more than a century previously by the cardinal's brother, Duke Henri du Plessis de Richelieu (c1579-1619). Duke Henri, a notorious libertine and duellist, was appointed Governor of Angers in 1619 but before he could celebrate his promotion, he bumped into the Marquis de Thémines, a political opponent and a rival for the governorship. Cross words were spoken, insults flung back and forth, swords drawn and the duke was killed in the ensuing row. The cardinal was devastated by the loss of his brother and even considered retiring from public life to a monastery, although he changed his mind.[7] The history of the French, involving princes of the Church and noblemen in the State is convoluted, especially if one is a Richelieu. The salient point is that Henri's death without surviving issue caused the headship of the family to pass to his younger brother Armand, who also became a cardinal in 1622, and then to François Armand, who did not live the celibate life of his ancestors who had taken holy orders.

In 1721, two of his lovers, the Marquise de Nesle and Madame de Polignac, who were also sisters-in-law, had a belligerent confrontation with each other resulting from the already mentioned *faux pas* by the duke's secretary who had carelessly scheduled assignations with both ladies at the same time and place. All three parties turned up. The duke was relaxed about the error, but not so the ladies who fell on each other, tugging at necklaces and tossing flowers plucked from one bosom in the face of the other. This was a mere brawl of a type which was socially frowned on, so when they were separated the ladies agreed to meet formally in the Bois de Boulogne. Pistols were the chosen weapon, which indicated that the duel was to be no mere gesture. The two women were to fire at will as they walked towards a scarf which marked the barrier between them. The marquise fired first but missed. Polignac's aim was better and her rival fell to the ground covered in blood, but it was discovered that the wound was superficial. Strangely the marquise claimed victory and proclaimed that a Richelieu was worth the shedding of her blood, but never was any victory more Pyrrhic since the contested lover declared his preference for Polignac.[8] He was not a man of great constancy and soon after transferred his affections to Charlotte Aglaé d'Orléans. As a coda, it could be added that in 1736 the duke himself killed a Comte de Ponterieder who had issued the challenge after the duke had seduced, ensnared, beguiled or in any case won over the comte's lover.[9]

In general duels between women did not end in death, but there was a particularly nasty exception in Russia in 1829, when two neighbouring landowners, Olga Zavarova and Ekaterina Polesova, who had been at loggerheads for years, decided the quarrel had to be settled once and for all. The story has been repeated many times, but it must be added that it is hard to trace a completely reliable source. As it has been handed down, the tragic, inter-generational plot would have tested even the vision of Aeschylus. The two women brought their daughters along with them to witness their encounter, and compelled the girls' governesses to act as seconds. The lighter rapier was generally considered easier for women to manipulate, but these two ladies chose the sabre. Olga was killed on the spot after being struck on the head, but before expiring she managed to stab Ekaterina in the stomach and she died a couple of days later. Five years later the same cast gathered at the same spot to see the daughters, Alexandra and Anna, take up sabres, perhaps the identical weapons used by their mothers, for their own duel. On this occasion, Anna Polesova perished.

There were several female duels in the nineteenth century which commanded public attention, but there is some value in focusing on one which existed in the same borderland between reality and imagination as the Paris of Balzac or the London of Dickens. In 1884, Emile-Antoine Bayard unveiled in Paris a painting entitled *Une affaire d'honneur*. The scene is suitably dramatic: two women, one still wearing a fashionable hat, are crossing swords in the Bois de Boulogne, although the woodland has something of the innocence of a rustic scene by Corot. There are no men in sight, but there are four female observers, one leaning languidly against a tree, two others huddled anxiously nearby and a fourth semi-concealed in the background. The main feature, which guaranteed the work's success and popularity, is that the two duellists are stripped to the waist, their upper dress neatly tucked into the skirts to avoid being unduly crumpled when pulled up for the next social event. The painting aroused great controversy, but so too had Manet's more tranquil depiction of the female nude in his *Déjeuner sur L'Herbe* some two decades previously. Bayard's work, however,

Emile-Antoine Bayard, *Une affaire d'honneur*, 1884 (National Fencing Museum)

was produced by an unusually fevered imagination and stands for a relationship between an eroticized imaginary dimension of life and events on the ground.

From the first emergence of feminism at around the time Bayard's painting went on display, feminists protested against such lurid portrayals of women, most famously with the attack on the Rokeby Venus in the National Gallery in London in 1914. Feminists also demanded women's right to manage their own lives and to redress on their own behalf any wrongs or indignities they suffered, by the duel if necessary. This right was demanded by Marie-Rose Astié de Valsayre, ardent feminist, secretary of the French League of Women's Freedom, campaigner for female suffrage, medical practitioner and advocate of the right to abortion. In addition, Astié ran a fencing school which she encouraged women to attend not only for purposes of self-defence but because, she believed, fencing strengthened the breasts and facilitated breast-feeding. In the same year as the unveiling of *Une affaire d'honneur*, we find her issuing challenges to a male journalist, De La Bretèche and later to a fellow feminist, Eugénie Pierre, but both refused.[10]

Her most famous encounter was in 1886 with a Miss Shelby, an American who was, like Astié, a qualified doctor and a campaigner for women's rights. As with their male counterparts, neither feminist sisterhood nor the banality of a disagreement was any bar to an indignant challenge. The two were well-educated and well-travelled women who had much in common, but they were also avid nationalists and differed over the merits of French and American female medicine. A duel would appear an odd way of settling a dispute over such a question, so a measure of scepticism is in order. The canonical version is that they agreed to fight it out and fixed a date a fortnight later, with the agreed weapon being the sword. Perhaps the delay was a gallant effort to give Miss Shelby time to sharpen her skills but, their convictions not having wavered in the interim, they met, swords in hand, at Waterloo, a choice of venue which seems unnecessarily melodramatic. It is said that each had the appropriate suite of seconds, medics and attendants, all women, and that when the Frenchwoman drew first blood she was declared winner. That was the end of the duel, and history does not record whether the outcome altered Miss Shelby's view of the superiority of French doctors, male or female.

Astié de Valsayre was not done with duelling, but it strains credulity to record that the next woman she challenged was Kate Booth, known in France as *La Maréchale*, daughter of Catherine and William Booth, co-founders of the Salvation Army.[11] Kate had been ordered by her father to take charge of the French mission and in 1881 established her HQ in Paris. By the following year she was able to publish the first French number of *War Cry* under the title *En Avant!* Something about these developments must have upset Astié since in 1886, a month after her duel with Miss Shelby, she posted a letter to Miss Booth in which she declared her distaste for the Salvation Army's 'pernicious doctrines', called on Kate Booth to remove all trace of it from France or else give her satisfaction. Perhaps Astié's blood was still hot after her victory over Miss Shelby, or perhaps she had misunderstood the connotations of the word Army in the case of General Booth's evangelical movement, but Kate Booth answered that she was a pacifist and declined the challenge.

The League for the Emancipation of Women met in Paris in 1890, and in the midst of discussions on inequality and injustice in patriarchal society its adherents found time to pass a motion of censure, proposed by the pugnacious Astié de Valsayre, on Caroline Rémy de Guebhard (1855-1929), a celebrated journalist who wrote under the *nom de plume* of Séverine. She was an anarchist, crusading left-wing journalist, defender of Dreyfus, advocate of woman's rights, founder of *Le Cri du Peuple* and thus France's first woman editor of an important daily newspaper. However, as dissidents and reformers of all ages have invariably found, she had enemies a little further to the left, who founded the rival *La Voix du Peuple* and used its columns to hound Séverine. Since there was no let-up of the attacks, Séverine and supporters among her journal's staff decided they had to react. Séverine seems to have been initially willing to fight herself, but clothes were a problem. She viewed it as impractical to fight in the long skirts worn by women of the time, and it was illegal for women to wear trousers. Her campaign to have that law changed was unsuccessful. The editorial board decided that a man had to take up the challenge, and a colleague, Georges de Labruyère, who was also by this time her lover, offered his services. He was probably the ideal candidate, having been in the hussars, and once he got into the swing of things he went on to fight a further five duels. The opponent who came forward, Prosper-Olivier Lissagaray, was another radical, a Republican-Socialist, and no novice at duelling. In 1868 he had faced his cousin and political adversary Paul de Cassagnac, both men armed with rapiers. On that occasion, Lissagaray emerged injured, alive but defeated.

De Labruyère had, in addition to his gallant wish to defend Séverine, a reason of his own for taking on Lissagaray. The latter had mocked him for using the name de Labruyère as his byline, suggesting that it concealed an unjustified claim at descent from the famous moralist Jean de la Bruyère. Such mutual effrontery could not pass unavenged, so de Labruyère and Lissagaray chose duelling pistols to set the matter straight. After the first exchange both were wounded, but not too severely, causing Lissagaray to demand that the duel continue. The seconds vetoed his request and when some days later de Labruyère sent word that he was willing to resume the fight, it was Lissagaray who declined. Astié next raised her voice. Her objection took no account of de Labruyère's hurt feelings and focused on Séverine's hypocrisy in allowing a man to defend her interests, thereby tacitly accepting women's inferior status. Undoubtedly Astié could point to her own experience as a duellist but the two women also loathed each other.[12]

The unlovely contamination of fact by conjecture, this time with a high dosage of drooling wish fulfilment, is apparent in an encounter in Vienna in 1892. This was a golden age in Austrian history with Franz Joseph on the throne, but with the seemingly unshakeable solidity of Hapsburg rule undermined by the competing psychoanalytic schools, by the Viennese *art nouveau*, by the Secessionists and by such writers as Robert Musil and Karl Kraus. It is said that in this climate two aristocratic ladies fought a duel, and in certain shops in the Austrian capital it is still possible to purchase miniature dolls of them wielding not rapiers but heavy sabres as they struggle with each other. Their dress is immaculately feminine - appropriately fashionable sandals, hair carefully set, necklaces neatly in place, skirts flying but then the shocking element: the blouses are neatly turned down leaving the contestants naked to the waist. No doubt any connection with the Bayard painting exhibited eight years previously is pure coincidence, but the piquant detail of the exposed breasts meant that the encounter has been recorded as the 'topless duel'.

The duel may well have taken place, if not in those circumstances. The contestants were of blue blood, Princess Pauline Metternich and Countess Anastasia Kielmannsegg. The immediate cause of the dispute was suitably genteel, a quarrel over the arrangements of flowers for an exhibition of which the countess was lady president, although some authorities allege that there were darker dynastic forces at work, and that the princess' ambition to rise to prominence in Viennese society was being frustrated by the countess. Whatever the truth, it proved impossible to reach an accommodation and they decided a duel was necessary. They chose swords which are always easier to control than imperfectly aimed pistols so it may be that neither one had any wish to inflict injury. Duelling was outlawed in Austria, but determined to go ahead with their plan, they fixed a venue in nearby Liechtenstein and hired the most eminent female doctor of the day, the Polish Baroness Lubinska, to attend. She pointed out that since they had no intention of fighting to the death but only to first blood, the main risk came not from bullet wounds but from the possibility of septicaemia if a piece of fabric ended up wedged under the skin. She recommended that they fight partially stripped. Both women contracted blood wounds, so neither claimed victory. They embraced, kissed and made up.[13]

So all's well that ends well in this enticing tale with a moralistic ending. Two empty-headed, conceited women from the upper reaches of society bicker over nothing, lose all sense

HONOUR AND THE SWORD

of proportion, fight in lascivious poses before being brought to their senses. The story has appeared in many reputable histories of duelling and cannot be completely dismissed, but then perhaps its popularity proves the power of erotic tittle tattle over the male imagination. The first account appeared in an Italian publication, *Tribuna*, but was denied shortly afterwards by someone claiming to be Princess Metternich herself.

Even such a revered figure as Marie Curie found herself embroiled in scandal and duelling, although at a distance. The defence of her honesty and honour was undertaken on her behalf by male friends. In 1903, she won the Nobel Prize for Physics jointly with her husband Pierre, but three years later he was killed in an accident. She subsequently entered into a relationship with Paul Langevin, a former student who went on to become a highly distinguished scientist in his own right. At the time of his relationship with Madame Curie he was also a married man. His wife grew suspicious, commissioned a break-in at the flat the couple shared for their trysts, and then leaked the information to a newspaper. It was 1911 and the affair caused a national scandal. While it was still headline news, it was announced that Madame Curie had been awarded a second Nobel Prize, this time for Chemistry. Her reputation in tatters, she was unsure whether or not to go to Stockholm to pick up her award, but was persuaded to travel by Albert Einstein. Meanwhile the scandal gave rise to two duels, although some accounts suggest that it was a factor in no fewer than five. In the principal one, Langevin challenged Gustave Tery, a journalist who had been particularly scathing in his criticism of the pair, but the event was an anti-climax. The two men arrived at the agreed location, only for Tery to declare he would not destroy a French genius, while Langevin retorted that he was not a murderer, so they both put their guns away. Swords were employed in the other duel occasioned by the scandal, this time between the editors of rival publications, Henri Chervet of the radical *Gil Blas*, who supported Curie, and Léon Daudet of the nationalistic *L'Action Française*, who execrated her. They fought until Daudet received an injury which brought the duel to an end. This event occurred in the early days of motion pictures and there is film footage of the encounter.

One further, totally fictional female duel, described in the novel *Belinda* by the Irish novelist Maria Edgeworth is of interest, not least because fiction offers a different order of truth from history, and the novel brings to the foreground some issues, not all comic, normally left in the background.[14] An acute, astringent and ironic observer of the manners and mores of her time, Edgeworth describes two duels in *Belinda*. As is clear, dress codes were always a problem for intending female duellists, but this had the capacity to heighten the potential comic element, since often, unlike the women in Ribera's work or in the Viennese 'topless duel', female duellists chose to disguise themselves as men. Lady Delacour held her husband in contempt and purely to torment him paraded in public what was no more than a social and platonic relationship with Colonel Lawless, for whom she had no greater love and only slightly more regard. To her dismay, Lord Delacour showed, in his wife's reports of the affair, a gentlemanly concern for 'his *honour and my own*' (italics in the original) and so challenged the unfortunate Lawless, whom he shot dead. Lady Delacour was moderately irked at this development, and turned her considerable energies to a by-election. She was motivated more by dislike of 'the odious Mrs Luttridge', whose husband was a candidate, than by belief in the policies of the candidate she supported. Relations between the two women deteriorated, but they agreed in bemoaning the fact that it was deemed unseemly for ladies to repair to the field of honour. Fortunately, change was in the air, and they were encouraged by the fact that a male acquaintance, 'one of the cleverest young men in England, and a man of fashion into the bargain, was just going to publish a treatise upon "the Propriety and Necessity of Female Duelling".' Given this authorization, the ladies chose pistols for their encounter and, dressed as men, met at the appointed time, only for Mrs Luttridge's second to announce that her principal had injured her trigger finger, and so would be under the handicap of having to fire with her left hand. Lady Delacour accepted that this would infringe the laws of honour, and so the two fired in the air, just before a gang of local men turned up intent on throwing the two women into the duck pond for indecorous behaviour. Although they had escaped unscathed, 'the want of petticoats had nearly proved (our) destruction'.

The duel in this novel is presented in a light, comic tone, and it is to be regretted that no other woman novelist of that age with a mind as acute as Edgeworth's took up the opportunity to explore the mindset of the female duellist.

1 Michael Grant, *Gladiators*, London: Pelican, 1971, pp. 34-5; https://www.museodelprado.es/en/the-collection/art-work/women-gladiators/ee076233-5858-4a35-a5c0-9ce631cd5382

2 Ignaz Matthey, 'A Stupid and Ridiculous hoax: The mythologisation around duelling by women', 2019, https://www.academia.edu/41220390/A_stupid_and_ridiculous_hoax_The_mythologisation_around_duelling_by_women

3 G.K. Chesterton, 'The Song of Right and Wrong', in *Collected Poems*, London: Methuen, 1967, p. 217.

4 J.G. Millingen, *The History of Duelling*, London: Bentley, 1841, vol.1, p. 270.

5 Madame de Villedieu, translated by Donna Kuizenga, *Memoirs of the Life of Henriette-Sylvie de Molière*, Chicago IL: University of Chicago Press, 2004.

6 Anne-France Dautheville, *Julie, chevalier de Maupin*, Paris: J-C Lattès, 1995: Théophile Gautier, *Mademoiselle de Maupin*, translated by Helen Constantine, London: Penguin, 2005.

7 Joseph Bergin, *The Rise of Richelieu*, Manchester: Manchester University Press, 1997, pp. 190-91.

8 Hugh Noel Williams, *The Fascinating Duc de Richelieu*, first edition, 1910, republished West Bloomfield MI: Franklin Classics, 2018, p. 50.

9 John Norris, *Pistols at Dawn: A History of Duelling*, Cheltenham, The History Press, 2009, p. 126.

10 Matthey, *op. cit.*

11 Roy Hattersley, *Blood & Fire: The Story of William and Catherine Booth*, London: Little, Brown, 1999, pp. 287-9; also https://it.fullersociety.com.

12 Séverine and Michael Shreve, *Rebel in a Black, Dress: The Life and Writings of Séverine*, retrieved 13 July 2020, https://rebelinablackdress.wordpress.com

13 *Pall Mall Gazette*, 23 August 1892.

14 Maria Edgeworth, *Belinda*, London: J. Johnson, 1809.

13

THE FACTS OF FICTION

LITERARY DUELS

Duelling has, sometimes reluctantly, fascinated novelists, dramatists and film-makers, and has also, sometimes hypocritically, horrified them, but the frequency of the duel on the page, stage and screen is probably second only to the love scene. Unlike a pitched battle, a duel focuses on and personalizes conflict in a way which reveals character warts and all, as well as being guaranteed to raise adrenaline levels by making the spectator a witness to the ultimate human struggle. The attitude adopted and the description offered vary according to the culture of the nation, the aesthetics of the writer and the sensibilities of the age, meaning that, deliberately or not, the duel has at times been made to seem valorous and heroic but at others merely the ridiculous conduct of buffoons.

Fictional duels can be divided into certain, admittedly porous, categories - dramatic, comic, tragic, heroic, altruistic, bizarre, incomprehensible, jealousy-driven, honour-centred, character-revealing or plot-enhancing. The heroes of Tobias Smollett, such as the eponymous hero of *The Adventures of Roderick Random* (1748), seem to view life as a series of combats in which they are pitted against devious enemies out to demean them. It may not be an exercise in over-interpretation to see Smollett's first published work, a poem entitled 'The Tears of Scotland' lamenting the condition of Scotland after the defeat of Culloden, as illustrating a recurrent mentality in his novels where a defeated individual finds himself engaged in the existential, ever-changing but never-ending war of each against all. A significant couplet reads, 'The wretched owner sees afar / His all become the prey of war.' Smollett denounced the duel in Letter XV in his *Tour of France and Italy*, but as a novelist he relished its value as a device to spice up a story or to enable his heroes to best knavish individuals, of whom there were many. Roderick Random and his kin take to duelling partly out of necessity but certainly with a will, and John Leigh has valiantly identified no fewer than eighteen duels or references to duels in the course of Smollett's first novel.[1]

Although it is commonly described as a picaresque novel, the frontispiece of an 1831 edition of *Roderick Random* drawn by George Cruikshank shows two men with swords drawn, but neither has the poise of a gentleman fencer. Roderick is singularly unfortunate in the people he meets, who have a uniform tendency to mistreat him. His first encounter is with a fellow Scotsman with the unfortunate name of Gawky, a Scots word meaning approximately 'clumsy', who fails to show up at the agreed time. Roderick will have ample opportunity to show his mettle both on land and sea, and even to provoke a duel between two female admirers, although this duel trails off into farce.

Cruikshank's 1831 frontispiece for *Roderick Random* (Wikimedia Commons)

Duelling is more serious business in *Clarissa, or The History of a Young Lady* (1748) by Smollett's contemporary, Samuel Richardson. The novel was an immediate international success and was still popular in Russia in the nineteenth century where it drew favourable comment from both Pushkin and Chekhov. The central theme is the unscrupulous pursuit of Clarissa by the intriguingly named Robert Lovelace, and the novel has won a new audience among modern feminist critics for its unvarnished depiction of harassment, as it would now be known, of Clarissa by her more powerful suitor. The author himself preferred to describe the progress of the plot as Clarissa's defence of her virtue. Since her own family attempted to coax or coerce her to accept Lovelace's proposal, she found herself increasingly isolated. Her brother James had fought a duel with Lovelace, but that had not caused him (James) to sympathize with Clarissa's plight. The pressure on her from her own family is so great that she agrees to flee with Lovelace, whom she still dislikes, but his conduct towards her is such that she eventually sickens and dies.

Clarissa does have some friends, notably her cousin Colonel Morden, who determines to make Lovelace pay for his malice. The closing letters in the book are taken up with the formalities of preparation for the 'interview' which will take place while both men are travelling on the continent. Anxious letters are forwarded, communications are missed, different cities from Florence to Munich visited, but all the while Lovelace assures his correspondent in England, John Belford, of his determination not to appear cowardly and to give Morden satisfaction. Lovelace still hopes for a friendly settlement. No other work of this kind so clearly chronicles the subtle mixture of forced bravado and nonchalance allied with subtly glimpsed fear which are combined in the outward display of gentlemanly honour.

The two men finally meet in Trento, then under Austrian rule. The evening before the meeting, they speak civilly about the weapons, decide swords are appropriate, ride out together to choose a suitable spot, appoint a surgeon who will be at the service of both, and then part 'with a solemn sort of ceremonious civility'. Richardson's description of the duel, as supposedly conveyed by a second in a letter to John Belford, is a masterly example of the genre:

> They parried with equal judgment several passes. My Chevalier drew the first blood, making a desperate push, which, by a sudden turn of his antagonist, missed going clear thro' him, and wounded him on the fleshy part of the ribs of his right side; which part the sword tore out, being on the extremity of the body. But, before he could recover himself, his adversary, in return, pushed him into the inside of the left arm, near the shoulder: And the sword, by raking his breast as it passed, being followed by a great effusion of blood, the Colonel said, Sir, I believe you have enough. My Chevalier swore by G-d, he was not hurt: 'Twas a pin's point: And so made another pass at his antagonist; which he, with a surprising dexterity, received under his arm, and run my dear Chevalier into the body: Who immediately fell: saying, The luck is your's, Sir - O my beloved Clarissa! - now art thou ... inwardly he spoke three or four words more. His sword dropt from his hand. Mr. Morden threw his down, and ran to him, saying in French Ah Monsieur, you are a dead man! Call to God for mercy! (Letter CXIII)

Belford records that even Lovelace's family agreed that 'his fate was deserved'. The duel was not vengeance but justice, even Divine justice, possibly the last time that the duel was presented in quasi-religious terms.

Duelling Heroes

The dandified, devil-may-care hero incarnated in early Hollywood films by Errol Flynn, had a long, reputable pedigree in literary history. This hero's duel provided the frisson of excitement, the whiff of danger, the allure of intrigue, the delight of melodrama, and dramatizes a casual disregard for self-preservation beyond the reach of the average sensual man. The sword not the pistol was the weapon of choice, the condescending smile not the sneer his most striking trait, elegance of personality his style, and the defence of personal reputation rather than the upholding of justice his aim. 'None dare meddle with me' could be the watchword, since his self-confidence had no bounds, as many a conceited upstart who had the impertinence to tangle with him in fiction or history, found to his dismay.

As in other spheres, the influence of Sir Walter Scott all over Europe, not just in Britain and America, was profound, as is evident in the number not only of translations but of theatrical and operatic adaptations of his work. In *The Fair Maid of Perth*, Henry Gow volunteers himself as champion of Magdalen Proudfute, while *The Monastery*, *The Antiquary* and *Kenilworth* all feature duels. The many duels in his narrative poems, such as 'The Lady of the Lake', which was transposed by Rossini to *La donna del lago*, or the Waverley Novels, such as *The Bride of Lammermoor*, the inspiration of Donizetti's *Lucia di Lammermoor*, had an incalculable influence on writers of succeeding generations.

Scott may have been the victim of a fruitful misunderstanding or misrepresentation for he himself stands at a turning point in literary representations of the duel, in that he lends it a certain romantic glamour (or at least was perceived as doing so) but simultaneously calls it into question.[2] He invented the historical novel and provided the prototype for the daring duellist found in Alexandre Dumas and Baroness Orczy, or even R.L. Stevenson. These novelists are substantially different one from the others, but the moral landscape in which the dashing supermen who appear in *The Master of Ballantrae*, *The Three Musketeers* or *The Scarlet Pimpernel* has much in common with that of Scott, and is radically different from that of Richardson and Smollett.

D'Artagnan, the fourth of the 'three' musketeers, is the ideal exemplar. He is a native of Gascony, exemplar of a people commonly identified from the Middle Ages onwards as swaggering braggarts. At his first stop *en route* for Paris where he aims to assert himself as a man to be reckoned with, an elderly stranger uses some disparaging words about his steed and causes him to issue his first challenge. That duel is thwarted, but on his arrival in Paris he contrives to irritate all three musketeers, Athos, Porthos and Aramis, and when they decline the invitation to a three-against-one duel, he insists on meeting them individually the following day. Not only does he survive all three duels but he acquits himself with such gallantry and grace that his acceptance into that high company is guaranteed. He will fight many more duels, and see off more villains, including those in the pay of Cardinal Richelieu, before his novitiate is complete.

The main duel in Orczy's *The Scarlet Pimpernel* series comes in *I Will Repay* and does not involve Sir Percy Blakeney directly, but its outcome will require his intervention. The lowly born Déroulède has thoughtlessly but not maliciously spoken slightingly of Adèle in the presence of the young Vicomte de Marny, who is in love with her. Being good at heart, Déroulède has no wish to fight, and fends off the indignant vicomte, but when the latter continues to goad him and insists he kneel to apologize, Déroulède can take no more and ends up killing him. The ramifications of the family desire for revenge will bring the Scarlet Pimpernel himself into the fray.

Advertisement for the 1923 film sequel - with American title - to *The Scarlet Pimpernel* (Wikimedia Commons)

The great Victorian novelists could not avoid bringing the duel into their novels, but in varying tones. For Thackeray, the duel was part of society as he observed it, so *The Luck of Barry Lyndon* (1844), adapted imaginatively for the cinema by Stanley Kubrick in his 1975 film, *Barry Lyndon*, gives prominence to the duels which measure out the rise in society of the eponymous Irish rogue. There are two duels in *The History of Henry Esmond Esq*, one invented and the other drawn from history, both involving the historical figure of Lord Mohun, presented in the novel as a thorough scoundrel but a man of a superficial charm which bewitches Lady Castlewood. The weak-willed Lord Castlewood runs up gambling debts to Mohun, which he manages to repay, but he is enraged by the allegation, which is in the public domain although false, that Mohun had seduced Lady Castlewood. He requires satisfaction. The two men meet in London with their respective seconds, with young Henry Esmond on hand as second to Castlewood. Before the duel they show the necessary equanimity of mind by attending theatre before repairing to an inn where Esmond does his best to provoke Mohun to challenge him and thus leave his master in the clear, but his attempted insults are disdainfully rebuffed. Since no reconciliation is possible, the entire company make for Leicester Fields for an immediate duel in which the wronged Castlewood is killed. Mohun makes his escape but Henry is sentenced to prison. Later, Mohun will engage the Duke of Hamilton in a duel in which both men perish, as recounted in an earlier chapter.

The encounter in *Pickwick Papers* (1836) is among the most comic in English, with the unfortunate Mr Winkle facing the unsavoury Dr Slammer and begging his second, Mr Snodgrass, to take action, any action, to prevent the duel, while the heedless Snodgrass considers it his duty to present his principal as a man of fearless bravery, desperate to show his mettle. The duel in *Nicholas Nickleby* (1839) is a more serious matter, bringing Lord Frederick Verisopht up against his former business partner, Sir Mulberry Hawk. Verisopht is killed, and Hawk has to flee to France.

Robert Louis Stevenson provides the classic portrayal
of a stirring duel in *The Master of Ballantrae* (1889), where a
long-festering dispute pits the two brothers of the House of
Durisdeer one against the other. The split between James and
Henry Durie has its origins in the decision made within the
family to safeguard their property after the landing of Bonnie
Prince Charlie in Scotland. The Master, James, would go out
with the Prince while the dull Henry would remain at home
and side with the Hanoverians. Smollett in the poem quoted
above wrote that the Jacobite rising meant that 'The sons
against their fathers stood / The parent shed his children's
blood,' and similar internecine bitterness is apparent here.
After Prince Charlie's defeat at Culloden, James flees abroad,
leaving behind Alison Graeme, who is in love with him. Out
of necessity, she marries Henry, meaning that the division
between the brothers is total and irreconcilable. When years
later, the Master returns surreptitiously to the family home,
a duel, already predictable, is made inevitable when Henry
calls his brother a coward, admitting it is 'the most deliberate
act of my life'. The duel is fought at night in an open space
endowed with the sacredness of a cathedral; 'the blackness
was like a roof over (our) heads', and a 'windless stricture of
frost had bound the air'. The setting is perfect for a duel of
unblemished purity: wild countryside beyond the reach of
civil society, a surround of darkness, a small arena of light, two
antagonists with a private resentment camouflaging a common
love of family. The moves are described in few words since
Mackellar, the servant and narrator, is 'no judge of the play'.
Henry is a trained fencer and gains the upper hand, leaving
the Master 'with shaken confidence', and causing him catch
his brother's blade with one hand, 'a practice not permitted',
before stumbling and being run through with the sword. Henry
and the servant go to find a stretcher but when they return to
carry the body away, they find it has disappeared. The Master's
adventures will continue.

'Victorian Compromise'

The climate changed. The motives and morals attributed to the characters of such later writers as Conrad, Chekhov, Fontane or, above all, Pirandello, all of whom scorn the duel while being unable to simply ignore it, display a new hierarchy of social and ethical values. Changes of sensibility, belief and culture are never easily dated with any precision, but the alterations in prevailing notions of honour and consequent shifts in views of the duel can be placed with a fair degree of confidence in the latter decades of the nineteenth century, variously denominated the *fin de siècle*, the era of decadentism, the *belle époque*, the days of the emergence of art for art's sake and aestheticism, *l'Italia umbertina*, the 'Victorian compromise' in Chesterton's term. The literary historian Holbrook Jackson coined for fiction in this period the arresting description 'Shocking as a Fine Art'.[3] Established nostrums in many fields were subjected to satirical questioning. 'The great thing is not to allow oneself to be frightened by the venerableness of an institution,' wrote Henrik Ibsen.[4] To many writers, muted or strident changes in cultural and ethical standards meant that the old codes and beliefs came to seem merely quaint and dated and therefore a worthy subject for irony or scoffing. The creative writer has a freedom denied to the historian or sociologist to explore recesses of the mind or to roam speculatively in the individual or collective subconscious, so insights can be more acute, or as Walter Benjamin expressed it, 'fiction has words and words conquer ideas.'[5] In this climate, honour became subject to mockery and the duel an empty ritual still practised but divorced from all connection with chivalric standards.

The duel in Theodor Fontane's novel, *Effi Briest* (1894), seems at first sight like a throwback to more traditional models, but the author's unease is made palpable in his description of the challenge and the duel itself, and especially in the very swiftness with which the offending party is dispatched. Effi's husband, Baron Innstetten, is pitted against her lover, Major Crampas, but Fontane's attitude speaks of a period of transition, when a new scale of values was coming into being but was not yet fully established.[6] The baron's act in killing his opponent in a duel still goes unpunished and tacitly commended by society, Effi is still made an outcast in society but the underlying tone is regretful and uncertain.

The novel has a well-made plot of the sort George Bernard Shaw railed against in theatre. No good can come from the marriage of Effi to the baron. Other late nineteenth-century heroines such as Emma Bovary, Hedda Gabler and Anna Karenina also find themselves in marriages to men who are not in any way wicked or oppressive, but who are much worse, that is, dull, stolid and bland. Their wives are on the contrary spirited and imaginative, given to fretting and chafing against the limits placed on them as women in conventional bourgeois society. Effi is only seventeen when the baron proposes marriage. Strangely, he had made the same proposal to her mother when they were both young, but Effi does not object to the marriage and gives no indication of higher hopes than of becoming a wife and, possibly, mother. Innstetten operates efficiently and reliably inside the barriers of his work as a civil servant in a newly united Germany. He is well thought of, will be promoted from the position of provincial governor to a superior posting in Berlin as is fitting for a pedestrian, predictable, good-hearted but feet-on-the-ground civil servant. Effi, in contrast, is a restive, lively, highly imaginative, quixotic, whimsical, head-in-the clouds young woman, qualities which render her plainly incompatible with her husband.

Initially, the couple are content. Innstetten is considerate and trusts that his wife will settle into life in the small town where he is doing service. She has a brief glimpse of a more glittering world when she attends a concert given by an Italian soprano, who then moves on. Effi's sleep is also disturbed by what may be a ghostly visitation from what she takes to be a Chinese man buried in the town and whose image she has seen in a miniature portrait in the unused upstairs floor of their house. With predictable good intentions, Innstetten brushes aside such childish fears but later makes the enigmatic remark that 'ghosts are never produced, they're natural'. Modern readers will turn to Freudian explanations of the spirits as emanations of frustration with married life.

The conjugal equilibrium is disturbed by the arrival of Major Crampas, himself unhappily married, endowed with a reputation as 'dangerous' and with a record as a duellist. He and Effi are allowed to associate and even go riding together under Innstetten's largely benevolent eye. Effi is attracted to the newcomer but seemingly wards off any insinuations she finds too risqué. Fontane is at his most Victorian in dealing with any developing relationship, implying some closeness in their rides in the country but never describing any intimacy. It is only when, after Innstetten has been promoted to the ministry in Berlin and when a new world of possibilities opens out before her, that it is made clear that Effi is suffering from pangs of conscience for reasons which are not clear to the reader. She has now broken all contact with Crampas and her past, and has a daughter to whom she is devoted, as she is to her husband, so has lived six years of contented if loveless married life. At this point a cache of yellowing letters between her and the major is accidentally discovered. The unstated implication is that the previous relationship had been adulterous.

At this juncture the Chestertonian expression 'Victorian compromise' is useful. Innstetten is left in a quandary over how to react, a dilemma unknown to previous generations of men. After due consideration, he decides he is obliged to behave in conformity with the traditional requirements of Prussian honour and duty. He requests a colleague, Wullersdorf, to act as his second, a decision he immediately regrets because the secret has thus been revealed and might be broadcast in society. The language of his thoughts is significant: 'we've become accustomed to judge everything, ourselves and others, according to its rules... I've no choice, I must do it.' There is no indication that he actually believes in the social rules, but he is a fastidious, conventional man of no great strength of will and must follow them. He must issue a challenge, he must dismiss his wife, whom he loves, he must ruin the happiness of both. Wullersdorf half-heartedly suggests that the passage of time means the matter could be now ignored, but they find it impossible to establish what the appropriate time would be. Innstetten respects no higher standard than the impulse to defer to tradition: 'talk about God's judgement is nonsense ... our own cult of honour is idolatry, but we must submit to it.'

Innstetten knows that the ritual he is about to enact is vacuous and will be destructive but he cannot make a stand against it. Crampas is of like mind, agreeing that 'it has to be done'. The two men meet, Crampas is killed on the spot, Innstetten returns to Berlin to make a confession to his superiors who show understanding. The duel had to be fought, however senseless the routine. Innstetten, not given to self-analysis, has no misgivings or regrets and pays no penalty. It is Effi who is left abandoned and who has to accept separation from her daughter. Her parents, originally censorious, accept her back home where she attains some form of resigned contentment, but is left ailing and dies while still young, the fate of the fallen woman.

Anton Chekhov's novella, *The Duel*, was written in the 1890s and set in a fairly recent past.[7] Duels and gunshots ring out frequently in Chekhov's work, causing him to joke, or half-joke, that he was incapable of writing a play without at least one gun being fired. In *Uncle Vanya*, Vanya fires at the Professor, Serebriakov, but misses, a sign of the futility of his very being. In *Three Sisters*, the duel is fought offstage but the shot, which signals the end of Tusenbach's life and of Irena's prospects of escape from a stifling existence in a remote place, is heard in the house. The characters in *The Duel* have an awareness of fictional duels in Russian fiction and this knowledge is indispensable when the two duellists meet, since the members of the party are comically unfamiliar with standard duelling protocols and have to summon imprecise memories of Pushkin as guidance. The place of the encounter is no longer a field of honour, but simply a secluded place where they will not be disturbed as they go about a dismal business which is not a duty but a reckoning between men who have a score to settle.

The differences between the two protagonists, von Koren and Layevsky, are of temperament and philosophy, but each also loathes the other. Von Koren, an energetic, opinionated scientist, well versed in the thought of Spencer and contemporary materialist thinkers, has turned up in the town in the Caucasus to pursue his entomological researches. His restless mind has led him to embrace a form of social Darwinism which justifies the rule of mere strength and causes him to deliver impassioned philippics in favour of the elimination of the weak, the purposeless and the drifters no matter how personable and harmless they may be. All his bile focuses on Layevsky, whom he denounces for his 'debauchery, ignorance and filthy ways', but also as 'a doomed victim of the epoch, of trends of opinion, of heredity and all the rest of it'.

Layevsky can be viewed as one of those louche 'superfluous men' who had been introduced into Russian literature by Lermontov and Turgenev. He has high hopes when he leaves St Petersburg for the Caucasus with Nadezhda, a married woman. Being an idealist, he had hoped to live a bucolic life close to nature, but predictably tires of it and tires too of Nadezhda. He is prey to that nameless dissatisfaction with himself and with life which afflicts many of Chekhov's characters and is filled with a yearning for some 'elsewhere', in this case St Petersburg, which he has earlier fled but where he now dreams life would be more fulfilling. Return would mean abandoning Nadezhda, but this creates no problem of conscience for him. A sad figure, Nadezhda suffers from Layevsky's neglect of her, and has left herself open to sexual blackmail by running up debts with the predatory Kirilin, owner of a local store. The relationship between her and Layevsky reaches a fresh crisis when news arrives that her husband has died, leaving her free to marry but creating in Layevsky a feeling of entrapment and an increased desperation to abandon her and escape.

In this disturbed state of mind, with time running out for him to find the cash for his travel, Layevsky behaves outrageously in the house of the mild mannered deacon Samoylenko, finally issuing to the company an unfocused, wild challenge, which von

Koren grasps. There is no mention of honour. The projected duel is simply the most extreme of the weapons available to men divided by rage, futility or antipathy. As he sinks into himself, facing a long sleepless night, Layevsky reflects on 'how stupid and senseless duels are', and around the same time von Koren, in the course of a harangue to his companions, announces that 'a nobleman's duel is essentially no different from a drunken tavern brawl', thereby overturning centuries of dignified theorizing. These conclusions change nothing in the mind of either man. Von Koren concludes, 'all the same, we'll go off and fight. That means there is a power which is stronger than all our discussions on the subject.' Neither man has any deep insight into the nature of that power, but neither has the force of will to liberate himself of it.

If there is also comedy in the situation, it is nihilistic, *fin-de-siècle* tragi-comedy. Von Koren may jeer at the idea of the duel, but his attitude, intent as he is on taking the opportunity to kill his opponent, is now quasi-psychopathic. At the field, Layevsky fires in the air, but von Koren takes careful aim and his shot is rendered harmless only when he is thrown off balance by a terrified scream from Samoylenko who has followed them to the field, and who realizes the seriousness of von Koren's intention. The duel is aborted. The futile, pointless encounter facilitates a statement of that specifically Chekhovian vision of life, that desperate optimism in the face of desolation expressed, for example, by Irena in the closing words of *Three Sisters*. Layevsky is compelled to reassess his life and values and like several of Chekhov's dubious characters undergoes a moral transformation which makes him assume responsibility for Nadezhda's sin and dishonour. He and von Koren are reconciled before the latter leaves to further his scientific research. Normality is re-imposed. The final words are bathetic: 'it began to drizzle', but there is no storm. In this post-*code duello* world, as conceived by Chekhov, the duel, however senseless in itself, provides a means of reconciliation and the transformation of life and character.

Interestingly, Joseph Conrad had some difficulty in having his novella, also called *The Duel* (1908), accepted by publishers.

Perhaps the duel as a subject seemed too passé, or perhaps the commissioning editors were incapable of seeing the work as a historical novel where the characters and mores were from another age, but the novelist's scepticism was of his own.[8] The Napoleonic Wars provide the background and the plot is based, however loosely, on the story of two French officers, Generals Fournier-Sarlovèze and Dupont de l'Etang, who over a period of nineteen years searched each other out whatever their posting, and fought perhaps thirty separate duels.

Their history inspired Conrad and the two men were transformed in his novella into Lieutenant Gabriel Feraud of the 7th Hussars and Lieutenant Armand d'Hubert of the 3rd Hussars, both officers in Napoleon's army. The obsessive drive of the two men becomes in Conrad's hands almost a parody of the duel and of the cast of mind, gone beyond recall in Conrad's day, which made it acceptable. The protagonists are driven as surely as Greek tragic heroes by an irresistible force which is in their case not cosmic fate but social fatalism. They are not psychopathic individuals; the drive that impels them to meet in duel after duel over the years does not spring from some individual flaw or idiosyncrasy of character, but rather from a need to live up to a code. Their changing feelings trace a descent from the initial irritation felt by one, Feraud, to a deepening, mutual antipathy which never quite sharpens into hatred before finally transmogrifying into a reluctant respect bordering on fraternal affection.

D'Hubert is given the unwelcome task of arresting a fellow officer, Feraud, who in a duel has inflicted a serious wound on the son of a prominent citizen of Strasbourg, where the company is posted. He locates him in Madame Lionne's elegant salon, but Feraud cannot see any wrong he has committed and is displeased at being apprehended, especially when in conversation with a lady. His reaction is belligerent from the outset, leaving d'Hubert bemused. At his apartment Feraud invites d'Hubert into the garden where he draws his sword, compelling d'Hubert to defend himself. In the ensuing struggle d'Hubert wounds the other and he faints. As he rushes off

THE FACTS OF FICTION

to summon a doctor, d'Hubert notes that he 'dreaded the discredit and ridicule above everything, and was painfully aware of sneaking through the backstreets like a murderer.' He has carried out orders, has found himself trapped into a sword fight, but already in conversation with the surgeon is beset with the feeling that 'the truth was confoundedly grotesque and embarrassing'. Feraud's resentment is, on the contrary, made stronger when he is put under house arrest and then demoted.

Conrad seems to have nurtured a fascination, evident in *Lord Jim* or *The Secret Agent*, with the decision which sets an irreversible, life-long course. Feraud and d'Hubert, the former vengeful and aggressive, the latter resigned and compliant, are bound together as securely as two lovers. The two men reach a strange form of comradeship, which does not, however, permit a reconciliation, although after the second duel when d'Hubert is injured their seconds encourage this solution. Theirs is a union of shared ideals, whose nature is obscure and has overtones of a grotesque comedy which do not escape the onlooking novelist. Conrad participates in the hunt the two men undertake over the years to find the other and re-engage in a duel. The changing panorama as the army engages in campaigns over Europe lends itself to cinematic treatment, a potential fully exploited by Ridley Scott in his film, *The Duellists*. Conrad probes the nature of the obsessive links between the two men, and intervenes to wonder about the point of it all. His style of story-telling is at the antipodes from that of the invisible novelist. He is a presence in his story, making his incisive bewilderment an element in the narrative.

D'Hubert's view that he 'had no option, no choice whatever, consistent with (my) dignity as a man and an officer' is accepted later by the old Chevalier de Valmassique, a soldier and gentleman of the old school, and uncle of Adèle, the woman d'Hubert falls in love with. When he explains his dilemma, the chevalier's only observation is that d'Hubert should have resolved the matter before considering marriage. D'Hubert reveals he has already fought three duels with Feraud, but has also been shoulder to shoulder with him on the retreat from Moscow, has intervened secretly to have his pension restored and even to have Feraud's name removed from the list of Napoleonic officers sentenced to death after the Restoration. D'Hubert's wedding date is fixed but his antagonist erupts back into his life with a demand for another duel which takes the atypical form of a chase with pistols in a wood. Feraud misfires with his two permitted shots leaving him at d'Hubert's mercy, which he does extend.

This is no fairy tale, but there is a happy ending for d'Hubert. Duellists often fought over a woman they both loved, but this storyline is reversed as d'Hubert realizes that he has found the love he has always craved and that he owes it to his antagonist, 'this stupid brute'. Feraud's fate, underscored in the final scene of the film which has him standing alone overlooking a grand but empty landscape, is to face a future of isolation. D'Hubert outlines the course of his former days to his newly wedded wife, who concludes, 'Isn't it funny? *C'est insensé* to think what men are capable of.' A very modern scepticism.

In Sicily too, with a culture and history where Mediterranean and European features mingle, writers were coming to the same conclusion. The traditional, jealousy-motivated duel made its last appearance in Giovanni Verga's *Cavalleria rusticana*, written in 1880 as a short story, recast in 1884 as a play, and then transformed in 1890 into an opera by the composer, Pietro Mascagni. When the play toured in northern Italy and the opera all over Europe, it offered audiences glimpses into the exotic folklore of an unfamiliar world. The tragedy is set in train when Turiddu returns from military service to discover that Lola, to whom he was engaged, has abandoned him to marry the wealthy Alfio. He begins seeing Santuzza as a cover for his renewed relationship with Lola, but the jealous Santuzza exposes the affair to Alfio, requiring him to issue a formal challenge which Turridu accepts in the startling form of a bite in Alfio's ear, the blood signifying a fight to the death. The weapons are daggers, and Turiddu's death is screamed out to the village by Lola with the wild, melodramatic closing line, '*Hanno ammazzato cumpari Turiddu*, They've killed Turiddu.' In the opinion of the Sicilian novelist, Leonardo Sciascia, that single line was responsible

The fateful ear-biting scene in *Cavalleria Rusticana*, c1890, anonymous,
attributed to Rauzzini; restored by Adam Cuerden (Wikimedia Commons)

for establishing the reputation of the Sicilians as people of
uncontrolled passion, whereas he believed that duelling and
punishment killings were motivated not by 'a passion of the
heart, but by sort of intellectual passion, from a passion or
concern for formalities of an almost juridical nature'.[9] Turiddu
and Alfio, in this view, were motivated not by uncontrollable
jealousy but by conformity with laws they recognized. Perhaps
that is the key to the *code duello* elsewhere.

The very notion of honour has a long afterlife in Sicily, where
members of the mafia refer to themselves as 'men of honour', a
description at odds with any reality. The laws of the duel are
unknown to the mafia, who will shoot a man in the back or lay
an ambush in numbers for an individual opponent.

The protocol of the duel seemed absurd to Verga's
contemporary and fellow Sicilian, Luigi Pirandello, who
had studied in Bonn and was cosmopolitan in outlook while
remaining Sicilian to the core. He was born in Agrigento in

southern Sicily, and experience of violence was part of his upbringing. Andrea Camilleri, later the highly successful author of detective novels, wrote in a biography of Pirandello that his father had been involved in 'seven armed conflicts and six duels'.[10] Pirandello's view of life is decidedly sombre and only partially tempered by his theories of *umorismo*, an idiosyncratic brand of humour which introduces 'decomposition, disorder and disharmony' into the vision of life. His earliest works are set in a Sicilian environment, and the contradictory demands of male and female honour are dramatized in, for instance, *Il beretto a sonagli* (*Bell and Candles*, 1917). Ciampa discovers not only that his young wife has had an affair with his employer, but that Beatrice Fiorica, his employer's wife, plans to publicize it, thereby undermining Ciampa's honour in public and compelling him in reparation to murder his wife, whom he loves. The compromise is that Beatrice is persuaded to declare herself insane, so her revelations can be disregarded and Ciampa freed of the need to execute the *delitto d'onore*, the honour crime.

There are many duels in Pirandello's theatre as well as in his novels and stories, all treated with derision in line with his *umorismo*. The early novel, *Il turno* (*The Turn*), written in 1895 but published in 1902, is focused on the plight of Stellina, whose father wishes her to marry for love and money, but these are incompatible objectives. Her love for young Pepè Alletto is fully returned but he is penniless, so her father devises a scheme which will see her marry the wealthy but elderly Diego Alcozèr in the expectation that he will die quickly and leave his widow wealthy and free to marry her true love. Alletto, in other words, will have to wait his turn, but obviously such a neat scheme is destined to go awry. The wedding reception turns into a brawl. Pepè is struck on the cheek by another guest, Luca Borrani, but has no idea of the appropriate reaction until he is instructed by a lawyer, Ciro Coppa, who tells him he must fight a duel. The gormless Pepè has no understanding of what that involves, and so is dismayed that he is being dragged into combat 'over a bit of nonsense', his dismay increasing when his opponent chooses the sabre, a weapon Pepè has never seen let alone held. The description of the duel is given by his seconds, who are plainly not impressed at Pepè's feckless display.

> Parry? Feint? Neither! Stock still like a puppet in a theatre booth ... so then nothing for it, whack, whack, and at first contact, bang! Just as well he did not get it on the head. Borrani would have cut him in two like a melon.[11]

Pepè emerges battered and bruised, but still alive, only to discover shortly afterwards that Stellina has changed her mind about her future. The marriage is annulled leaving her free but she sets up home with Ciro Coppa, who has a profession and an income.

The short story, *Ma non è una cosa seria*, (*It's Not Serious*), written in 1910 but rewritten in 1917 with the same title for the stage, features Perazzetti, a Casanova figure who finds himself fighting a duel with his best friend over his sister whom Perazzetti has seduced with a promise of marriage, on which he has reneged. Neither Perazzetti nor his opponent believes in what they are doing, but they have no option. In the play the same but renamed character, having narrowly escaped from the duel, decides that matrimony offers him the safest route to a calmer life while permitting him to continue on the primrose path of dalliance. The marriage he plans will be of a unique type, since the chosen woman will live apart from him, but his legal status as husband means that no future lover can expect matrimony and no busybody brother can intervene to demand that status for a misused sister.

Il giuoco delle parti (1918) is normally known in English as *The Rules of the Game*, although a more satisfactory translation would be *The Game of Roles*. The tragic-humorous outcome is brought about by a duel, itself produced by a devious ruse. Silia is living with a lover, Guido, she seems to despise, while her wily husband, Leone, the incarnation of the Pirandellian humourist, continues to visit her every day out of external respect for the roles foisted on him as husband by the bourgeois society he despises. A gang of boors, headed by a marquis who is also a master fencer, invades her home while she is alone, jostling and insulting her, an offence which requires satisfaction. To everyone's surprise Leone, goaded by Silia, issues the standard challenge required of a husband in such circumstances, but in his own mind while he is officially the husband, that role is in reality taken by Guido, so Leone sends him out to the duel and to death. Far from being a chivalric rite, the duel is an absurd but tragic game, manipulated by a nonchalant cynic, played by idiots, and ending in bloodshed and death.

The duel as elaborate game, where only the outward protocols are observed, was pushed to its extremes by G.K. Chesterton. He was politically devoted to quasi-medieval values in the political philosophy he and Hilaire Belloc named Distributism, and imaginatively enchanted in his fiction by chivalry and its paraphernalia. The sleuthing activities of his detective, Father Brown, twice bring him into contact with duellists, the first time with the Sicilian Prince Saradine who has been constrained to flee from Sicily and take up residence in England. Chesterton's view of 'savage Sicilian loyalty' brings him closer to Verga than to Pirandello, although the tale is concluded in terms Pirandello would have recognized. In Sicily, the prince had abducted a woman and murdered her husband, and is dismayed when years later their son Antonelli arrives in England with two rapiers for a revenge duel. Regrettably Antonelli is unaware that Saradine has swapped places with his impoverished brother, giving his brother the title and himself taking on the role of retainer. The description of the duel glitters like the sun on the water on the lake in the estate:

> Evening above them was like a dome of virgin gold, and. distant as they were, every detail was picked out. They had cast off their coats, but the yellow waistcoat and white hair of Saradine, the red waistcoat and white trousers of Antonelli, glittered in the level light like the colours of the dancing clockwork dolls. The two swords sparkled

from point to pommel like two diamond pins. There was
something frightful in the two figures appearing so little
and so gay. They looked like two butterflies trying to pin
each other to a cork.[12]

The wrong man is killed, and the real villain goes scot-free. A
later duel observed by Father Brown in Paris has the savour of
a Jekyll and Hyde mystery, with the two supposed opponents
being revealed as twin sides of the one character. The duellist's
real opponent is himself.

'They will not meet on the Day of Judgment,' said the
priest. 'If God Almighty held the truncheon of the lists,
if St Michael blew the trumpets for the swords to cross
- even them if one of them stood ready, the other would
not come... They are the opposite of each other, they
contradict each other. They cancel out, so to speak.'[13]

There is one other, enigmatic and paradoxical, duel in
Chesterton. *The Man Who Was Thursday* is a tale of a cabal of
anarchists named after the days of the week, but it transpires
that all the members are police infiltrators apart from one, the
Marquis, whom Gabriel Syme, who is Thursday, engages in a
duel to prevent him boarding a train to Paris to explode a bomb.[14]
The chapter is entitled simply 'The Duel', and the encounter
is described with brio and panache before it is revealed that
the anarchist-marquis is also a policeman in disguise. The
duel between the two men is no more than a hoax, an empty
ceremonial fought by two imposters. Even for GKC, nothing
remained of the old code of honour.

1 John Leigh, *Touché!: The Duel in Literature*, Cambridge MA: Harvard University Press, 2015, pp. 140-2
2 I am grateful to Prof Graham Tulloch for these points on Scott.
3 Holbrook Jackson, *The Eighteen Nineties: A Review of Art and Ideas at the Close of the Nineteenth Century*, London: Penguin, 1950, pp. 125-33.
4 Quoted by Michael Meyer in *Ibsen*, London: Penguin, 1974, p. 354.
5 Quoted by Vincenzo Ruggiero, *Crime in Literature: Sociology of Deviance and Fiction*, London: Verso, 2003, p. 4.
6 Theodor Fontane, translated by Douglas Parmée, *Effi Briest*, London: Penguin, 1967.
7 Anton Chehkov, translated by Ronald Wilks, *The Duel*, London: Penguin, 1984, pp. 17-119.
8 Joseph Conrad, *The Duel*, in *A Set of Six*, New York: Doubleday, 1924.
9 Leonardo Sciascia, *The Day of the Owl*, London: Granta Books, 2001, p. 94.
10 Andrea Camilleri, *Biografia del figlio cambiato*, Milan: Rizzoli, 2000, p. 27.
11 Luigi Pirandello, *Il turno*, Rome: Newton Compron, 1993, p. 47. Translation mine.
12 G.K. Chesterton, 'The Sins of Prince Saradine', in *The Innocence of Father Brown*, London: Penguin, 2013, pp. 160-83.
13 G.K. Chesterton, 'The Duel of Dr Hirsch', in *The Wisdom of Father Brown*, London: Penguin, 2012, p. 61.
14 G.K. Chesterton, *The Man Who Was Thursday*, London: House of Stratus, 2001.

14

THE ROMANTIC DUEL
THE DEATH OF PUSHKIN

The duel in the early 1800s was both a fixed point in the cultural
landscape and also, for a refined elite, a symptom of a Romantic
aesthetic sensibility, a temperament widespread in Europe at
the time. There were many literary duellists and even more
duels in literature, but the entire tangled, contorted and self-
aggrandizing complex of factors that drove men to issuing and
accepting challenges are more strongly present in the life and
work of Alexander Sergeyevich Pushkin than in any other man.
As a cultural force the *code duello* imposed on him obligations,
while as an aesthetic tenet it offered dramatic embellishment.
Pushkin in his life submitted to the first and in his poetry
exalted the second.

He fought many duels and narrated many more, attaining one
climactic moment of absolute, literary tragedy in *Eugene Onegin*
and a similar moment of existential tragedy on 27 February 1837
in the duel in St Petersburg with Georges d'Anthès which cost
him his life. Pushkin was the greatest victim - but the word is
inadequate for a willing participant - in the history of duelling,
and Europe's greatest loss in the centuries-long carnage that was
the gentleman's duel. His was the duel of duels, the Armageddon
of single combat. The depiction of the duel in his fiction and
the inexorable journey towards the meeting which would end
his own life bring to the fore the beliefs which constituted the
pillars of civilization for the men of his time and all the follies

which people of later generations saw in the same act. Pushkin's final duel demonstrated the power of forces such as jealousy, honour, bravado, the femme fatale and rumoured infidelity, as well as the dramatic appeal of society balls, power play, whispers and rumours, shadowy intrigue, anonymous letters, fate foretold in gnomic utterances, mysterious foreigners, complexity of motives, all resulting in genius destroyed, or self-destroyed.

'May I present, as we set sail / The hero of my current tale?' run the opening lines of *Eugene Onegin* in James E. Falen's translation.[1] Let me introduce Pushkin in the idiosyncratic idiom he employed, at least in translation, when bringing forward the protagonist of his novel in verse. The informality of these lines is unsettling, but the style throughout combines geniality and genius. It has often been said that it is impossible to reproduce the mixture of sublimity and simplicity in Pushkin's verse in another language, but the dazzling swagger of the poem remains visible. This quality owes a great deal to Lord Byron, whose portrait hung in both Pushkin's and Onegin's studios and whose name recurs in the stanzas. The casual familiarity of tone in the poetry, but perhaps not the prose, allows the writer to appear to lean forward over his desk as he writes, and makes the reader feel more like a listener in a closed circle. The first hero of the tale to be told here is Pushkin himself. He was a member of the aristocracy of Russia but an exotic creature of partly African descent and features, sometimes at home in the endless round of balls and receptions that made up patrician life in St Petersburg, but at others an outsider of dissident beliefs. His discomfort in court circles was echoed in that of the protagonists of some of his stories, and emphatically so in the unease of Onegin himself, but when Pushkin was exiled to the south of the Russian Empire by Tsar Alexander I, who was suspicious of his seeming sympathy with the Decembrist rebels, many of whom had copies of Pushkin's works in their possession when they were rounded up, he pined and complained.

Every critical study designates him as the father of Russian literature, whose formative influence was recognized by subsequent geniuses such as Tolstoy and Dostoevsky. As poet, he was the quintessential Romantic, 'half in love with easeful death' in the words John Keats addressed in London to a baffled nightingale, living in a tempestuous zone between the Freudian drives of Eros and Thanatos. The death with which Pushkin was more than half in love took the form of the duel. For other duellists whose story has been told in this book, it is possible to compartmentalize their life, to separate to some extent the man from the final folly, even while recounting the backstory, placing the doleful march to the field in the context of their times or careers, discussing in the context of a life-long rivalry the animus which separated the protagonist from their ultimate antagonist, as was the case with Hamilton and Burr, or illustrating a sudden but irremediable dispute, as with Casanova and Branicki, or even describing the act of folly in terms of the prevailing manners and mores of the age, as with the Duke of Wellington. But the case of Pushkin is unique.

The idea or ideal of the duel was embedded in the complex psyche of Pushkin, making it more than a secular social-political belief but giving it the status of a near-religious creed and inserting it firmly as an intricate and integral part of his being. It is generally futile to attempt to bring the man from behind the book, but in Pushkin's case the distance is shorter than with most writers. His human and literary biographies seem almost a preparation for the final encounter. He was by temperament a duellist as much as a poet. He described duels in other works apart from the celebrated encounter in *Eugene Onegin*. Let us consider two instances. The first novella in the *Tales of the Late Ivan Petrovich Belkin* (1831) is entitled *The Shot* and is set in a military establishment where an outsider, known only as Silvio, lives on the margins of the camp but is a generous host to its residents. Etymologically, Silvio designates a native of the woods, someone not at home with the ways or even in the abodes of humans, and the only daytime activity of this Silvio is honing his marksmanship by firing bullets at cards. The skill he displays wins him recognition in the army environment, and in the evenings he is a convivial host, all of which makes it a matter of surprise to the company that when he is grossly insulted at his own table by an officer he does not immediately reply with a challenge. His failure to do so means he is branded a coward, but he explains to the unnamed narrator that he has sworn to fire only one more shot in his life and that this is not the appropriate moment. Shortly afterwards, a message arrives which requires him to pack and leave immediately, and he delays only to set out the reasons for his sudden departure to the narrator. In an earlier life, prey to a wild, unjustified jealousy of a man who seemed equipped with all the bounty life could confer, Silvio gave way to this jealousy and hatred. He deliberately offended the man, accepted the inevitable challenge but planned to fire in the air. He was taken off guard when his antagonist shot first, the bullet piercing his bonnet. The adversary insisted that Silvio should exercise the right of second shot and took up a stance which made him an easy target, but Silvio was dismayed at the sight of the other casually eating cherries, showing a nonchalance towards life or death which proved his superiority to the common run of humankind. Why kill such a man in those circumstances when his attitude showed his indifference to his fate?

The message received in the military camp announces that his ex-adversary is about to marry a woman of great charm, and Silvio chooses this as the moment to exercise his right to fire his one remaining shot. He sets off and makes no further contact with his former friends. Chance is often a feature in Pushkin's tales, so when the narrator goes on his travels he ends up one night in a remote town where he is invited to the home of a local count. A curious feature of his library is a portrait with two bullet holes. The count tells of a man called Silvio with whom he had once fought an uncompleted duel, and who had pursued him years later demanding his right to one shot, but granting the count the privilege of firing first. They faced each other in the library. The count missed and hit the portrait, but was reduced to a state of terror at forfeiting the happiness of his new life. The countess heard the fracas and rushed in to beg Silvio to show mercy, in spite of her husband's call to her to desist. Silvio shot to miss, his bullet entering the canvas alongside the count's. He was satisfied at witnessing the count's fear and agitation. He had chosen to fire his one shot when love endowed the life of his hated adversary with value, but baulked at mere murder.

The Captain's Daughter (1836), a historical novel still being written when *Eugene Onegin* was published, follows the adventures of Pyotr Andreich Grinyov who at the age of sixteen is dispatched by his father to serve in the army in the remote Belogorsk Fort.[2] The core of the novel recounts the Pugachev uprising of 1773-75 which Pushkin had been researching and on which he left an uncompleted work, but it is also a coming-of-age story recounting the developing relationship between Pyotr and Maria, the daughter of the commandant. On arrival, Pyotr also strikes up a prickly friendship with a fellow officer of his own age, Shvabrin, who has been sent to the fort as a disciplinary measure after killing a man in a duel over an issue no one can understand. The commandant's wife explains that the two men had gone out together but then drew their swords. Shvabrin dispatched his opponent. 'What can you do?' asks the woman. 'It's a good horse that never stumbles.'

Pyotr falls in love with Maria, but the friendship between the two men falters when he shows Shvabrin a love poem he has written. To his dismay, Shvabrin is dismissive both of the poem and of the girl with whom he claims to have had a prior relationship. Pyotr accuses him of lying, which leads Shvabrin to demand satisfaction. The man whom Pyotr requests to act as second reports them to the commandant, so when the two come together at the agreed hour they are arrested. The commandant's family are appalled at Pyotr's conduct, but the two men are still determined to fight. They meet by the riverside where Pyotr has the upper hand until he is distracted by his loyal serving man, whose arrival allows Shvabrin to stab Pyotr in the chest and cause him to lose consciousness. He remains unconscious for days, but is tended by Maria. The couple will have to endure the perils of the uprising before they can finally come together.

Over the descriptions of these and other duels, there lingers the spirit not of the moralist but of the epicurean, even of the premature exponent as art for art's sake. Pushkin offers no lessons, or none he was capable of following himself. Unapologetic and unabashed, he is fascinated by the scene. His draws on his own experiences as a duellist, making him more than the poet who extracts every blood-stained drop of drama from his depiction. William Hazlitt, a near contemporary, wrote of the 'pleasure of hatred', the delight that we can still feel 'when the spirit of the age ... no longer allows us to carry our headstrong and vindictive humours into effect', but does permit us to 'try to revive them in depiction'.[3] Pushkin's case was more complex. The spirit of the age was wholly in tune with duelling, and Pushkin depicted the duel with uncritical relish, nowhere more so than in *Eugene Onegin*.

There is an element of cruelty, not entirely concealed by the surface whimsicality of the tale, in the initial desire of Silvio in *The Shot* to dismantle his opponent's self-respect, and it may be that this same offhand sadism, identified by Mario Praz as a component of late Romanticism, supplies the motive which critics had failed to find as an explanation of Onegin's behaviour towards Tatyana, who loves him, and towards Lensky, his friend and fellow poet.[4] *Eugene Onegin* is set in 1820 but was written between the years 1825-32 and has a linear plot of no great complexity whose free flow allows for quirky or reflective digressions. The central point is the duel in Chapter 6, the previous action being preparatory and the remaining cantos the requital for Onegin's misconduct. Onegin is a society fop who squanders his talents in frivolity and debauchery in St Petersburg until he grows tired of it all and retires to a country estate he has inherited from his uncle. His character is established from the outset by the description of him waiting with pitiless impatience for his aged relative to die, 'while thinking under every sigh / Devil take you, Uncle, die!' He finds life in the country somewhat surprisingly to his taste - he is a Romantic - and makes friends with a younger poet, Lensky, who is imbued with the *joie de vivre* which the jaded Onegin has lost.

There are two sisters in a nearby family. Lensky falls in love with Olga, while the more reserved and bookish Tatyana falls in love with Onegin. Lensky and Olga are engaged to be married, but when Onegin fails to make any advance to Tatyana, she takes an initiative not normally permitted to her sex and writes a love letter to him. He remains unmoved and tells her a man like him is unsuited to the married life, and in any case she should set aside nebulous dreams nurtured by the novels she has been reading. Sometime later, the two men go together to the women's home for an evening of socializing and dancing, and it is on this occasion that the events, minor in themselves, are set in the motion which will lead to the tragedy. Onegin is not wholly heartless, and is dismayed to see Tatyana's evident pain at seeing him there but disregarding her.

> By being at this feast he hated,
> And noting how poor Tanya shook,
> He barely hid his angry look
> And fumed in sullen indignation;
> He swore that he'd make Lensky pay
> And be avenged that very day.

His revenge takes the form of monopolizing Olga's attention and inviting her to dance.

> She blushes in appreciation,
> Her prim conceited face alight,
> While Lensky rages at the sight,
> Consumed with jealous indignation.

The final blow for Lensky is her refusal to partner him for a mazurka because she has already promised that privilege to Onegin. Lensky storms off, and the following day issues a challenge to his former and present friend. To oversee the encounter they appoint one Zaretsky, ironically described as a 'man of honour' but in reality

> ... a rowdy clown,
> chief gambler and arch rake in town,
> the tavern tribune and a liar.

The presence of this man only partially strips the duel of its allure, because in every respect the rituals are respected. Lensky even realizes on meeting Olga that he was mistaken in believing she no longer loved him, but he is obliged to go on. The Rubicon has been crossed.

> The foes! How long has bloodlust parted
> And so estranged these former friends?
> How long did they, warmhearted,
> Share meals and pastimes, thoughts and ends?
> And now, malignant in intention,
> Like ancient foes in mad dissension
> As in a dreadful senseless dream
> They glower coldly as they scheme.

The description of the duel is meticulously detailed. Pushkin had already been involved in a sufficient number to know the script. The two men are placed thirty paces apart, at liberty to fire when they wish as they advance towards each other, but Onegin fires first and shoots Lensky dead. Onegin flees the land, but is not pursued by any legal force. Years later he meets Tatyana at a society ball in St Petersburg, but she is married and although she declares she is still in love with him, she chooses marital fidelity and rejects Onegin's advances.

Eugene Onegin is not *Othello*, even if jealousy is a force in both works. There is not in the protagonist any primal fault, nor any sign of some tragic, internal *hamartia*, merely the obstinacy of individual men, their unthinking submission to the imperatives of the ego and to the demands of the time. There is no irresistible passion, no trace of the wild jealousy that impelled Othello, but rather the softer Romantic emotionality. Onegin and Lensky had been soul mates until a quarrel over a trifle drove them apart, and made them act in conformity to the ethics of the day. In other times, the remedy would have been confession, submission to a wiser authority, a delay until moods changed, but in their day satisfaction was required, and immediately. The novel in verse is, in the receptive imagination of the sympathetic reader, a painful display of excess and of the penalties of excess, although Pushkin is neither moralist nor philosopher. The course of events leading up to the duel is uncannily prescient of the forces which would lead Pushkin to his own fatal duel a few years later, and there are even parallels between Olga's coquettish behaviour and that of Natalya, Pushkin's wife, but probes into the future and speculation on some unseen hand are best left to a dramatist. To do justice to Pushkin's case, such a dramatist would require the insights of an Aeschylus or Shakespeare. Pushkin's poem appeals to thoughtful spectators in the wings who study the mischances and misdeeds of life, and the enigma is that Pushkin offered himself the occasion for such reflection but did not take it.

All the enigmas of the *code duello* and its grip on humans in all their fallibility and foolishness are crystallized in the poem. The deep motive for the split and the duel eluded both Vladimir Nabokov and the critic Edmund Wilson in the famous quarrel - whose ferocity would in other times have led these former friends to the field of honour - occasioned by the publication of Nabokov's 'literal' translation of Pushkin's work.[5] The debate over the validity of the translation itself does not concern us, but it is worthwhile to examine what Wilson called Nabokov's 'most serious failure', that he finds himself

> unable to account for Evgeni Onegin's behaviour in first giving offence to Lensky by flirting with Olga at the ball and then, when Lensky challenges him to a duel, instead of managing a reconciliation, not merely accepting the challenge, but deliberately shooting first and to kill.

Nabokov believes that this act is 'quite out of character', while Wilson analyses Onegin as being 'nasty, *méchant*', and proves his point by referring to Onegin's offensive impatience as he waits for his ailing uncle to expire and allow him to inherit his estate and wealth. This malignant side of his character is further evidenced, Wilson believes, by his flirtatious behaviour towards Olga at the ball which led to the challenge and duel. Wilson alleges that Nabokov 'has simply not seen the point', but perhaps both had missed the point in looking for internal flaws of character rather than in external social protocols. Pushkin gave credence to a kaleidoscope of beliefs, but he was an unflinching adherent of the *code duello*, and both he and Onegin acted in accordance with its demands. The truth they recognized was of the fragile sort Francis Bacon indicated, born of time and not of authority, but it was strong enough to determine life and death. Onegin behaved frivolously and unfeelingly in playing the gallant with Lensky's fiancée at the ball, and thereafter the two found themselves in a cultural *cul de sac*. A duel was inevitable. Lensky read Schiller, another fashionably Romantic poet, the night before facing Onegin. Lensky perished. Onegin was left to contemplate the body of the man he had killed. Art and life often overlap in Pushkin.

> In anguish, with his heart forsaken,
> The pistol in his hand like lead,
> Eugene stared down at Lensky, shaken,
> His neighbour spoke; 'Well then, he's dead.'
> The awful word, so lightly uttered,
> Was like a blow. Onegin shuddered,
> Then called his men and walked away.

A Death Foretold

Pushkin completed *Eugene Onegin* in the early 1830s, and the following year he married Natalya Goncharova. After an initial period of nuptial happiness he was plunged into a state of intermittent emotional insecurity and jealous turmoil centred on, and largely caused by, one man, Georges d'Anthès. The complicated personalities of the parties involved and their relationships can only be sketched out here, but one underlying fact bears repetition. Pushkin was an inveterate duellist and in this a child of his times. Serena Vitale, in her magnificent, meticulous reconstruction of the last year in Pushkin's life, dedicates a chapter to the duels which had measured out his existence.[6]

She lists twelve which took place or were narrowly averted but there were certainly others. Born in 1799, he was only eighteen when he issued his first challenge to an elderly relative, Peter Gannibal, after they quarrelled over a girl at a country dance. No duel ensued. As a youth in St Petersburg, while producing his magnificent poetry he lived a life of goliardic roistering, spending his evenings in gambling, drinking, falling in love and frequenting brothels. Elaine Feinstein quotes the wife of the historian Karamzin as writing, 'Pushkin has a duel almost every day,' and although Feinstein dismisses this view as exaggerated, she does give examples of duels. He challenged a Guards Major, who refused to fight such a callow youth, but did face a colleague who was offended by an epigram Pushkin had written. On that occasion his antagonist fired and missed, while Pushkin's gun failed to go off because snow had caused the trigger mechanism to jam.[7] In one he stood casually eating cherries, like the character in *The Shot*, leaving his opponent disconcerted.

Pushkin had never lived a tranquil life, but any possibility of domestic harmony was ruined by the presence in Russia of the Frenchman, Georges-Charles d'Anthès, and of the Dutch ambassador, Jacob Heeckeren, who made d'Anthès his adopted son and heir. It is possible that the two met by chance when d'Anthès was making his way to Moscow to make a fresh start in Russia after setbacks to his career at home. The two were also in all probability lovers. Heeckeren is a deeply unattractive character but d'Anthès was an opportunist who needed little encouragement to take advantage of any situation. Bisexual is an inadequate term to cover the complexity of d'Anthès' situation when he was emotionally and perhaps sexually involved with a man and a woman. He fell in love with Pushkin's wife, Natalya, but then everyone did, including Tsar Nicholas I. She was by all accounts an alluring woman of Botticellian beauty. D'Anthès was infatuated and she did nothing to cool his ardour. He courted her assiduously in public and attempted to do so in private, but the lady, although flattered by his attention and willing to indulge in coquettish behaviour, behaved like Tatyana in keeping him at a certain, but minimal, distance. The two probably did not become lovers, although the gilded society of St Petersburg was rife with rumours to the contrary, but they showed no discretion in seeking out each other's company in the receptions and feasts which were a feature of the season in the palaces of the capital city. In addition to having to cope with this public scandal, Pushkin was also beset by financial difficulties, and was disappointed by the commercial failure of a periodical, *The Contemporary*, he had set up. His friends and acquaintances, who were assiduous letter-writers, record that his demeanour showed unsurprising signs of deep instability. Perhaps it was predictable that he would call someone out, but the recipient of his challenge was unexpected. Irked by an innocuous comment by the friendly Count Sollogub, he issued the challenge. The dispute was patched up and the benevolent Sollogub came to Pushkin's assistance as he came under increasing pressure.

The final toxin was the circulation to selected members of the aristocracy of a venomous, satirical document written in faltering French announcing that Pushkin had been admitted to the Order of Cuckolds. The author of this missive has never been identified, although investigations have never ceased. It provoked shock and perhaps some malevolent delight in high society, and left Pushkin aghast. Irreverent he may have been, but he did care about his honour and his public standing. After a delay of some days, he issued a challenge to d'Anthès,

Georges-Charles d'Anthès, Pushkin's nemesis, lithograph, National Pushkin Museum, St Petersburg (Wikimedia Commons)

not on the basis of the anonymous document but on account of his overall behaviour towards Natalya. The *cartello* fell into the hands of Heeckeren, who was horrified. It was he who replied in d'Anthès' name, formally accepting but requesting time for reflection. This news electrified St Petersburg society from the tsar down, but this society was further rocked by the revelation that d'Anthès had proposed to Natalya's sister, Catherine, who was not endowed with any of her sister's attractiveness and had no obvious compensating gifts of personality.

Pushkin was not the only one left bemused by this development which was and remains more unfathomable than the plot twists of the great nineteenth-century European novels, *Anna Karenina*, *Effi Briest* or *Madame Bovary* on the emotional and social predicaments created by infidelity. Did d'Anthès have any feelings for Catherine? Was his move a cynical ruse to ward off Pushkin's threats and also allow continued access to the member of the Goncharov family who really interested him? Posterity is still divided on that question, but d'Anthès' suit was accepted by Catherine and peace-makers scurried between the three men centrally involved - Pushkin, d'Anthès, Heeckeren. They negotiated an armed truce rather than a cessation of hostilities. The wedding took place, but Pushkin was not among the guests.

D'Anthès and Natalya continued to meet and converse intimately at the many balls thrown by the aristocracy in St Petersburg, to the consternation of Pushkin who plainly felt the humiliation deeply. The next step is puzzling. Pushkin poured out his bile not to d'Anthès but to Heeckeren, sending him a letter with a summary of all he endured at the hands of d'Anthès and addressing him in vile, insulting terms which could only be answered by a duel. This time it was d'Anthès who took on himself the duty to reply on his 'father's' behalf and issue the challenge. Pushkin accepted, and conditions were readily agreed - a distance of twenty paces with an imaginary barrier separating them, the two to advance towards each other on a given signal and fire at will. There is no doubting the bitterness of Pushkin towards his opponent but, as is customary

Aleksej Naumov, *Duel of Alexander Pushkin and Georges d'Anthès*, 1885
(Wikimedia Commons)

with duels, it is impossible to ascertain if either was firmly intentioned to kill the other. Pushkin loathed d'Anthès, and perhaps the sight of his ferocity unnerved d'Anthès. It was he who fired first, just possibly to forestall a shot from Pushkin. Perhaps he did mean only to wound him, but his bullet struck his adversary in the stomach. Pushkin did not die on the field but was carried off and lingered on the settee at his home in agony for two days. There was no remedy for wounds of such gravity. Friends and colleagues came and went, the tsar was in contact and communicated a promise that he would ensure the wellbeing of Natalya and the children.

Afraid of unrest at Pushkin's funeral, the tsar ordered a quiet ceremony and burial at Pushkin's estate in the country. D'Anthès was put on trial and, duelling being a capital office in Russia, was condemned to death, but no one expected the sentence to be carried out. He was expelled from Russia, and later became a senator in France. He lived to the age of eighty-three. Heeckeren was reinstated into the Dutch diplomatic service and continued a successful career.

A Fading Fashion

If the killing of Pushkin represents the culmination of duels of honour, it was not the end of the duel. The gates of hell remained open yet a while. There were later duels in Russia and elsewhere, the most celebrated of which took place on 15 July 1841 and ended with the death of Mikhail Lermontov at the age of twenty-six. Lermontov, who almost certainly never met his older contemporary, was regarded as Pushkin's literary heir and mourned his death in a poem which circulated in St Petersburg. It was a spontaneous if imprudent outpouring of grief and anger, and its call for divine retribution on unnamed figures in court circles whom Lermontov blamed for Pushkin's demise attracted unwelcome attention. Like Pushkin, Lermontov frequented aristocratic palaces before growing bored with the superficiality of that life and joined the military. He saw active service in Chechnya, where he was praised for his bravery, but his prickly temperament made him few friends, while his acerbic verses on powerful contemporaries and his increasing opposition to the tsar's despotic regime saw him twice sent into internal exile. He was already established as a poet when he attained greater national celebrity in 1840 with the publication of the novel, *A Hero of Our Time*, featuring Pechorin, the 'superfluous man', a figure of clearly Byronic origins. Pechorin indulges insouciantly in a number of affairs, but when asked what he has been doing, his answer is 'being bored'. Like Onegin, Pechorin is driven to fight a duel in which he kills his opponent, departing the scene with the laconic comment, *finita la commedia*. In the same year as the publication of the novel, Lermontov insulted Ernest de Barante, son of the French Ambassador, and fought a duel with him close to the spot where Pushkin had faced d'Anthès. The ambassador had attempted to negotiate a solution to the d'Anthès/ Pushkin dispute to ward off the duel, but did not obstruct his son. Lermontov was wounded and was sent again into exile.

Allowed briefly back to St Petersburg after appeals were made on his behalf, he enjoyed a burst of creative activity when, much to his dismay, he was ordered to re-join his regiment. On the way he stopped at Pyatigorsk possibly to receive medical treatment, but he became embroiled in a quarrel with Nikolai Martynov, a fellow officer resident there whom he had known since their days as army cadets. Martynov had acquired a taste for extravagant Circassian dress, and invariably wore a large dagger in his belt. The two men saw each other frequently during Lermontov's sojourn in the town, and the two entered into an exchange of epigrams which were either sardonic or robustly jocular. Relations were ruptured at a party at which Lermontov delivered to some lady a jibe about the need to beware 'a man from the mountains with a large dagger'. Martynov took this remark amiss, although Lermontov attempted to laugh it off, but to no avail. The duel took place and Lermontov died on the spot.

1 Alexander Pushkin, *Eugene Onegin*. There are seemingly eight translations of this poem in English, including the much-debated, literal version done by Vladimir Nabokov. I have used the translation by James E Falen, Oxford: Oxford World's Classics, first edition, 1995.
2 Alexander Pushkin, translated by Alan Myers, *The Queen of Spades and Other Stories*, Oxford: Oxford University Press, 1997.
3 Iliam Hazlitt, *The Pleasure of Hating*, London: Penguin, 2004, p. 106.
4 Mario Praz, *The Romantic Agony*, Oxford: Oxford Paperbacks, 1970.
5 Edmund Wilson, 'The Strange Case of Pushkin and Nabokov', *New York Review of Books*, 15 July 1965.
6 Serena Vitale, translated by Ann Goldstein and Jon Rothschild, *Pushkin's Button*, London: Fourth Estate, 1999, pp. 266-72.
7 Elaine Feinstein, *Pushkin: A Biography*, London: Phoenix, 1999, pp.36&39.

AFTERWORD

THE SNOWS OF YESTERYEAR

'When a song belongs to ploughing,' writes Eric Hobsbawm, 'it cannot be sung when men do not plough; if it is sung, it ceases to be a folksong and becomes something else.'[1] This shrewd judgment is applicable not only to the popular, oral culture of craftsmen, the beat of whose songs once kept time to the rhythms of their work and whose lyrics expressed their frustrations and hopes, but also to the hegemonic culture of the upper classes. Cultural turns of mind sometimes survived the lifestyle which gave rise to them but at others they vanished, leaving as their only trace terms now divorced from the activities and ways of thought which once produced them. What is honour today? What is the meaning of duel?

There is always some mystery over the factors and timing of the appearance, acceptance and final disappearance of cultural standards. The air of Europe is heavy with the smell of decaying cultures, beliefs, ideologies, philosophies and creeds which once shaped life and were dogmatically impervious to all challenge. Some linger in mutilated form, but others evaporate. *Mais où sont les neiges d'antan?* (But where are the snows of yesteryear?), in François Villon's melancholy query. Medieval debates on angels balancing on pins, Rosicrucian quests for esoteric truths, quasi-Biblical disputes on the timing of the Flood, Catholic-Protestant wars over religious hegemony, royalist apologias of the divine right of kings, Jacobite questions over rights of succession were never, could never be, settled and are now of interest only to the archaeologist or the pure historian, viewed as eccentric curios of other less enlightened days. Is the code of honour and sword now another of this list? Is it possible to say when the last duel was fought? What remains of the old jargon and ritual?

Yet the past is never quite dead. The philosopher Jacques Derrida coined the term 'hauntology' to denote occasions where notions from other times are summoned up to haunt, or dignify, actions in the present. A clear, if ignoble, example was provided by Rudy Giuliani, ex-Attorney General of the United States, ex-Mayor of New York and Donald Trump's personal lawyer, in Washington on 6 January 2021. In the course of a speech to a crowd which had assembled to support Trump's claim that the 2020 election had been rigged, Giuliani called on his listeners to engage in 'trial by combat'.[2] What made that term come to his mind? It may have been plucked from some dark recess of his memory, and he would not care if it ran counter to any reliable notion of honour or of the rules of chivalry. The words may have had little meaning for the excited mob but they heard 'combat' and the speech was followed by the invasion of the Capitol. In the ensuing tumult, offices were ransacked, property thieved and five people lost their lives. There were no knights at hand to ensure fairness. Trial by combat was never anarchy, and the historical grandeur of Giuliani's words was at odds with the contemporary brutality of the unfolding riot.

Other incidents involving noted figures are grotesque or risible, or simply at odds with time and culture. In 1839, at the height of the Victorian Gothic revival, the Earl of Eglinton organized on his estate in Ayrshire a complete medieval tournament with knights in armour and jousts in lists competing for the hand of a Queen of Beauty, but it descended into farce when the rain poured mercilessly down on the ardent competitors.[3] In 1862 Turgenev challenged Tolstoy but Tolstoy apologized for the offence he had given.[4] Ernest Hemingway was challenged to a duel in Cuba in 1954, but declined.[5] James Joyce jeered at a fellow student, George Clancy, who was struggling to construe a passage from French, causing Clancy to challenge Joyce to a duel, which might have occurred had not

Professor Edouard Cedric intervened to calm tempers.[6] In one of his early satirical pieces, Dario Fo, the Italian actor-author and Nobel Prize winner, showed some disrespect to the Italian Army. To his surprise, a spluttering officer contacted him with a challenge. Dario accepted, provided that the duel was fought in accordance with ancient Korean traditions, which ended with the ceremonial sodomizing of the defeated party by the victor. No one checked works of Korean history to verify this tall tale, but the challenger fell silent.[7]

There have been a certain number of duels in the twentieth century, but they are historical throwbacks, out of time and out of place, like colonial-era churches in downtown Manhattan. An element of harlequinade was inevitably attached to such encounters which may have used traditional and even ritual language. In August 1926, two Italian writers, the poet Giuseppe Ungaretti and the novelist and playwright Massimo Bontempelli, fought a duel in the garden of the house belonging to Luigi Pirandello. Ungaretti had a low view of Bontempelli and attacked him mercilessly in print, provoking the latter to slap him in public in a Roman café frequented by the literary set. As in the days of yore, a challenge was issued and the two engaged with swords, until Ungaretti received an injury to his arm which was slight but sufficient to satisfy honour. When word got out, the two men were treated with scorn and ridicule.

The last Italian duel, also with swords, occurred in 1952 in Palermo between two Sicilian aristocrats, Baron Arcangelo Salvatore Alù and Raimondo Lanza di Trabia, playboy, soldier, sportsman and president of Palermo Football Club. When Lanza resigned from that office, Alù announced his availability, but was prevented from casting his vote by Lanza who mendaciously told him his son had been injured in an accident. Alù rushed off, thus unable to be present for the vote, and when he discovered the deceit he decided not to raise a legal action but to challenge Lanza to a duel with sabres. The event was covered in the colour supplement of the *Domenica del Corriere*, with a sketch of the two facing each other, sword in hand. They met in the garden of an aristocratic villa, the one stripped to the waist and the other wearing a vest, surrounded by conventionally attired seconds and spectators. Reports indicate that there were thirty-three exchanges until Alù was wounded in the shoulder. First blood had been drawn, so the seconds ordered an end to hostilities and the two men shook hands. This was not the *Sicilia mafiosa* of modern times, but the more ancient aristocratic Sicily portrayed by Tomasi di Lampedusa in *The Leopard*. The scene could have unfolded anywhere in Europe in the seventeenth or eighteenth centuries, but the reporter was surely right to suggest that in 1952 such an event was more of a carnival show.[8]

It was not the last such in Europe. That dubious honour must go to Gaston Defferre, French socialist politician and long-serving Mayor of Marseille, who on 20 April 1967 used decidedly unparliamentary language in the National Assembly in Paris to an opponent, René Ribière. The words, *taisez-vous, abruti!*, can be translated as 'Shut up, moron!' Ribière was not mollified by the president's rebuke to Defferre and issued the classical challenge, which was accepted. Swords were the agreed weapon, and the two met the next day on the outskirts

Gaston Defferre duels with René Ribière, 21 April 1967 (Rare Historical Photos)

of Paris, with Jean de Lipkowski, who was then serving as Secretary of State for Foreign Affairs, as officiating officer. It may be indicative of the underlying frivolity of the event that Ribière was due to be married the following day, but photographs show the two in shirt sleeves, with outstretched swords and solemn expressions, clashing in the style of Dumas' musketeers. Ribière even has his free hand held neatly behind his back. He suffered the first wound but insisted that the fight continue, which it did until Defferre drew second blood, ending the show. Ribière was patched up and enabled to make it to the church on time. The affair was widely reported but the state prosecutor brought no charges.

There was one supposed attempt at a challenge in the twenty-first century which is worth recording. In the polemical exchanges which preceded the Second Gulf War, Iraq's vice president, Taha Yassin Ramadan, gave an interview broadcast by CNN challenging President George W. Bush to a personal duel with Saddam Hussein. Ramadan did not recall the many historical precedents of medieval European monarchs, but did suggest that in this way 'we would be saving both the American and Iraqi people'. He explained the proposal. 'Let the American president and a selected group with him face a selected group of us and we choose a neutral land, and let Kofi Annan be a supervisor and both groups should use the same weapon.' The White House replied that this was an 'irresponsible statement' that did not merit a 'serious reply'.[9]

A British court was obliged to hear a bizarre request. *The Times* reported that a judge had

> rejected a 60-year-old man's attempt to invoke the ancient right to trial by combat, rather than pay a £25 fine for a minor motoring offence. Leon Humphreys remained adamant yesterday that his right to fight a champion nominated by the Driver and Vehicle Licensing Agency (DVLA) was still valid under European human rights legislation. He said it would have been a "reasonable" way to settle the matter. Magistrates sitting at Bury

St Edmunds on Friday had disagreed and instead of accepting his offer to take on a clerk from Swansea with "samurai swords, Gurkha knives or heavy hammers", fined him £200 with £100 costs.[10]

It was an unnoticed irony that the town where the court sat was Bury St Edmunds where centuries previously a famous trial by combat, mentioned in an earlier chapter, took place.

It is an even greater curiosity that trial by combat has never been officially removed from the tenets of English Common Law which form part of the United States' legal inheritance from colonial days. In 2016, it was reported that one Richard A. Luthman demanded his 'common law right to Trial by Combat against the Plaintiffs and their counsel'.[11] Mr Luthman noted that 'in 1774, as part of the legislative response to the Boston Tea Party, Parliament considered a Bill which would have abolished appeals of murder and trials by battle in the American colonies. It was successfully opposed by a Member of Parliament John Dunning, who called the appeal of murder "that great pillar of our constitution".' Mr Luthman concluded by arguing that the Ninth Amendment preserved the right to trial by combat as one of the rights 'retained by the people'. Justice Philip Minardo of the New York Supreme Court, while agreeing with the plaintiff on the point of historical fact that trial by combat had never been repealed in the US, still refused the request for a duel.

But that was not the last plea made on the question.[12] In a court in Harlan, Iowa, David Ostrom also appealed for the right to trial by combat, and referred to the judge's *obiter dicta* in the 2016 case as a valid precedent. Embroiled in a divorce case with his wife Brigitte, Mr Ostrom had grown exasperated by the law's delays and by legal vexations which had, he claimed, 'destroyed him legally'. He cast the blame on the lawyer Matthew Hudson, and filed documents challenging either Brigitte or her lawyer as her champion to meet him 'on the field of battle', where he would 'rend their souls from their corporal bodies'. In his reply, Hudson eschewed legal jargon but took fastidious issue with the use of the term 'corporal', arguing that the correct term was 'corporeal'. He also wondered whether the possible death of one party should in modern law outweigh the property tax and custody issues which were at the heart of the dispute. The judge cited irregularities with both motions and declined to rule on either, although he did suggest that Ostrom undergo a sanity test. The issue thus remains unresolved in American law, and perhaps two modern American citizens will one day be permitted to enter the lists, clothed in armour, armed with lances or swords, and call on God to resolve their dispute in truth and justice. Maybe the Giuliani case will finally clarify the legal status of trial of combat in American law.

Whatever attitude is adopted, the plain fact is that the codes of honour and the practice of duelling have vanished, like Villon's snows, and are found only in pitifully debased form as 'something else', principally as a mere metaphor. The word duel recurs in the most varied of contexts - duelling banjos, Chelsea-Arsenal duel, Hitler-Stalin duel, duel between the Beatles and the Rolling Stones, the long duel between Coca-Cola and Pepsi, cat and mouse duel and many more. Gauntlets are now thrown between competing commercial firms more frequently than they ever were between knights at arms.

The decline of respect for honour with the consequent end of duelling was due to change in habits of mind, and perhaps to nothing more serious than fashion, however injurious that term is to human self-respect. The notion of gentlemanly honour did not survive the First World War and was ridiculed by subsequent generations who preferred a mundane form of cynicism towards all creeds. The change of attitude towards duelling itself can be measured in the very title of two works which have acquired the status of classic in this field, and which have been quoted several times in the present study. In 1836, an author who maintained a convenient anonymity by signing himself A Traveller gave his work the title *The Art of Duelling*. The term 'Art' did not denote an aesthetic category, and the work viewed duelling as a craft, regrettable but necessary, to be practised in accordance with rules which could be learned. Some three decades later, in a sober work by Andrew Steinmetz, *The Romance of Duelling in*

All Times and Countries (1868), the opening lines read: 'The Age of duelling, like that of chivalry, may be said to be past for ever in England; but there is a lingering romance about the subject, which will always invest it with interest.' The age of duelling was in fact dying but not yet dead, but the practice was beginning to acquire that romance or glamour, however monstrous, which time confers on medieval castles or even dungeons. The heroic-romantic tone of the novels of Alexandre Dumas, Walter Scott or Robert Louis Stevenson attest to the new culture.

Duels now also serve the tourist industry. There are several commemorative monuments celebrating figures who fought and died in duels, or which mark places where duels were fought. One of the most arresting is the plaque, already mentioned, erected in Campo S. Stefano in Venice in honour of Felice Cavallotti (1842-98) who fought in many duels and was finally killed by an opponent. Near the town of Kirkcaldy in Fife some citizens felt it necessary to erect a memorial tablet with the words, 'Near this site, the last duel in Scotland was fought on 23rd August, 1826.' On that date David Landale, a businessman, killed George Morgan, a bank manager. The monument stands in a windswept spot in the countryside and suffered the ravages of time, but the local authority felt it worthwhile to replace it.[13] There is a plaque in Weehawken in New Jersey, where Hamilton father and son fought and died, but none at such other established sites such as Hyde Park, the Bois de Boulogne or St Stephen's Green in Dublin, where many duels were fought. The most famous of all such monuments carries an outright lie. The statue of Louis XIV outside the palace of Versailles, which he built, carries on its base a list of his achievements, one of which was to suppress duelling. The Sun King had indeed issued his *Edit du Roy portant règlement général sur les duels* in 1679 to make made duelling a crime punishable by death for principals and seconds, but duelling in France outlived the man who claimed to have abolished it.

The changing spirit which did lead to the ending of duelling is best expressed by Alexander Herzen (1812-70), an acquaintance of Lermontov from their days at Moscow

University. Herzen's revolutionary socialism, his bitter hatred
of serfdom and of the absolutist rule of the tsar meant that
he spent much of his life either in confinement inside
Russia or, after 1847, in exile abroad, mainly in London. It is
worth noting that in his student days Herzen too embraced
Romanticism, although he quickly abandoned that outlook for
the more rigorous philosophy of Hegel and later Proudhon. He
married Natalya Zakharina in 1838 and was distraught when
he discovered she was having an affair with Georg Herwegh,
a German poet of great popularity in his own lifetime and a
revolutionary of the same kidney as Herzen. The affair between
the couple lasted from 1849 until Natalya's death in 1852. In
1851, Herwegh challenged Herzen to a duel, but he declined,
explaining his reasoning in his autobiographical *My Past and
Thoughts*:

> It is not worthwhile to try to prove the absurdity of the
> duel: no one tries to justify it theoretically except a few
> bullies and fencing-masters; but a practice everyone
> submits to in order to prove - the devil knows to whom
> - his courage.
> The worst thing about the duel is that it justifies any
> blackguard either by giving him an honourable death,
> or by making him an honourable man-killer... It is an
> invitation belonging to that pugnacious social circle on
> whose hands the blood is still so far from being dry that
> the wearing of deadly weapons is looked on as a sign of
> nobility and practice in the art of killing as an official
> duty.
> While the world is governed by military men,
> duelling will not be abolished... How many men have
> passed with proud and triumphant faces through all
> the misfortunes of life, prison and poverty, sacrifice
> and toil, inquisitions and I do not know what and have
> been lopped off by some impudent challenge from some
> mischievous scoundrel?[14]

And how many other men who did not experience prison or poverty, sacrifice or toil, who did not attain fame but who lived their lives in the modest or vainglorious pursuit of happiness that the American Declaration of Independence proposes as the best humankind can hope for, were 'lopped off' by malice or mischief, fatuousness or inanity, or in deference to that will o' the wisp called honour?

1 Eric Hobsbawm, *The Age of Revolution: Europe 1789-1848*, London: Abacus, 1988, p. 330.
2 *The Times*, 7 January 2021.
3 Ian Anstruther. *The Knight and the Umbrella: an Account of the Eglinton Tournament 1839*, Gloucester: Alan Sutton, 1986.
4 Letter by Turgenev to Afanasy Fet, 7 January 1862.
5 Arthur Krystal, 'En Garde!', *The New Yorker*, 9 May 2007.
6 Richard Ellmann, *James Joyce*, Oxford: Oxford University Press, 1959, p. 62.
7 Erminia Artese (interviewer), *Dario Fo parla di Dario Fo*, Cosenza: Lerici, 1977, p. 67.
8 Gabriello Montemagno, 'Il Tempo dei Duelli', in *La Repubblica*, 20 July 2011. See also, Marcello Sorgi, *Il grande dandy: vita spericolata di Raimondo Lanza di Trabia*, Milan: Rizzoli, 2011.
9 CNN.com/World, 3 October 2002. Accessed at http://archives,cnn.com/2002/World/meast/10/03/iraq.bush.duel/
10 *Daily Telegraph*, 16 December 2002.
11 *The Washington Post*, 6 August 2015.
12 *The Times*, 16 January 2020.
13 James Landale, *Duel: A True Story of Death and Honour*, Edinburgh: Canongate, 2005, p. 136.
14 Alexander Herzen, *My Past and Thoughts*, Berkeley CA: University of California Press, 1982, vol. II, p. 904. I am grateful to Neal Ascherson for bringing this passage to my attention.

GLOSSARY OF DUELLING TERMINOLOGY

Blaze	Irish colloquial synonym of duelling.
Brawl	A fight between members of the lower orders: spontaneous, lacking all decorum, not regulated or disciplined by any code of conduct or *politesse*; quite unrelated to the duel of honour between gentlemen.
Call out	To respond to an insult, usually by issuing a challenge.
Cartel	The missive used to deliver a challenge; from the Italian *cartello*, a little note; the wording to be polite and pithy, not scornful or expansive.
Challenge	An invitation issued by an offended party to the offender calling on him to settle the dispute and/or erase the offence by recourse to arms.
Choice of Weapons	Privilege of challenged party.
Clonmel	Town in County Tipperary, Ireland; meeting place in 1777 of a group of gentlemen who drew up the *code duello*, or Clonmel Code, intended as guide for duelling practice in Ireland but recognised throughout the English-speaking world as setting the basic standards and protocols.
Cowardice	The ultimate slur on the character of a gentleman: the deepest inner fear of gentlemen; 'for all men would be cowards, if they durst.' (Earl of Rochester, *A Satyr against Reason and Mankind*)

Death	Surprisingly rare in duelling; statistics differ but rarely higher than 25 per cent and usually much lower.
Delope	To fire in the air; sometimes agreed in advance by both parties, but a practice frowned on by the Clonmel Code; cause of fatal misunderstandings, perhaps in the Hamilton-Burr duel, or in the fictional case of Barry Lyndon, who deloped but suffered injury which led to amputation of one leg.
Difficulty	Understatement indicating a dilemma, or disagreement which has not quite reached the stage of a challenge; euphemism for an offence expected to lead to a duel; more commonly used in the US, e. g. by George Washington in reference to the preliminaries of the Hamilton- Burr duel.
Distance	No fixed rule over appropriate distance between duellists, decision to be made by agreement between seconds; very rarely paced out from back to back position.
Duel	Single combat between two opponents, both gentlemen of same or similar rank; fought with identical weapons; in response to a real or imaginary offence; conducted in accordance with a mutually accepted complex or code of regulations, rituals and protocols; 'The last reasoning of men'. (A Gentleman, *The British Code of Duel*) 'A formal preliminary to a reconciliation between two enemies. Great skill is necessary to its satisfactory observance; if awkwardly performed the most unexpected and deplorable consequences sometimes ensue. A long time ago a man lost his life

in a duel.' (Ambrose Bierce, *The Devil's Dictionary*)
'Thunder against it. Not a proof of courage. Prestige of the man who has had a duel.' (Gustave Flaubert, *Dictionary of Received Ideas*)
'Ridiculed by certain smart people, (but) in reality one of the most dangerous institutions of our day. Since it is always fought in the open air, the combatants are nearly sure to catch cold.' (Mark Twain, *A Tramp Abroad*)

Encounter	Euphemism for duel.
Field of honour	Place where duel is enacted; preferred location some way from city centre but not so far as to make access difficult.
Fire-eater	Irish term for enthusiast for code of honour, with multiple duels to his credit; flourished in late eighteenth century
First blood	Agreement to end duel with first wound, not fight to the death.
Friend	Alternative term for a second.
Friendship	Fragile condition among men, easily shattered but promptly formed or restored after an exchange of fire.
Gauntlet	Throwing down of; legendary medieval gesture signifying challenge.
Gentleman	In rank less than a nobleman, but above proletarian; holder of honour; one entitled to dismiss with contempt challenge from person of lower status; later a bourgeois.
Honour	The prestige of rank; a variably defined collection of virtues and qualities; self-esteem and public reputation; the hallmark

of a gentleman, prized above life itself, especially in fiction.

Horsewhipping Punishment inflicted by a gentleman on a person whose lowly rank excludes him from those worthy of receiving a gentlemanly challenge.

Interview Euphemism for duel.

Leeching Stepping up to the point from which it is permissible to fire, the distance between duellists having been agreed beforehand between the seconds.

Lie Give the lie to: offence undermining honour and leading inevitably to challenge and duel; 'perhaps the commonest cause of a gentleman challenging another to a duel.' (James Kelly, *That Damn'd Thing Called Honour*)

Meeting Euphemism for duel.

Nose Pulling or tweaking of; a means of degrading another man; a gross offence even if in response to an insult.

Posting Publicizing of offence endured; naming the party responsible for the offence in a public place, or in a news-sheet; a device employed mainly when the other party declines to accept a challenge and engage in duel.

Preparations Night before: drawing up last will and testament; final loving letters to family. State of mind; 'Declare war on all nervous apprehensions; a few friends to dinner and laugh away the evening over a bottle of port; avoid drinking to excess or food which tends to create bile.' Reading; 'one of Sir Walter's novels, if a lover of the romantic, or Byron's *Childe*

	Harold if a lover of the sublime' (*The Art of Duelling*).
Principal	The duellist, as distinct from seconds or surgeons in attendance.
Provocation	Assault on honour of whatever kind; rivalry over women; accusations of cheating; financial impropriety; seduction of female member of family; accusation of lying; etcetera as deemed appropriate by the individual gentleman.
Releager	Agreed meeting place for the duel.
Satisfaction	Redress sought for injury or offence: term originally indicating 'dissatisfaction' of one party with a situation and demand that it be rectified and he thus 'satisfied'; came to be synonym for challenge.
Second	Appointed by intending duellist from among his close associates: much sought-after honour whose final perk was possibility of incrimination for murder if one party is killed; 'requires an acquaintance with arms and a mind capable of negotiation' (*The British Code of Duel*); 'the first duty is to prevent, if possible, the affair coming to a serious issue, without compromising the honour of his friend' (Steinmetz); responsible for coordinating all arrangements with other party's second, time and place, weapons, distances between principals; loading of pistols: overseeing fairness at field.
Seduction	'The one unhappy case in which no apology whatever can be received'; however, the gentleman connected with the family of

the seduced must be '*thoroughly convinced that the fault lay with the male*' (*The British Code of Duel*); in practice, the assumption invariably was that the female of the speices was innocent and led astray by a lusty, immortal adventurer.

Signal
Normally given by dropping a handkerchief; 'the period most trying to a duellist is from the time the word "ready" is given until the handkerchief drops' (*The Art of Duelling*).

Tomb
Scene of solemn celebration of life and glory of deceased gentleman: cause of death in these circumstances unmentionable.

Victim
Term wholly inapplicable in cases of death by duelling.

SELECT BIBLIOGRAPHY

This bibliography includes only published books. References to articles in journals and newspapers or consulted online are given at the end of the chapter in which they are cited.

Classic Studies

Anon, *The British Code of Duel*, London: 1824: republished Slough: Richmond Publishing Co., 1971.

'A Traveller', *The Art of Duelling*, London: 1836: republished Slough: Richmond Publishing Co., 1971.

Bacon, Francis, 'Of Revenge', in *Essays or Councils Civil and Moral*, edited by Brian Vickers, Oxford: Oxford University Press, 1996.

Brantôme, Seigneur de, *Discours sur les duels*, Paris: Librairie des Bibliophiles, 1887.

Cauchy, Eugène, *Du duel considéré dans ses origines et dans l'état actuel des moeurs*, Paris: Charles Hingray, 1846.

Cockburn, John, *A History and Examination of Duels*, second edition, Edinburgh: 1888.

Douglas, William, *Duelling Days in the Army*, London: Ward & Downey, 1887.

Lea, Henry Charles. *The Ordeal*, parts I & II of *Superstition and Force* (1866), Philadelphia PA: University of Pennsylvania Press, 1973.

The Duel and the Oath, part III of *Superstition and Force* (1866), Philadelphia PA, University of Pennsylvania Press, 1974.

Letainturier-Fradin, Gabriel and Tavernier, Adolphe, *Le Duel à travers les âges; histoire et législation*. Paris: Marpon et Flammarion, 1892.

Millingen, J.G., *The History of Duelling*, 2 vols., London: Bentley, 1841.

Neilson, George, *Trial by Combat* (1890), Clark NJ: The Lawbook Exchange, 2009.

Sabine, Lorenzo. *Notes on Duels and Duelling*, Boston: Crosby, Nichols & Co., 1885.

Steinmetz, Andrew, *The Romance of Duelling in All Times and Countries*, 2 vols., London: Chapman & Hall, 1868.

Truman, B.C., *The Field of Honour: Being a Complete and Comprehensive History of Duelling in All Countries*, New York: Fords, Howard & Hulbert, 1884.

Modern Histories

Baldick, Robert, *The Duel: a History of Duelling*, London: Spring Books, 1965.

Banks, Stephen, *A Polite Exchange of Bullets*, Woodbridge: Boydell Press, 2010.

Duels and Duelling, Oxford: Shire Library, 2012.

Informal Justice in England and Wales, 1760-1914, Woodbridge: Boydell Press, 2014.

Billacquois, François (translated by Tristan Selous), *The Duel: Its Rise and Fall in Early Modern France*, New Haven CT, Yale University Press, 1990.

Cardini, Franco, *Onore*, Bologna: Il Mulino, 2016.

Cavina, Marco, *Il sangue dell'onore*, Bari: Laterza. 2005.

Espramer, Francesco, *La biblioteca di Don Ferrante: duello e onore nella cultura del Cinquecento*, Rome: Bulzoni, 1982.

Farquhar, Michael, *A Treasury of Great American Scandals*, New York: Penguin, 2003.

Frevert, Ute, *Men of Honour: A Social and Cultural History of the Duel*, Cambridge: Polity Press, 1995.

Hobsbawm, Eric, *The Age of Revolution 1789-1848*, London, Abacus, 1988.

Holland, Barbara, *Gentlemen's Blood: A History of Dueling from Swords at Dawn to Pistols at Dark*, New York: Bloomsbury, 2003.

Jacoby, Susan, *Wild Justice: The Evolution of Revenge*, London: Collins, 1985.

Kelly, James, *That Damn'd Thing Called Honour: Duelling in Ireland 1570-1860*, Cork: Cork University Press, 1995.

SELECT BIBLIOGRAPHY

Kiernan, Victor G., *The Duel in European History: Honour and the Reign of the Aristocracy*, Oxford: Oxford University Press, 1988.

Leigh, John. *Touché!: The Duel in Literature*, Cambridge MA: Harvard University Press, 2015.

Monorchio, Giuseppe, *Lo specchio del cavaliere*, Ottawa: Biblioteca di Quaderni d'Italianistica, 1998.

Norris, John, *Pistols at Dawn: A History of Duelling*, Cheltenham, The History Press, 2009.

Peltonen, Markku, *The Duel in Early Modern England: Civility, Politeness and Honour*, Cambridge: Cambridge University Press, 2003.

Narrative and Theatre

This section contains only works discussed or mentioned in the text.

Chekhov, Anton. *The Duel* (translated by Ronald Wilks), London: Penguin, 1984.

Chesterton, G.K., *The Sins of Prince Saradine*, in *The Innocence of Father Brown*, London: Penguin, 2013.
The Duel of Dr Hirsch, in *The Wisdom of Father Brown*, London: Penguin, 2012.
The Man Who Was Thursday, A Nightmare, London: House of Stratus, 2012.

Conrad, Joseph, *The Duel*, in *The Complete Short Fiction of Joseph Conrad*, London: Pickering & Chatto, 1993.

Edgeworth, Maria, *Belinda*, London: J. Johnson, 1810.

Fontane, Theodore, *Effi Briest* (translated by Douglas Parmée), London: Penguin, 1967.

Lermontov, Mikhail, *A Hero of Our Time* (translated by Martin Parker and Neil Cornwell), London: Alma Classics, 2009.

Miller, Arthur, *A View from the Bridge*, London: Penguin, 1961.

Ouida, *Under Two Flags* (1867), Oxford: Oxford University Press, 1995.

Pirandello, Luigi, *Il turno*, Rome: Newton Compton, 1993.
Ma non è una cosa seria (It's Not Serious) (play 1910)
The Rules of the Game (play, 1912)

Pushkin, Alexander, *Eugene Onegin* (translated by James E. Fallon), Oxford: Oxford University Press, 1990.

The Shot, in *The Queen of Spades and Other Stories* (translated by Alan Myers), Oxford: Oxford University Press, 1997.

Richardson, Samuel, *Clarissa, or The History of a Young Lady* (1748), London: Penguin, 1992.

Sciascia, Leonardo, *The Day of the Owl*, London: Granta Books, 2001.

Smollet, Tobias, *Humphry Clinker* (1771), London: Penguin, 1967.

Stevenson, Robert Louis, *The Master of Ballantrae* (1889), London: Heinemann, Tusitala edition 1924.

Scott, Walter, *Tales of a Grandfather, Being Stories Taken from Scottish History*, 3 vols., Glasgow: Gowans & Gray, 1923.

Thackeray, William M., *The Luck of Barry Lyndon* (1844), London: Penguin, 1973.

The History of Henry Esmond Esq (1852), Oxford: Oxford University Press, 1996.

Verga, Giovanni, *Cavalleria rusticana*, (1880), translated by G.H. MacMillan, London: Penguin, 1997.

Waugh, Evelyn, *Sword of Honour* (1952-61), 3 vols., London: Penguin, 1999.

Introduction

Galante Garrone, Alessandro, *Felice Cavallotti*, Turin: UTET, 1976.

Chapter 1

Casanova, Giacomo. *Il duello* (1780), Genoa: ECIG, 1991.

The Duel (translated by J.G. Nichols, with Foreword by Tim Parks), London: Hesperus Press, 1990.

Histoire de ma vie, Paris: Librairie Plon, 1961.

The History of My Life (edited by Peter Washington), London: Everyman's Library, 1966.

Baccolo, Luigi, *Vita di Casanova*, Milan: Rusconi, 1994.

Childs, J. Rives, *Casanova, A New Perspective*, London: Constable, 1989.

Flem, Lydia (translated by Catherine Temerson), *Casanova or the Art of Happiness*, London: Allen Lane, 1998.

Masters, John, *Casanova*, London: Michael Joseph, 1969.

Chapter 2

Chrétien de Troyes, *Yvain, the Knight with the Lion*, in *Arthurian Romances* (translated by W.W. Comfort), London: Everyman's Library, 1965.

Lancelot, in *Arthurian Romances* (Ibid)

Crouch, David, *Tournament*, London: Hambledon and London, 2003.

Hope Moncrieff, A.R., *Romance and Legend of Chivalry*, London: The Mystic Press, 1987.

Huizinga, Johan, *The Waning of the Middle Ages*, London: Penguin, 1968.

Jager, Eric, *The Last Duel: A True Story of Trial by Combat in Medieval France*, London: Century, 2005.

John of Salisbury (edited by Cary J. Nederman), *Policratus*, Cambridge: Cambridge University Press, 1990.

Llull, Ramon (edited by Marina Gustà), *Llibre de l'orde de cavalleria*, Barcelona: Edicions 62, 1980.

Saul, Nigel (ed.), *Age of Chivalry: Art and Society in Late Medieval England*, London: Brockhampton Press, 1995.

The Song of Roland (translated by C.K. Scott Moncrieff), London: Chapman & Hall, 1919.

Tristan and Iseult (translated by Hilaire Belloc (1913)), London: George Allen & Unwin, 1961.

Chapter 3

Ariosto, Lodovico (translated by Barbara Reynolds), *Orlando Furioso*, London: Penguin, 1975.

Boiardo, Matteo Maria. *Orlando Innamorato* (translated by Charles Stanley Ross as *Orlando in Love*), Anderson SC: Parlor Press, 2004.

Burckhardt, Jacob, *The Civilization of the Renaissance in Italy* (1860), London: New English Library, 1960.

Castiglione, Baldassare (translated by George Bull), *The Book of the Courtier*, London: Penguin, 1967.

Della Casa, Giovanni (translated by R.S. Coffin), *Galateo*, London: Penguin, 1958.

Durridge, Robert, *The Figure of the Poet in Renaissance Italy*, Cambridge MA: Harvard University Press, 1965.

Frugoni, Chiara, *Inventions of the Middle Ages*, London: The Folio Society, 2007.

Fubini, Riccardo, *L'umanesimo italiano e i suoi storici*, Milan: Franco Angeli, 2001.

Garin, Eugenio, *Italian Humanism*, Westport CT: Greenwood Press, 1975.

Jardine, Lisa, *Worldly Goods: A New History of the Renaissance*, London: Macmillan, 1996.

Tasso, Torquato, *Gerusalemme Liberata* (translated by Anthony Esolen as *Jerusalem Delivered*), Baltimore MD: Johns Hopkins University Press, 2000.

Wade Labarge, Margaret, *Medieval Travellers: The Rich and the Restless*, London: Hamish Hamilton, 1982.

Chapter 4

Renaissance Treatises

Alciati, *De Singulari Certamine* (with additional section by Mariano Sozzini), Venice: 1544.

Ashley, Robert, *Of Honour* (edited by Virgil B. Heltzel), San Marino CA: The Huntington Library, 1947.

Gessi, Berlingero, *La Spada di Honore*, 1671.

Lo Scettro Pacifico, 1676.

Muzio, Girolamo, *Il duello*, Venice: 1550.

Possevino, Giovanni, *Dialogo dell'Honore*, Venice: 1565.

Romei, Annibale. *Discorsi del Conte Romei, divisi in Cinque Giornate*, Venice: 1585.

Saviolo, Vincentio (edited by Jared Kirby), *A Gentleman's Guide to Duelling*, London: Frontline Books, 2013 (contains edited version of *His Practise, In two Bookes. The first intreating of the use of the Rapier and Dagger. The Second of Honor and Honorable Quarrel*, London: 1595.)

Studies

Benedict, Ruth, *The Chrysanthemum and the Sword*, Boston MA: Houghton and Mifflin, 1946.

Burke, Peter, *Culture and Society in Renaissance Italy*, New York: Scribner, 1972.

The European Renaissance: Centre and Peripheries, 1420-1540, Oxford: Wiley-Blackwell, 1998.

Dodds, E.R., *The Greeks and the Irrational*, Berkeley CA: University of California Press, 1951.

Erickson, Carolly, *The First Elizabeth*, London: Macmillan, 1983.

Goodman, Ruth, *How To Behave Badly in Renaissance Britain*, London: Michael O'Mara Books, 2018.

Shapiro, James, *1599: A Year in the Life of William Shakespeare*, London: HarperCollins, 2006.

Chapter 5

Bacon, Francis, *Essays*, London: The Folio Society, 2002.

Buchan, James, *John Law: Scottish Adventurer of the Eighteenth Century*, London: MacLehose Press, 2018.

Chamberlain, John, *The Letters of John Chamberlain*, edited by E.N. McClure, Philadelphia PA: American Philosophical Society, 1939.

Fraser, Antonia, *King James*, London, Book Club Associates. 1974.

Glesson, Janet, *Millionaire: The Philanderer, Gambler and Duelist Who Invented Modern Finance*, New York: Simon & Schuster, 2016.

Pepys, Samuel, *The Diary of Samuel Pepys, a new and complete transcription*, edited by Robert Latham and William Mathews, 11 vols., London: Bell & Hyman, 1977.

Jardine, Lisa & Stewart, Alan, *Hostage to Fortune*, London: Victor Gollancz, 1998.

Stone, Lawrence, *The Crisis of the Aristocracy*, Oxford: Oxford University Press, 1965.

Chapter 6

Beccaria, Cesare (translated by Richard Davies), *On Crime and Punishments*, Cambridge: Cambridge University Press, 1995.

Bentham, Jeremy, *An Introduction to the Principles of Morals and Legislation* (1780), edited by J.H. Burns and H.L.A. Hart), Oxford: Clarendon Press, 1999.

Boswell, James, *The Life of Samuel Johnson*, London: Everyman's Library, 2000.

The Journal of a Tour to the Western Isles of Scotland, London: Everyman's Library, 2002.

Buchan, James, *Adam Smith and the Pursuit of Perfect Liberty*, London: Profile Books, 2006.

Paley, William, *The Principles of Moral and Political Philosophy*, London: 1785,

Smith, Adam, *The Theory of Moral Sentiments* (1750), New York: MetaLibri, 2005.

Smollett, Tobias. *Travels through France and Italy* (1766), Oxford, Oxford World's Classics, 1999.

Swift, Jonathan. *The Journal to Stella* (edited by George A. Aitken), London, Methuen, 1901.

Chapter 7

Byron, Lord George (edited by Leslie A Marchand), *Selected Letters & Journals*, London: Pimlico, 1993.

O'Toole, Fintan, *A Traitor's Kiss: The Life of Richard Brinsley Sheridan*, London: Granta Books, 1998.

Stater, Victor *High Life Low Morals: The Duel That Shook Stuart Society*, London: John Murray, 1999.

White, T.H., *The Age of Scandal*, London: Penguin, 1966.

Chapter 8

Anon, *The Great Duellist: a Sketch of the Duelling Practices of the Hon Henry Clay*, Boston MA: J. Leavitt & Alden, 1841.

Freeman, Joanne B., *Affairs of Honour*, New Haven CT, Yale University Press, 2002.

Martineau, Harriet, *Society in America*, 3 vols., London: Saunders & Otley, 1837; reprinted by Cambridge University Press, 2009.

Parton, James, *Life of Andrew Jackson*, New York: Mason Brothers, 1860.

Seitz, Don C., *Famous American Duels*, New York: Thomas Y Crowell Company, 1929.

Stevens, William Oliver, *Pistols at Ten Paces*, Boston MA: Houghton Mifflin Co., 1940.

Truman, Major Ben C,. *The Field of Honour* (1884); the sections relating to America edited by Steven Randolph Wood as *Duelling in America*, San Diego CA: Joseph Tabler Books, 1992.

Williams, Jack K., *Dueling in the Old South: Vignettes of Social History*, College Station TX: Texas A&M University Press, 1980.

Wyatt-Brown, Bertram, *The Shaping of the Old South*, Chapel Hill NC: University of North Carolina Press, 2001.

Young, Alexander, *Chronicles of the Pilgrim Fathers,* New York, Cosimo Classics, 2005.

Chapter 9

Adams, John Quincy, *Diaries 1799-1821*, edited by David Waldstreicher, New York: Library of America, 2019.

Mitchell, Broadus, *Alexander Hamilton*, New York: Macmillan, 1962.

Chernow, Ron, *Alexander Hamilton*, New York: Penguin Press, 2004.

Ellis, Joseph J., *Founding Brothers: The Revolutionary Generation*, New York: Random House, 2000.

Fleming, Thomas, *Duel: Alexander Hamilton and Aaron Burr, and the Future of America*, New York: Basic Books, 2018.

Rogow, Arnold A., *A Fatal Friendship, Alexander Hamilton and Aaron Burr*, New York: Hill and Wang, 1998.

Sylla, Richard, *Hamilton: The Illustrated Biography*, New York: Sterling, 2016.

Vidal, Gore, *Burr*, London: Abacus, 1973.

Chapter 10

Anon, *A Chapter on Duelling by One of those People Called Christians*, 2nd edition, London: James Fraser, 1840.

The Trial of James Thomas Earl of Cardigan for Felony, Published by Order of the House of Peers, London: William Brodie Gurney, 1841.

The Poetical Works of Sir Alexander Boswell, Glasgow: Maurice Ogle & Company, 1871.

Chalmers, John, *Duel Personalities: James Stuart versus Sir Alexander Boswell*, Edinburgh: Newbattle Publishing, 2014.

Geoghegan, Patrick M., *King Dan: The Rise of Daniel O'Connell 1775-1847*, Dublin: Gill and Macmillan, 2008.

Harvey Wood, Harriet, *Lockhart of the Quarterly*, Edinburgh: Sciennes Press, 2018.

Hunt, Giles, *The Duel: Castlereagh, Canning and Deadly Cabinet Rivalry*, London: I.B. Tauris, 2008

McAllam, D., *Friend of Peace*, Edinburgh: 1816.

Moss, Michael, *The Duel between Sir Alexander Boswell and James Stuart*, Newcastle upon Tyne: Cambridge Scholars, 2019.

Woodham-Smith, Cecil, *The Reason Why*, London: Constable & Co, 1953.

Chapter 11

Attard, Joseph, *The Knights of Malta*, Malta: PEG, 1993.

Barrington, Sir Jonah, *Recollections and Sketches*, London: Henry Colburn, 1827.

Dumas, F. Ribadeau, *Cagliostro*, London: George Allen and Unwin, 1967.

McCallan, Iain, *The Seven Ordeals of Count Cagliostro*, London: Century, 2003.

The Correspondence of William I & Bismarck: With Other Letters from and to Prince Bismarck, vol. 2, London, F.A. Stokes & Co, 1903.

Select Bibliography

Chapter 12

Bergin, Joseph, *The Rise of Richelieu*, Manchester: Manchester University Press, 1997.

Dauthville, Anne-France, *Julie, chevalier de Maupin*, Paris: J-C Lattès, 1995.

Gautier, Théophile, *Mademoiselle de Maupin* (translated by Helen Constantine), London: Penguin, 2005.

Grant, Michael *Gladiators*, London: Pelican, 1971.

Hattersley, Roy. *Blood & Fire: The Story of William and Catherine Booth*, London: Little, Brown, 1999.

Madame de Villedieu, translated by Donna Kuizenga, *Memoirs of the Life of Henriette-Sylvie de Molière*, Chicago IL: University of Chicago Press, 2004.

Williams, Hugh N., *The Fascinating Duc de Richelieu* (1910), West Bloomfield MI, Franklin Classics, 2018.

Chapter 13

Camilleri, Andrea, *Biografia del figlio cambiato*, Milan: Rizzoli, 2000.

Jackson, Holbrook, *The Eighteen Nineties: A Review of Art and Ideas at the Close of the Nineteenth Century*, London: Penguin, 1950.

Ruggiero, Vincenzo, *Crime in Literature: Sociology of Deviance and Fiction*, London: Verso, 2003.

Chapter 14

Binyon, T.J., *Pushkin, A Biography*, London: HarperCollins, 2002.

Feinstein, Elaine, *Pushkin: A Biography*, London, Phoenix, 1999.

Kelly, James, *Lermontov: Tragedy in the Caucasus*, London: Robin Clark, 1983.

Lermontov, Mikhail (translated by Martin Parker and Neil Cornwell), *A Hero of Our Time*, London: Alma Classics, 2009.

Pushkin, Alexander, *Eugene Onegin* (translated by James E Falen), Oxford: Oxford World's Classics, 1995.

Pushkin, Alexander, *The Queen of Spades and Other Stories* (translated by Alan Myers), Oxford: Oxford University Press, 1997.

Praz, Mario, *The Romantic Agony*, Oxford: Oxford Paperbacks, 1970.

Vitale, Serena (translated by Ann Goldstein and Jon Rothschild), *Pushkin's Button*, London: Fourth Estate, 1999.

Afterword

Anstruther, Ian, *The Knight and the Umbrella: an Account of the Eglinton Tournament 1839*, Gloucester: Alan Sutton, 1986.

Herzen, Alexander, *My Past and Thoughts*, Berkeley CA: University of California Press, 1982.

Landale, James, *Duel: A True Story of Death and Honour*, Edinburgh, Canongate, 2005.

Sorgi, Marcello, *Il grande dandy: vita spericolata di Raimondo Lanza di Trabia*, Milan: Rizzoli, 2011.

INDEX